Passenger Liners
Scandinavian Style

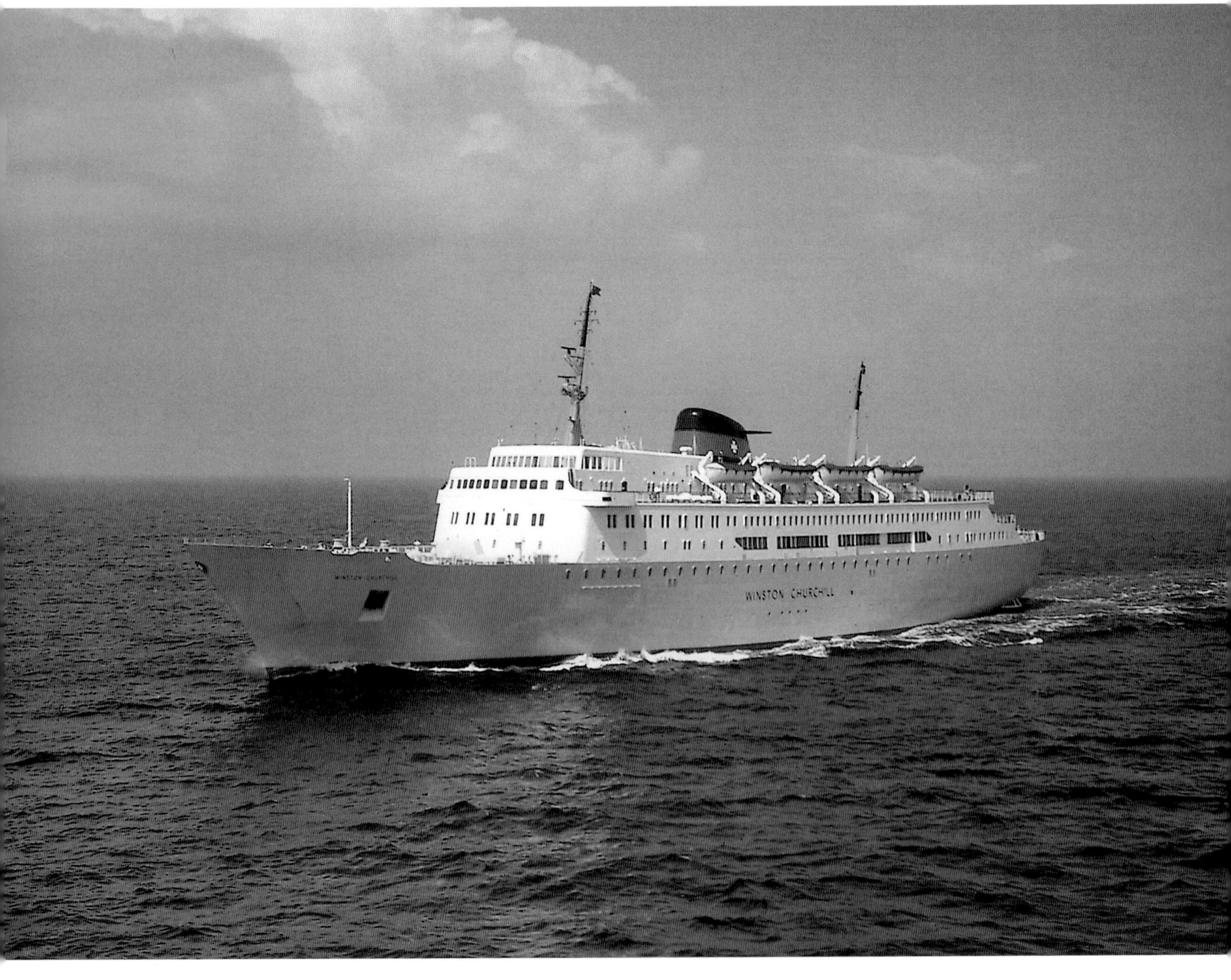
WINSTON CHURCHILL

PassengerLiners Scandinavian Style

by
Bruce Peter

Published by
Carmania Press
Unit 212, Station House, 49, Greenwich High Road, London, SE10 8JL.

All rights reserved. No part of this publication may be reproduced or transmitted in any form
or by any means without the prior permission of the publisher.

© Bruce Peter and Carmania Press.
ISBN 0-9543666-1-1. First published, 2003.
British Library Cataloguing for Publication Data.
A Catalogue Record for this book is available from the British Library.
Artwork production by Alan Kittridge.
Printed by The Amadeus Press, Cleckheaton, West Yorkshire.

Contents

Acknowledgements 5
Bibliography 5
Introduction 6
1. **The Danish Liners** 12
   Det Forenede Dampskib Selskab (DFDS) - The United Steamship Company
   Østasiatiske Kompagni - The East Asiatic Company
2. **The Norwegian Liners** 36
   Den Norske Amerikalinje - Norwegian America Line
   Det Bergenske Dampskibsselskab (BDS) - The Bergen Line
   Fred. Olsen Line
   I.M. Skaugen
   Jahre Line
3. **The Swedish Liners** 79
   Svenska Amerika Linien - Swedish American Line
   Svenska Lloyd - Swedish Lloyd
4. **The Sun Vikings** 129
   Norwegian Caribbean Line
   Royal Viking Line
   Royal Cruise Line
5. **Effjohn International Companies** 145
   Sundance Cruises
   Crown Cruise Line
   Commodore Cruise Line
   Sally Cruises
6. **The Smaller Cruise Lines** 151
   Pearl Cruises of Scandinavia
   Scandinavian World Cruises
   Nordline
   Flagship Cruises
   Cruising Yachts and Expedition Ships
7. **Royal Caribbean Cruise Line** 157
   Admiral Cruises
   Celebrity Cruises
8. **Consolidation, Globalisation and New Directions** 166
Fleet List 168
Index 177

FRONT COVER
Norwegian America Line meets Swedish American Line in the Caribbean in this fine painting by Stephen Card. The *Sagafjord* passes the *Gripsholm*. *Stephen Card*

FRONTISPIECE
The graceful lines of the *Winston Churchill* are shown to advantage as she crosses the North Sea at the beginning of her DFDS career. Throughout her long service with the company, she was very reliable and performed remarkably well in all weathers, even on stormy Atlantic crossings to the Faroe Islands. *Author Collection*

BACK COVER
Modern romanticism: Two striking pre-War colour views of the 1928 *Gripsholm*'s interiors, the work of Carl Bergsten. *William Tilley*

Acknowledgements

I must express my thanks to the following people and organisations who have been so generous with their time, information and photographs. Without their help there would have been no book.

John Adams, Micke Asklander; Dag Bakka, jr.; Captain Rolf Bassenberg; the Bergen Maritime Museum; Anders Bergenek; Aris Bilalis; Jonathan Boonzaier, Klas Brogren; Stephen Card, who has allowed us to use one of his most beautiful paintings on the cover of this book; Captain David Carr of Cunard; Bryan Corner-Walker; Tim Dacey; Shawn Dake; Jane Allan and Nicholas Oddy and my other colleagues at the Glasgow School of Art; Laurence Dunn; Claes Feder; Jørgen Fink of Det Danske Erhvervsarkiv, Århus; Ross Furlong of Saga Holidays; Dr. Andrea Ginnante of Fincantieri, Riva Trigoso; Ambrose Greenway; Dr. Ann Glen; Stephen Gooch; Ingrid Guse; Göteborg Maritime Museum; Knud E. Hansen A/S; Clive Harvey; Lars Hemingstram; David Hodge at the National Maritime Museum, Greenwich; Søren Lund Hviid; Per Jensen; Røyne Killingstad; Knut Klippenberg of Fred. Olsen Lines; Peter Knego; Peter Kohler; Stephanie Kokkali; Bård Kolltveit; Kay Kørbing; Captain Bo Lewenhagen; Mick Lindsay; Henrik Ljungstrom; Cara Lubbock of Fred. Olsen Cruise Lines; John McFarlane; Frank Manders; Richard and Susan Maren; Georg Matre; Eric Messerschmidt; the late Vincent Messina; Peter Newall; Flemming Nielsen of Aalborg Stadsarkiv; Thomas Noregaard Olesen; Captain Pantelis Papageorgiou; Alastair Paterson; Ebbe Pedersen of DFDS; Keld Helmer Petersen; Paolo Piccione; René Taudal Poulsen; Pauline Power; Paul Pålsson; Anna Scafa-Wagener of Flender Werft, Lübeck; Ian Shiffman of Table Bay Underway Shipping; Henrik Segercrantz and Tarja Koskinen of Kvaerner Masa Yards; Tony Smith of World Ship Society; Søren Thorsoe; Bill Tilley; David Trevor-Jones; Ivor Trevor-Jones; Tyne and Wear Archives; Henrik Vaupel of DFDS; Tage Wandborg; Catarina Westerlind and Per-Olov Wirén of Broström A/B; Thomas Wigforss; Alan Zamchick; Michael Zell.

Above all, my especial thanks go to Anthony Cooke for his patience, kindness and hard work. As a result of his good counsel and thorough editorial skills, this book has been a joy to write and publish.

Bibliography

Brogen, Klaas: *Designs 1987 – Designs 1999*, Shippax, Halmstad, 1987-99.
Brogen, Klaas: *Guide 1988 – Guide 1999*, Shippax, Halmstad, 1988-99.
Cooke, Anthony: *Liners & Cruise Ships – 3*, Carmania Press, London, 2003.
Dawson, Philip: *British Superliners of the 1960s*, Conway Maritime Press, London, 1990.
Dawson, Philip: *Cruise Ships: An Evolution in Design*, Conway Maritime Press, London, 2000.
Eliseo, Maurizio and Piccione, Paolo: *The Costa Liners*, Carmania Press, London, 1997.
Harvey, W.J.: *Stena, 1939-1989*, World Ship Society and Stena Line, Gothenburg, 1989.
Hutchings, David: *Caronia – Legacy of a 'Pretty Sister'*, Shipping Books, Market Drayton, 2000.
Jacobsen, E. and Johnsen, P.E: *Skipsfarten På Oslo – Bilder Gjennom Femti Är*, Tangen Maritime Forlag, Naersnes, 1999.
Keilhau, W.: *Norway and the Bergen Line*, A/S John Griegs Boktykkeri, Bergen, 1953.
Kludas, Arnold: *Great Passenger Ships of the World Today*, Patrick Stephens, Sparkford, 1992.
Lange, Ole: *Logbog For Lauritzen, 1884 – 1995*, Lauritzen, Copenhagen, 1995.
Lloyd's Register of Shipping.
Mattson, A: *De Flytande Palatsen – The White Viking Fleet*, Tre Böker, Gothenburg, 1983.
May, John: *Greek Ferries*, Ferry Publications, Narberth, 1999.
Maxtone-Graham, John: *Liners to the Sun*, Macmillan, New York, 1985.
Middlemiss, Norman L.: *Fred. Olsen – Bergen Line*, Shield Publications, Newcastle upon Tyne, 1990
Miller, William H.: *The Cruise Ships*, Conway Maritime Press, London, 1988.
Miller, William H.: *The Fabulous Interiors of the Great Ocean Liners in Historic Photographs*, Dover Publications, Mineola, New York, 1985.
Miller, William H.: *Great Cruise Ships and Ocean Liners from 1954 to 1986 – A Photographic Survey*, Dover Publications, Mineola, New York, 1988.
Miller, William H.: *Modern Cruise Ships, 1965-1990*, Dover Publications, Mineola, N.Y., 1992.
Pedersen, B. and Hawks, F.W.: *Norwegian America Line*, World Ship Society, Kendal, 1995.
Thorsøe, S., Vaupel, H., Simmonsen, P. and Krogh-Andersen, S.: *DFDS, 1866-1991*, Skibsudvikling Gennem 125 År, World Ship Society and DFDS, Copenhagen, 1991.
Lloyd's List.
Lloyd's Ship Manager Cruise and Ferry Quarterly.
Marine News (World Ship Society).
The Motorship.
The Naval Architect.
Sea Breezes.
Sea Lines (Ocean Liner Society).
The Shipbuilder and Marine Engine Builder.
The Shipping Record.
Shipping World and the Shipbuilder.
Ships Monthly.
Steamboat Bill (Steamship Historical Society of America).

Introduction

As a youngster, the highlight of my year was the annual family holiday in Denmark. Because my father is Danish, this was a brief opportunity to see my family, to enjoy the warm Scandinavian summer weather and, above all, to sail across the North Sea on a beautiful DFDS or Fred. Olsen – Bergen Line ship. Would we be sailing on the *England* or the *Winston Churchill*, the *Venus* or the *Jupiter*? On arrival in Newcastle, we would see the streamlined funnel and well-raked masts protruding above the terminal building. As we climbed the gangway onto the teak promenade deck, smiling blonde stewardesses greeted us and directed us to our cabins. With the family luggage safely stowed, there was time to explore the ship before going out on deck to watch as we cast off and headed down river, past Tynemouth and into the North Sea.

With our appetites sharpened by the sea air, we would retire indoors and make for the restaurant, where traditional Scandinavian dishes were on the menu. There, one could look through glass partitions and gently-lit saloons to vistas of the sea and waves and sometimes spray running down the windows at the front of the superstructure. The use of beautiful natural materials – in particular, dark wood panelling - and soft lighting created what the Danes and the Norwegians call a "hyggelig" atmosphere, warm, intimate, friendly and relaxed. The types of clothes and jewellery worn by the passengers, the sounds of Danish, Norwegian or Swedish being spoken, the aroma of Scandinavian cooking, the smoke of Scandinavian tobacco brands and the ping-pong tannoy announcements in dusky corridors were ephemeral qualities which added to the ships' distinctive character.

The Scandinavian passenger ships were unique and special – from purposeful North Sea vessels at one end of the scale to the most glamorous transatlantic liners and international cruise ships at the other. These delightful vessels, their design, operation and subsequent careers fascinated me. The North Sea ships may not have been as big as the great transatlantic liners and cruise ships, but all Scandinavian passenger ships shared the same high standards of design, maintenance and reliability. In recent years, I have visited and, when possible, sailed on all those which have survived, except the former *Stella Polaris*, which is now preserved in Japan. This book is the result of this lifelong love affair.

TECHNICAL AND AESTHETIC ADVANCEMENT

The Scandinavian deep-sea liners were neither Atlantic greyhounds, nor were they remarkable for their great size. They were modestly-proportioned, comfortable ships which did not rely on unimaginable glamour and statistical superlatives, as did their French, British, Italian and, later, American competitors. Without the government subsidies enjoyed by rival companies on the transatlantic run, they had to be profitable as well, which meant the efficient use of space and economical propulsion. For example, they were among the first to make widespread use of diesel engines.

The Burmeister & Wain shipyard and engineering works in Copenhagen developed the world's first-ever marine diesel engine for an ocean-going ship: the passenger-cargo liner *Selandia* was delivered to the East Asiatic Company, also of Copenhagen, in 1912. (The first Burmeister & Wain marine diesel engine had been tested in 1898.) Later, in the 1920s, B&W, as they were often known, developed an uprated diesel which, after further development, became the most widely-used marine power plant. Diesels were more economical than steam turbines and took up less space, leaving more for profitable passengers or cargo; and so the vast majority of Scandinavian liners were motorships. Furthermore, unlike Britain, which still built many coal-fired steamships until the Second World War, the Scandinavian countries had virtually no coalfields of their own; and coal was bulky and expensive to import.

The use of motor propulsion also had implications for the appearance of ships. Remarkably, the *Selandia* and most of her later sisters for the East Asiatic Company had no funnels and the exhaust went instead up pipes attached to one of their three or four masts. Most other motor passenger liners had shorter, wider funnels than steamers as these could also house generators, ventilators and other unsightly machinery, giving these ships a more orderly and purposeful appearance. Such innovation, linking technical expertise with aesthetic creativity, has made the Scandinavian countries famous the World over for their design and architecture. These disciplines have become renowned for their understated elegance, for their skilful manipulation of space and light, for their attention to exquisite detailing and, above all, for their innate sense of tradition and cultural continuity.

The Scandinavian liners of the early twentieth century were principally emigrant-carriers. Consequently, their interiors were largely for the use of third class passengers and were of perfunctory design. A small and exclusive first class section carried diplomats, businessmen and a few wealthy holidaymakers. Later, between the two World Wars, tourism became a rapidly growing trade. When emigration from the Scandinavian countries to America declined in the 1920s, a second generation of altogether more luxurious liners was commissioned. The shipowners aimed to attract a new clientele of prosperous American tourists – often the descendants of the original migrants – who wanted to visit family in Scandinavia and to travel there in comfort. The Swedish American Line's *Gripsholm* of 1925 and *Kungsholm* of 1928 were the outstanding Scandinavian liners of the period and each, in her own way, expressed Swedish culture and heritage through her interior design. The former was a grand Gustavian "floating palace", while the latter, designed by Carl Bergsten, was a showcase for Swedish modern romantic decoration, tinged with classicism. Yet, many of the qualities that made Scandinavian passenger liners of the 1920s so distinctive were continued in those of the 1930s, by which time modernism was in its ascendancy.

In Scandinavia, the modern movement developed from a felicitous combination of vernacular traditions and neo-classicism, combined with new architectural ideas, emanating mainly from the European avant garde. Significantly, would-be modernists drew inspiration from what they saw as the clean-lined purity and technical functionality of ship design and the first large-scale example of Scandinavian modernism, the Stockholm Exhibition of 1930, obviously owed much in its architectural expression to ships. Designed by Eric Gunnar Asplund, Nils Einar Eriksson and other progressive Swedish architects, the exhibition received massive and enthusiastic coverage in the European architectural press. The Swedes took to the new look very quickly, realising that simple white-rendered buildings looked very well in the bright Scandinavian sunlight. From then on, the modern movement dominated the Scandinavian architectural scene and critics wrote articles and books which publicised not only the buildings themselves but also the wider social agenda and the emphasis on good modern design improving the quality of life for everyone. (Eriksson was later commissioned by the Swedish American Line to design remarkably forward-looking interiors for its tragically short-lived flagship, the *Stockholm* of 1941 – see below.)

The modern designer believed in the importance of 'total form'. Buildings and objects should be thought of as complete entities, in which modern aesthetics would appear seamless and in which the exterior would reflect what was happening inside. Modern architects admired the external forms and masses of passenger ships for their apparent functionality, but were horrified by what they felt to be their excessively ornate interior decoration. Shipowners, on the other hand, believed that decorative interiors which reflected those on terra firma would impress passengers and help them to forget that they were actually at sea. Traditionally, they would select a firm of naval architects to design their vessels and separate interior designers to decorate them. For there to be a truly modern passenger ship, like-minded naval architects and interior architects would have to co-operate on an unprecedented scale to achieve the 'total form' required by modernism.

THE ARCHITECTS AND DESIGNERS

Inevitably, as each of the Scandinavian countries has its own traditions and sense of heritage, each nation's ships displayed distinct cultural nuances in their design. While Denmark and Sweden came to embrace 'the functional tradition' in architecture and design, Norway (which only gained full independence from Sweden in 1905) was swept by successive waves of National Romanticism which continue even today. Arnstein Arneberg (1882-1961), one of Norway's most significant twentieth century architects, was a leading proponent. Trained as a draughtsman at the Royal School of Design in Kristiania (now Oslo) from 1899 to 1902 and as an architect at the Royal Polytechnic in Stockholm from 1904 to 1906, he is best known as the designer of Oslo's magnificent City Hall (initially proposed in 1916 and finally completed in 1951). Significantly, Arneberg also designed interiors for several of Norway's most important passenger liners of the late 1930s and the 1950s. His first such projects were the outstanding Fred. Olsen vessels *Bretagne*, *Black Prince* (I) and *Black Watch* (I), the interiors of which were superbly crafted and adorned with generous displays of Norwegian folk art in the form of paintings, wood carvings, tapestries and embroidery. After the Second World War, Arneberg was commissioned to design interiors for Norwegian America Line's prestigious transatlantic liners *Oslofjord* and *Bergensfjord* and for Fred. Olsen's new *Blenheim* and *Braemar*. After his death in 1961, the practice continued and his former assistants Finn Nilsson and Kaare Skjaeveland took over the design of ship interiors, contributing to Norwegian America's *Sagafjord* and Fred. Olsen's 1966 *Black Watch* and *Black Prince*.

While Norwegian passenger ships were characterised by their relatively ornate interiors, Denmark and Sweden came to embrace a more rational approach. In 1934, the Dampskibs-Selskabet paa Bornholm af 1866 (popularly known as the 66 Company), which traded between Copenhagen and the island of Bornholm in the southern Baltic, employed the distinguished Danish architect Kay Fisker to work on the design of their new vessel. A modern movement pioneer, Fisker had previously designed the Danish Pavilion at the Exposition des Arts Décoratifs et Industriels Modernes held in Paris in 1925, which, among much else, was a brilliant showcase for the talents of many innovative Scandinavian designers. As Professor of Architecture at the Royal Academy of Fine Arts Architecture School at Charlottenborg in Copenhagen, Fisker was among the leading proponents of the modern movement in Denmark during the 1930s and, having also designed several important buildings on Bornholm, he was admired by the 66 Company's technical director, Thorkil Lund.

At that time, the most radical of the modernist theoreticians were arguing that architecture had to deal with such pressing social problems that there could be no room for historical references: hence the desire for functionalism. Fisker corrected this revolutionary view with an evolutionary explanation, "the functional tradition". He found that the beauty of traditional building forms was achieved over many generations, eliminating what proved superfluous until what remained was the pure utilitarian form, perfect in its simplicity. To him, Denmark's traditional architecture of yellow bricks and tiled, pitched roofs was nature transformed into culture, born of a clear sense of the Danes' place in history and the world. Fisker designed on a readily accessible, human scale and with an egalitarian social outlook, emphasising deep-rootedness, significance and sobriety. It was a kind of Darwinism applied to design, which closely mirrored the evolutionary approach used by naval architects, refining existing precedents and building on prior knowledge. Not surprisingly, Fisker's vision of modernity proved to be well-suited to the design of passenger ships.

The motorship *Hammershus* was delivered to the 66 Company in 1936 and, although very small at only 1,726 tons, provoked much interest on account of her strikingly modern design. The DFDS company of Copenhagen was so impressed by her that they asked Fisker to design the equally trend-setting *Kronprins Olav*, introduced in 1937

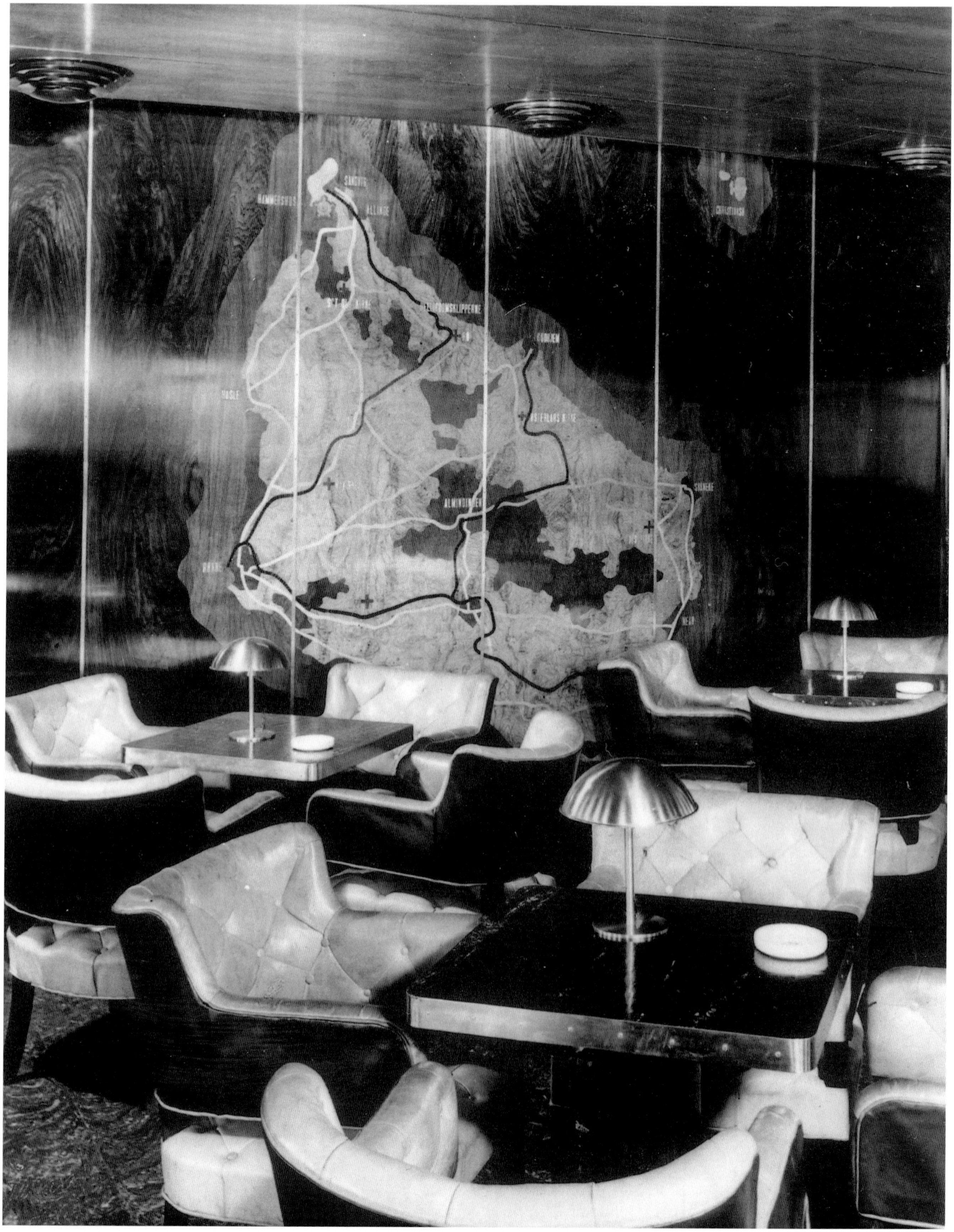
HAMMERSHUS
SANDVIG
ALLINGE
HASLE
ALMINDINGEN

on the important Copenhagen – Oslo route. At the Helsingør shipyard, itself a DFDS subsidiary, Fisker was introduced to a young and innovative naval architect called Knud E. Hansen. Working in close co-operation, the two devised a strikingly curvaceous silhouette for the new DFDS ship. This was made possible by recent advances in steel technology. Fisker and Hansen were a formidably creative duo and thanks largely to their precedent, Scandinavian passenger ships were at the forefront of modernity on the high seas in the following decades and they set the design trends which others followed.

The Bergen Line's *Venus* of 1931 had been one of the ships Hansen had already been involved in at Helsingør and her forward-looking design had obviously influenced his own thinking. 1937 saw not only the introduction of the *Kronprins Olav*, but also of Larvik – Frederikshavnferjen A/S's *Peter Wessel*. This ship, built by Aalberg Vaerft, had been designed by Hansen on a freelance basis and was widely acknowledged to be one of the first modern car-carrying passenger ships. Building on the success of these first vessels, Knud E. Hansen established his own naval architectural and engineering consultancy in Copenhagen. Hitherto, a shipowner would typically have invited bids from any shipyard capable of building a new vessel, with each yard's drawing office submitting a design. Thus, the final selection was inevitably a compromise between the quality and appropriateness of the design submissions and their respective costs. In contrast, Knud E. Hansen's firm was independent and could thus work closely with each shipowner to develop designs precisely tailored to their needs, before going out to tender for construction. Knud E. Hansen thus found a lucrative niche which greatly benefited Scandinavian shipping companies and often gave their ships that vital competitive advantage.

Later, in the post-War era, one of Hansen's most important assistants was Tage Wandborg, who remains a pre-eminent naval architect even to-day. Wandborg recalls that 'Hansen was a very refined and sensitive man, softly-spoken and genteel in manner. He paid great attention to the details of his work and he discussed what was being done by each person in the office at the beginning and end of the day, questioning the development of an individual's ideas and offering suggestions of his own. Hansen wanted originality from his people and would reassign work he thought did not measure up creatively.'

In 1960, Knud E. Hansen's life came to a tragic end. He fell overboard accidentally and drowned while sailing his yacht. Thereafter, Tage Wandborg became a leading light in the company and, as we shall see, designed a succession of outstanding passenger vessels throughout the 1960s and 1970s. He had been born near Helsingør in Denmark in 1923. Having worked for a time as an apprentice at the Helsingør shipyard, he attended the local Technicum (technical college), graduating in 1944. As Denmark was still under occupation and shipbuilding had ground to a halt, he first found employment with the train

Kay Fisker's interiors on the *Hammershus* made extensive use of fine wood veneers for wall and ceiling finishes - especially notable is the marquetry map of Bornholm in the ship's smoking room. Even the furniture and table lamps were specially designed. The most effective use of space was made by the elegant staircase and gallery in the entrance foyer. *Author Collection*

Of only a modest 1,726 tonnes, the Danish *Hammershus*, pictured in Copenhagen in the late-1950s, appeared attractive, yet workman-like, externally but caused much interest on account of her innovative internal design. *World Ship Society*

builder Skandia of Randers. Thereafter, he served in the Royal Danish Guard as the regiment's youngest Second Lieutenant before finally returning to the world of shipbuilding when he joined the technical staff at the Finnboda yard in Stockholm in 1947. Eight years later, he returned to Denmark and took up a senior position in the rapidly expanding firm of Knud E. Hansen.

It was Tage Wandborg who developed 1960s Scandinavian car ferry designs into the first purpose-built mass market cruise ships using the latest prefabrication techniques to cut costs and enhance build quality. Such vessels were relatively shallow-draughted, easily manoeuvrable and economic, but, when designed by Wandborg, they were not only ground-breaking in design but also aesthetically pleasing. They were easily distinguished from existing liners by their assertively sculptural silhouettes and harmoniously resolved design details. Building upon this pioneering work, Wandborg was largely responsible for the subsequent transformation of the modern cruise liner into the large and glamorous floating resorts enjoyed by so many today.

While Knud E. Hansen's firm designed for a wide variety of Scandinavian shipowners, the larger and well-established lines had their own in-house technical departments, which also produced outstanding and pioneering work. The Swedish American Line, for instance, employed first Eric Christiansson and, later, Gösta Kaudern and Claes Feder to co-ordinate the design of its vessels. Christiansson was born in 1901 and went to sea at the age of fourteen. In the 1920s, while studying marine engineering, he worked as a plater at the Lindholmens shipyard in Gothenburg. On graduation, he joined the Broström group, serving as their technical director between 1934 and 1965 and designing a succession of famous passenger liners and cargo ships. Norwegian America, meanwhile, benefited from the talents of its technical director and chief naval architect, Kaare Haug, to produce its post-War liners. In the 1930s, Haug had studied at King's College, Newcastle University, literally at the doorstep of the Swan, Hunter shipyard, where he and his classmates were indoctrinated in shipbuilding procedures. Appointed by Norwegian America immediately after World War II, Haug went on to design a great number of exceptionally beautiful streamlined cargo vessels, tankers and four outstanding passenger liners – the *Oslofjord*, *Bergensfjord*, *Sagafjord* and *Vistafjord*.

John Johnsen at Fred. Olsen produced that company's intriguing multi-purpose ferry liners of the 1950s and 1960s. Born in 1925, he studied naval architecture at the University of Durham, from which he graduated in 1953. Keen to return to Norway, and preferably to his native

Oslo, he initially found employment by day in the Sjøfartsdirektoratet and by night in the Oslo office of MacGregor – the famous manufacturers of hatches, davits and other shipboard fixtures and fittings. At the time, MacGregor were supplying equipment for a number of projects for the Fred. Olsen group as it gradually rebuilt its fleet after the War. It was by this mode that Johnsen was spotted by the company and employed to rationalise its cargo handling systems, as traditional cargo liners were felt to be rather inefficient. Fred. Olsen himself kept a close eye upon technical matters and between 1954 and 1960 no less than twenty new cargo ships were delivered to the group, all of which demonstrated increasing innovation in freight handling, loading goods on pallets through side hatches and, later, going over to full containerisation. This gave Fred. Olsen a crucial advantage over some competitors, especially in the transportation of delicate cargoes such as fruit – an important business for the firm.

Technical developments and efficiency savings aside, Johnsen was also a great aesthete. The first post-War Olsen passenger liners, *Blenheim* and *Braemar*, had been designed by Johnsen's predecessor, Leif Steineger, and their remarkable streamlined design set the tone for what followed.

The 1966 *Jupiter/Black Watch* and *Black Prince*, designed by Johnsen, combined distinctive streamlined exteriors with highly innovative cargo handling systems which enabled them to carry passengers and cars in the summer North Sea service and fruit from the Canaries and Madeira in the winter (see below). *Black Prince*, in particular, has been an enduring (and endearing) vessel and she still serves her original owners thirty seven years later. By the time Johnsen retired in 1990, he and his team had designed a huge number of new ships for Fred. Olsen – from giant oil tankers to small coasters – in addition to overseeing many conversions, making him one of the unsung greats of modern naval architecture.

Whilst the majority of Scandinavian liners were designed by Danish, Swedish or Norwegian naval architects who had trained in Britain, paradoxically, the DFDS design team was led by an Englishman trained in Denmark - Bryan Corner-Walker. He was in the Royal Navy when the Second World War ended for him with Denmark's liberation. Rather than returning to Britain, he settled in Copenhagen, where he studied naval architecture, before being appointed to DFDS in 1960, initially as its Chief Superintendent Engineer and, later, as its Technical Director. The first ship his technical department designed was the *England* of 1964 and almost every new DFDS ship from then onwards until 1974 demonstrates his influence and also that of the drawing office of the company's Helsingør shipyard.

As we have seen, shipping lines often employed their own designers, to work on consecutive ships, each being an improvement on its predecessor, to give fleets family resemblances. To examine these national and corporate identities, this book is arranged by country with the development of each shipping line described chronologically within that framework.

As the ramifications of Scandinavian passenger shipping are so immense and some areas have already been well-documented, this volume is not intended to be a comprehensive survey of the whole Scandinavian passenger shipping scene. Therefore the Norwegian Hurtigrute coastal service and the cross-Baltic ferry services, about which a number of publications exist, have been omitted. Many Scandinavian passenger-ships, however, were designed for dual roles: liner-cum-cruise ship or liner-cum-ferry. I have therefore concentrated on Transatlantic liners and their smaller cousins on the North Sea routes in the first section, while the more recent generation of Scandinavian cruise vessels, mainly purpose-built for the American market, is described in the second section. Stylistically less interesting than the larger ships, the small expedition cruisers and cruising yachts have been covered more briefly.

I hope you will enjoy this survey of the design and operation of the Passenger Liners Scandinavian Style.

Bruce Peter,
Airdrie,
Lanarkshire,
June, 2003.

1
The Danish Liners

Det Forenede Dampskib Selskab (DFDS) The United Steamship Company

Nowadays, the DFDS group is best known for its dense network of passenger and ro-ro services between North Sea and Baltic ports. At different times, though, its ships have traded to the Americas, the Mediterranean and the Middle East. The company is actually one of the World's longest established shipping lines, having been founded in 1866 through the amalgamation of a number of existing concerns – hence "The United Steamship Company".

DFDS was founded by a young and dynamic Danish merchant and financier called Carl Frederik Tietgen. Born in Odense in 1829, he moved to Manchester when he was twenty and there his interest in trade began. Tietgen returned to Denmark in 1855 and, settling in Copenhagen, he quickly demonstrated his intellect and apparently inexhaustible enthusiasm for business by setting up a large number of companies and overseeing the amalgamation of shipping interests which created DFDS. In those early years, DFDS ships sailed on routes similar to the company's present network – from Denmark to Britain, Norway, the Low Countries and the Baltic. There were also significant domestic routes connecting Denmark's principal cities and coastal towns.

In 1880, Tietgen joined the board of the Thingvalla Steamship Company which introduced a service to America. DFDS eventually took the company over in 1898 and ran the service under the name Scandinavian America Line. Thus, when Tietgen died in 1901, the DFDS fleet comprised a large number of small passenger and cargo steamers, but they also had on order some much more imposing transatlantic liners. Indeed, DFDS could by then claim to be among the World's ten largest shipping lines. One reason for the company's rapid expansion at this time was the opening in 1894 of the Copenhagen Free Port, enabling goods to be transferred from ship to ship without becoming liable to taxation.

As with the later Norwegian America and Swedish American Lines, emigrant traffic was very important to DFDS's transatlantic service and the directors decided to order a new ship for the American route. The *Oscar II* was built by Alexander Stephen & Son of Glasgow and delivered in 1902. Two sister ships were ordered from the same yard, the *Hellig Olav* and the *United States*. All three were single screw steamers of about 10,000 gross tons and carried 123 passengers in first class, as many in second class and 837 in a very basic third class. The 8,173-ton *C. F. Tietgen*, which had been built as the *Rotterdam* by Harland & Wolff for the Holland America Line in 1897, was bought to supplement the service in 1906. In 1914, she was replaced by the new *Frederik VIII* of 11,850 tons, which was delivered by the Vulcan shipyard at Stettin.

The *Frederik VIII* was a stately flagship with tastefully restrained first class accommodation, designed by the Danish neo-classical architect Carl Brummer. He became arguably the first Scandinavian architect to specialise in ship interior design. While German and French liners of the early years of the twentieth century were characterised by their lavish baroque decoration – especially in their first class spaces – Brummer instead developed a highly refined and distinctly Danish approach to ship interiors, which mirrored the architecture of the period on terra firma. The interiors of the *Frederick VIII* featured highly polished marquetry panelling with restrained classical details and white-painted ceilings with ornate strapwork in low relief. The first class dining saloon and smoking room were particularly outstanding with their high domed ceilings punching through to the deck above. Her tourist and third

The *Hellig Olav* glides serenely up the Hudson River to New York. During the First World War, the merchant ships of non-combatant countries carried neutrality markings on their hulls, hence the large Dannebrog flags painted fore and aft and the name and country of origin amidships. *Ambrose Greenway Collection*

The imposing *Frederik VIII* also carries First World War neutrality markings. Until the mid-1930s, she was a highly popular liner – but was gradually eclipsed by newer Swedish tonnage. *Ambrose Greenway Collection*

class spaces were less impressive, but even these compared favourably with those of liners run by competing companies.

When the United States began introducing progressively more severe immigration quotas in the 1920s, the Scandinavian America Line started to struggle and the Great Depression compounded its problems in the early 'thirties. Its vessels had relatively little first and second class accommodation and they were less easily adapted for the growing tourist trade to Scandinavia than those of the rival Norwegian and Swedish companies. Consequently, DFDS began withdrawing its transatlantic liners in the early 'thirties. Nevertheless, although finance was in short supply, the company did try to order a new liner in 1928 and again in 1934, applying for a loan from the Danish government. Unfortunately for the company, the government then asked the Danish Shipowners Association if it approved. Two rival owners, A. P. Møller and East Asiatic Company, objected – so, with no prospect of being able to afford a large and luxurious new ship, DFDS decided to close the New York passenger service. After the *Frederik VIII* completed her final voyage for the company and was sold in 1935, there was not another ship in the fleet to exceed 10,000 tons until 1974 when the *Dana Regina* was introduced (see below).

THE SWITCH TO MOTORSHIPS

The 'thirties may have seen the abandonment of the transatlantic passenger service but the company was expanding its freight operations and many of its larger cargo ships could carry a handful of passengers. It was, however, on the North Sea and on the ferry routes round Scandinavia that the greatest modernisation took place.

DFDS's head office at Kvaesthusbroen in Copenhagen looked across the busy harbour towards the Burmeister & Wain shipyard in Christianshavn, famous for its experience of building motor ships. The possible advantages of motor propulsion in saving space and weight could not have been lost on the DFDS directors, and they had ordered two similar cargo liners to make comparative trials – the motorship *California* delivered by Burmeister & Wain in 1913 and the steamer *Maryland* which came from the Tecklenborg shipyard at Bremerhaven in 1914. The *Maryland* was torpedoed in 1914 after only a few months of service, but the *California*, which could also carry 12 passengers, was an outstanding success and remained in the DFDS fleet until 1959. Even so, the early motorships were noisy, slow (the *California* could manage just 10 knots) and tended to vibrate, so steam was still the preferred choice for passenger vessels.

With the rapid improvement of the Burmeister & Wain diesel engine, however, DFDS took delivery of a large number of passenger motorships after 1925, both for its routes to Britain and its domestic services. The *Parkeston*, *England*, *Jylland* and *Esbjerg* were all built at Helsingør for North Sea service, the *C. F. Tietgen* sailed overnight from Copenhagen to Århus and the *Vistula* traded to the Baltic ports, while the tough little 1,854 ton *Dronning Alexandrine* ploughed her way through the often turbulent Atlantic waters to Greenland. Apart from those lost in the Second World War, the majority of these sturdy vessels continued in service well into the 1960s. Then as now, DFDS ships

The sister ships *Parkeston* (right) and *Esbjerg* are seen in the Port of Esbjerg in the early 1930s. Spartan and hard-working ships, the *Parkeston* and her three sisters did much to develop DFDS's North Sea routes to Britain between the wars and the *Parkeston* herself remained in service until 1964. *Author Collection*

were very well maintained and tended to have long careers with the company.

In 1937, the revolutionary 3,038-ton *Kronprins Olav*, built by the Helsingør Skibsvaerft was introduced on the company's prestigious 'capital cities route' between Copenhagen and Oslo. As we have already seen, she came from the drawing boards of Knud E. Hansen, whose own firm later became one of the most innovative designers of ferries and cruise ships, and Kay Fisker, one of Denmark's most eminent architects and urban planners. She was sleek and streamlined, with a high bow profile, a cruiser stern and a long, low superstructure with a tapering funnel.

Within, Fisker abandoned the traditional approach to shipboard design in favour of open-plan interiors, the saloons being separated by glass doors. The walls were simply panelled in sycamore and palisander, which were chosen for their distinctive figuring, the intrinsic beauty of which avoided the need for any superficial decoration. Fisker designed a new range of furniture for the *Kronprins Olav* – high-backed armchairs with winged headrests and long, curved banquettes. In the first class hallway, there was a magnificent spiral staircase with a portrait of the Norwegian Crown Prince hanging in the void behind. Because of their lightness and lack of cluttering decoration, the new ship's interiors gave the impression of being far more spacious than they actually were and, once in service, she was immediately popular both with passengers and with the architectural press. With everything specially designed – from the overall profile to clocks and ashtrays – the *Kronprins Olav* was a wonderful advertisement for modern Danish design and had a great influence on subsequent ships. The successful formula was repeated and refined in all subsequent passenger vessels for DFDS and other Scandinavian companies.

KRONPRINS FREDERIK and KRONPRINSESSE INGRID.

With the popular *Kronprins Olav* well-established, DFDS next turned its attention to providing better ships for the important Esbjerg – Harwich route, to cope with the growing tourist and business traffic between Denmark and Britain. The four existing ships on this route were essentially cargo vessels with some passenger space.

To familiarise themselves with what the competition were offering, DFDS's directors invited Kay Fisker to accompany them on an 8-day fact-finding tour, sailing on a variety of recently introduced overnight ferries. That way, they hoped to become aware of contemporary design practice in other countries. (In fact, because of work and teaching commitments, Fisker had to withdraw from the trip, but he sent his young assistant Poul Kjaergaard instead.) First, they sailed from Gothenburg to London on Swedish Lloyd's *Suecia*, a ten-year old steamship built on the Tyne in the traditional British style, with saloons fore and aft and machinery spaces between. The DFDS directors reported that she resembled an English manor house. In Liverpool, they examined the motor ship *Munster* of the Liverpool – Dublin route. In comparison with the stately *Suecia*, they thought the *Munster* very austere. Next, they sailed from Newcastle on the Bergen Line's new Italian-built *Vega*, reporting that her design was 'varied and in the slightly pretentious style of the Italian Atlantic liners'. Having returned to Copenhagen on their own *Kronprins Olav*, the directors concluded that DFDS's own standard of design was already far superior to that of any other shipping line and that the new Esbjerg – Harwich ship should also be entrusted to Fisker.

An order was placed with Helsingør Skibsvaerft in the spring of 1939, but by the time the superb new 3,895-ton *Kronprins Frederik* was delivered in June, 1941, Denmark had been invaded by the Germans and the ship was laid up in Copenhagen. Unlike much of the rest of the DFDS fleet, she neither saw war service nor was seized by the German army. Henrik Vaupel of DFDS explains why:

In these 1950s views, the *Kronprins Olav* shows off her sleek, streamlined profile, so revolutionary when she was first introduced back in 1937. During her peacetime career, she served mainly on the Copenhagen-Oslo route and is seen leaving Copenhagen. Towards the end of her DFDS career, she was switched to the Faroe Islands and Iceland services.
World Ship Society

15

The *Kronprins Olav*'s interiors were simple and refined. The hallway had pale veneers on the walls, which glowed in the reflected light of the specially-designed wall lights, while the ceiling was panelled in teak. In contrast, the balustrades were of brushed steel and the flooring was black linoleum. *Author Collection*

'This ship was really to be the pride of the Danish merchant navy and nobody in Denmark wanted to see her used by the hated Nazis, so it is said that the Resistance organised for a number of vital engine parts to be removed and hidden in Copenhagen's rubbish tip. Anyway, the Germans left her to sit in Copenhagen harbour for the entire duration of the War, ironically still with neutrality markings painted on her hull. In November, 1945 she was towed to Helsingør for final fitting out. It was a mercy that she was spared destruction for a lot of the Company's fleet was scattered around the World and many ships were lost. The ones seized by the Nazis were in a terrible condition and took time to rebuild. But with the *Kronprins Frederik* we had a beautiful new flagship which was still far ahead of its time.'

In appearance, *Kronprins Frederik* was very much an enlarged version of the *Kronprins Olav* and looked particularly handsome in the Company's livery of pale grey hull with red boot-topping and buff masts. The low, streamlined funnel was black with a broad red band, but as the bottom was hidden behind lifeboats, it appeared to be red with a black top.

Within, the ship had very high quality accommodation for only 358 (and later, 311) passengers, spread almost equally between first and second class. The elegant semi-circular first class smoking room filled the forward part of the superstructure and to the rear there was a small, curving cocktail bar. The hallway had a grand double staircase and immediately aft was the first class dining saloon, panelled in teak. Second class public rooms were located towards the stern. The ship was a triumph of miniaturisation and no space was wasted. The stairways were steep and the corridors were narrow, and cabins were squeezed into all kinds of unlikely corners around the engine room and cargo holds. There were even two luxury staterooms with separate sleeping and sitting areas.

The *Kronprins Frederik* was such a success that an identical sister ship was quickly ordered. The *Kronprinsesse*

The curvature of the *Kronprins Olav's* superstructure was reflected in the interior of her forward first class lounge with its dramatic cove-lit ceiling and red leather armchairs, specially-designed by Kay Fisker. *Author Collection*

April, 1953 that the *Kronprins Frederik* suffered a terrible fire which began in the engine room. She was badly damaged and the local fire brigade pumped in so much water that the next day she keeled over at her berth. It was four months before the wreck could be refloated and it appeared that she would be a write-off. Instead, the *Kronprins Frederik* was towed to Helsingør for a thorough rebuild from which she emerged as an almost brand new ship.

This work ensured that she outlived her younger sister in DFDS service and the *Kronprinsesse Ingrid* was sold to Greek owners in 1969. Meanwhile, the *Kronprins Frederik* was cascaded from the Harwich – Esbjerg service to the seasonal Newcastle-Esbjerg route, with alternate sailings to Thorshavn in the Faroe Islands and even to Greenland. Before her use on these North Atlantic routes, she was fitted with anti-roll tanks and a bow thruster to make her more easily manoeuvrable in the confined Faroese harbours. Between 1966 and 1971, she traded between Copenhagen and Thorshavn, Klaksvig, Trangisvaag and Rekjavik. Ann Glen remembers the *Kronprins Frederik's* sailings from Newcastle to Esbjerg in the mid-1960s:

'At Newcastle, you had to hand over the keys of the car to the stevedores who drove it into a kind of open-sided steel box in a harness. This was lifted by crane into the ship's hold and it was hair-raising for drivers to see their cars being treated in this way. The *Kronprins Frederik* had a captain called Neilsen who was an old sea dog. He was tall, slim and sun-tanned, with a craggy face and a slightly wild look. He used to sit in the lounge when off-duty and entertain the first class passengers with tales about sailing through storms to Greenland. He absolutely loved the *Kronprins Frederik* and told us that she knew when he was onboard.

'Sometimes, the *Kronprins Frederik* would race the

Ingrid entered service in June, 1949, just in time for the busy summer tourist season. When at Harwich Parkeston Quay on alternate days, the two ships provided a stark contrast to the Hook of Holland-bound railway steamers. Even the newest of these seemed antiquated in comparison with the sleek and brightly coloured Danes.

It was while tied up at Parkeston Quay on the 19th

The *Kronprins Frederik* was almost ready to enter service between Esbjerg and Harwich when Denmark was invaded. She is seen here laid up in Copenhagen's Free Harbour in 1945, still bearing her wartime neutrality markings. *Author Collection*

After the Allied victory, DFDS was finally able to complete its new flagship, the *Kronprins Frederik*, which was towed to Elsinore for final fitting out. With its vertically ribbed woodwork creating a sense of greater height and a gracefully curved staircase, the first class hallway was the epitome of Scandinavian elegance. *Author Collection*

The first class smoking room had a masculine air with its high-backed leather armchairs, while its curving sweep of windows gave a wonderful panoramic view over the bow. *Author Collection*

After her disastrous fire at Harwich in April 1953, the *Kronprins Frederik* was returned to her builders for a complete rebuild. Kay Fisker's second interior scheme for her was much less austere. The first class smoking room featured two-tone blue tapestry rugs, specially woven in Iran to Fisker's design. *Author Collection*

A first class cabin on the *Kronprins Frederik*: the dressing table, with its ergonomic styling and three-piece mirror, was another beautifully resolved small-scale design detail. *Author Collection*

newer Harwich boat to see who could get to the buoyed channel at Esbjerg first. I remember sitting out on deck with the deck chairs scraping from side to side as the ship rolled, creaked and vibrated as we raced for the harbour. You'd see the *England* or one of the other ships from Harwich appear on the horizon and we'd go as fast as possible as it was a matter of pride that the *Kronprins Frederik* should win. These escapades came to an end when one day she didn't slow down in time and grounded on a sandbank. After that, the company changed the schedules so that racing became impossible.'

The *Kronprins Frederik* continued in the DFDS fleet until August, 1974 when she was laid up at Esbjerg. Two years later, she was sold to Egyptian owners for use as a pilgrim ship in the Red Sea. It was only a brief new career for in December, 1976, after only eight months in service as the *Patra*, she caught fire and sank, killing 102 passengers. The former *Kronprinsesse Ingrid* continued in Mediterranean service, first as the *Mimika L* and then, from 1978, as the *Alkyon*, sailing from Piraeus to the Greek islands. She was laid up in 1983 and sold for scrap in Pakistan two years later. Of the three, it was the *Kronprins Olav* which lasted the longest, being sold by DFDS in 1967 to Italian owners for use as a ferry to Corsica and, later, across the Bay of Naples. It was not until December, 1986 that she was sold for scrap after a career of nearly fifty years.

PRINSESSE MARGRETHE and KONG OLAV V

At the Royal Academy Architecture School, one of Professor Kay Fisker's students was Kay Kørbing, who went on to become perhaps the best-known Scandinavian architect involved in ship design. Kørbing was born in Copenhagen in 1915, the son of J. A. Kørbing, who was technical director of DFDS from 1921, its managing director from 1935 until 1955 and subsequently its chairman. Kørbing senior did not encourage his son to become involved in shipping, so he worked instead as a bricklayer in Copenhagen – a beginning which, he says, first got him so interested in the raw materials of building and which taught him the importance of good architectural detailing. His interest in design led him to join the Kunstakademiets Arkitektskole under Professor Fisker from 1938 to 1942, where he was in the same class as Jørn Utzon, later the architect of the Sydney Opera House. The school was a hotbed of creativity.

When Kay Kørbing graduated, Denmark was under German occupation and work was scarce, so he left for Sweden, finding employment with the highly respected architect and urban planner Cyrillus Johanson. There, he produced the competition-winning design for a church in the Stora Essengen district of Stockholm. He returned to liberated Denmark and his first job was the rebuilding and interior design of Denmark House in London's Piccadilly, the headquarters of the Danish Tourist Office.

Kørbing's first ship design was a smoking room for the DFDS cargo liner *Naxos*, built in Frederikshavn in 1953-5, which could carry 12 passengers. Kørbing remembers how he got the job:

'It so happened that my godfather was a director of Helsingør Skibsvaerft, which built almost everything for DFDS. He tried several architects and then asked me to do some sketches because "you know your father's taste". I initially declined, but one of his fellow directors, a man called Garde, persuaded me and I did some sketches. As it happened, my father liked the drawings and he asked Garde "who drew these?" So that's how I got to do my first ship.'

Next, he worked on the cabins and saloons of two DFDS passenger and cargo liners for the North Atlantic trade – the *Oklahoma* and the *Ohio*, both built at Helsingør and delivered in 1956. After the cargo liners, Kørbing was asked to design the passenger vessel *Prinsesse Margrethe*, another fine ship for the Copenhagen – Oslo route.

The *Prinsesse Margrethe* was introduced in 1957 and was immediately hailed as being among the most beautiful of her type. She represented perhaps the ultimate development of the small motor liner for overnight service before the advent of car ferries. According to Kay Kørbing: 'To give the most spacious feeling to what was by today's standards a fairly small ship, I decided to create 'service

The graceful *Prinsesse Margrethe* catches a beam of late-autumn sunlight as she leaves Copenhagen in October 1964. *Ambrose Greenway*

The *Prinsesse Margrethe's* first class lounge was spacious and airy by day and attractively lit at night. Adjacent in a starboard wing was the cocktail bar with its contemporary abstract murals. *Keld Helmer Petersen*

towers' through the different decks to contain the plumbing, the wiring and staircases. These were located well within the shell of the ship, so you could see all around them. The *Prinsesse Margrethe* had truly open plan interiors and we had to work carefully round the existing design regulations. I wanted fully-glazed bulkheads between the saloons to give a greater feeling of space, so we developed retractable firedoors which folded away into the ends of the service towers. When you looked along the length of the ship, there was a continuous vista from one room to the next; and on the end walls there were specially commissioned abstract murals by Danish artists whom I knew.

'The modern furniture you could buy in Denmark at the time was very refined, but hopeless for ships as it would tip over in bad weather, while the ship furniture that was available was usually so heavy and old-fashioned. The moulded fibreglass cafeteria chair I designed for the ship was just about the first of its kind anywhere. Everything had to be good-looking but very hard wearing and easily maintained. I also did tubular steel-framed chairs for the lounges and special lighting was manufactured by Orrefors to give the right subdued effect.'

Externally, the *Prinsesse Margrethe* marked a further stage in the gradual development of the very distinctive style which characterised DFDS passenger ships for many years. She was a great success, so much so that a sister ship was ordered from the Aalborg Vaerft for delivery in 1961. The *Kong Olav V* was equally popular but DFDS had underestimated the growth in motor traffic which took place in the 1960s and neither ship was designed to carry more than a couple of dozen cars. Within seven years, they were replaced by larger car ferries with the same names.

After a few years on the Newcastle – Esbjerg route with her name abbreviated to *Prinsessen*, the *Prinsesse Margrethe* was sold to the Åland Islands-based Birka Line, becoming the *Prinsessan*. The *Kong Olav V* had her name shortened to *Olav* and was sold to the British-owned China Navigation Co. in 1969, becoming the *Taiwan* and sailing between Hong Kong and Keelung. In 1972, she was back in Scandinavia and joined her sister ship at the Birka Line as the *Baronessan*. Both operated 24-hour cruises from

The *Prinsesse Margrethe's* aft hallway featured a fully-glazed rear bulkhead, another innovation, here giving a fine view of an assortment of DFDS ships tied up at Kvaestbroen in Copenhagen harbour with the company headquarters in the background. *Keld Helmer Petersen*

Stockholm to Mariehamn. In 1978, the *Prinsessan* was sold to Saudi Arabian owners who placed her in the Red Sea pilgrim trade as the *Wid*. She was broken up in Pakistan in 1987. The *Baronessan*, meanwhile, headed out east again after being sold to the Chinese government. Until recently, she was in service from Hong Kong as the *Nan Hu*, but was reported to be in a very scruffy condition.

THE CAR FERRY ERA AND THE ENGLAND

Car traffic grew rapidly on DFDS's North Sea routes and the time-consuming crane-loading of vehicles into the holds of the *Kronprins Frederik* and the *Kronprinsesse Ingrid* was no longer satisfactory, especially as the Danish government was keenly promoting the country as a destination for British tourists. In 1962, DFDS went back to Helsingør Skibsvaerft to order a new passenger liner with drive-on car capacity. The 8,221-ton *England* was a side-loader through doors towards the starboard bow and stern quarters. She was innovative in many respects, as Kay Kørbing remembers:

'I was very pleased to get the job of designing the *England* as this really was to be something special in the Danish fleet – a floating first class luxury hotel. Ships of this kind are designed around their passengers, so the starting point for the whole process was the interior. Ship interiors tend to be designed in multiples of 210cm, the width of a table with a chair on either side and space to pull each chair back. Conveniently, this dimension is also the width of a typical cabin. Every table at the periphery of the room and every outside cabin needs to have a window, so this governs where the vertical structural members go. All this was carefully thought out on the *England* to make the ship as enjoyable as possible from the passenger's point of view.

'In appearance, the *England* was very elegant and modern. I remember a meeting in DFDS's boardroom

Models pose at the cocktail bar on the port side of the *England's* first class lounge in this DFDS publicity photograph. Note the ribbed ceiling, which contained a sophisticated air conditioning system to make sure her interiors remained fresh and evenly heated throughout. *Author Collection*

where company directors and technical people, all the design team from the shipyard and my interior architects sat around a mock-up model of the ship. A director of the shipyard pulled this carefully shaped lump of wood from his bag and stuck it on top of the model. "How would that be as a funnel?" It was streamlined and with fins to stop the smoke being sucked down onto the deck. Everyone agreed that it looked good and it was a design we used subsequently on other DFDS passenger ships – in fact, it was also used as a company trademark in publicity material.'

Bryan Corner-Walker, who headed the DFDS technical department, remembers: 'The company's chairman, J. A. Kørbing, while recognising the need to cater for the rapidly increasing car traffic, believed that ferries of the kind then being introduced all over Scandinavia would not be sufficiently robust for North Sea conditions. He therefore requested that we build a ship with the sleek hull lines of a conventional passenger liner instead. This was a wise course of action as the *England* proved to be an outstanding performer in all weather conditions.' The *England's* hull design was, in fact, developed from that of the Portuguese-owned liner *Funchal*, completed at Helsingør the previous year. Two Burmeister & Wain diesels gave a service speed of 21 knots with reserve power to catch up in case of storm delays – very important on the treacherous North Sea.

Not only was she a great beauty, she was also one of the best appointed ships of her type and it was rumoured that she would be used on cruises as well as for ferry work. In the event, she did make some cruises, but with limited success. As a ferry, she carried 155 first and 244 second class passengers and 100 cars, loaded through doors in the sides of the hull.

Forward on the saloon deck was the first class smoking room, later known as the Saga Lounge, which was decorated in warm beige and brown tones. It was panelled in rosewood and, like all the passenger spaces, was fully air-conditioned with ribbed ceilings specially designed by Kørbing and his team to blow in cool air and extract stale air all over to keep the ship fresh and evenly heated. The wall panelling followed the curved and slanted shape of the superstructure. Again, the furniture was specially designed. There were distinctive cubist lounge chairs and Orrefors glass light fittings, set into the ceiling to cast a warm glow. Behind was the first class dining saloon, later the Tivoli Restaurant, with a decorative panel in yellow by Arne L. Hansen. In between was a hallway. Floor-to-ceiling plate glass bulkheads and doors without frames, to give an uninterrupted expanse of glazing, separated the rooms. On the port side, there was a copper panelled cocktail bar adjoining the smoking room and, to starboard, a writing room.

The first and second class areas were separated by the galley, which served both restaurants, and, incidentally, the one in second class was very similar to its first class counterpart. Overlooking the stern and the second class sun deck was the second class smoking room, later known as the Hansa Bar, which was light and airy thanks to floor-to-ceiling windows in the rear bulkhead. One deck below were the *England's* first class cabins, shops and playroom – the latter was a first on a North Sea passenger ship, showing DFDS's concern that everyone should enjoy their trip. There were covered promenades on either beam and extensive teak sun decks. That for the first class was above the bridge and was sheltered by glazed screens to allow passengers to see the ship docking – always a fascinating experience. In stormy weather, the spray sometimes came right over the *England's* superstructure, so the space was soon enclosed with a glass fibre roof, becoming a kind of winter garden.

Quite apart from the introduction of the *England*, 1964 proved to be a momentous year for DFDS. Knud Lauritzen, of the J. Lauritzen shipping company, who had increased his shareholding in DFDS to 50%, was elected to the board of directors. Although the two companies remained independent at first, the Lauritzen group eventually became DFDS's parent company.

THE SPLENDID WINSTON CHURCHILL

On the 4th June, 1964, the *England* left Harwich on her maiden trip to Esbjerg and, after she had successfully completed a short period in service, the delighted DFDS directors quickly turned their attention to the building of a sister ship. DFDS was approaching its centenary and was celebrating in style with an unprecedented expansion and a newbuilding programme. At the time, DFDS's favoured shipyard at Helsingør was fully occupied with a series of

Locals look on as the *Winston Churchill* is launched into the Gulf of Genoa in almost complete condition on 25 April 1967. Those in small boats are perilously close to her hull and are about to feel the full force of her displacement. *Author Collection*

The *Winston Churchill's* interiors were, as with all of Kay Kørbing's designs, very elegantly detailed. In this vista though her first class hallway, which was panelled in palisander, we see Urup Jensen's tapestry panel on the rear bulkhead of the dining saloon. Notice how such details as the fire alarms (on the right hand wall) have been neatly arranged in recesses.
Author Collection

large cargo liners for the company's North Atlantic services and could not meet a quick delivery schedule. The next acceptable bid was from an unusual source – the Italian company Cantieri Navali del Tirreno e Riuniti at Riva Trigoso near Genoa. This family-owned yard built ships literally on the beach and launched them in almost completed condition. It was there that what proved to be one of DFDS's most popular and long-serving ships was laid down in January, 1966. She was one of no less than seven vessels which the Danish company had ordered from the Italian yard.

According to Bryan Corner-Walker, then DFDS's technical director: 'We carried out the initial design work for these ships ourselves and a naval architect by the name of Modeweg-Hansen drew up the contract drawings. Once the contract was signed, the shipyard then worked on the designs using their own technical expertise. At Riva Trigoso, there was a very talented chief naval architect called Gio Melodia, who refined the hull forms and gave the ships their distinctly Italian look.'

Dr. Andrea Ginnante joined the shipyard as the ship was nearing completion and he confirms that Melodia was influenced by Nicolò Costanzi, who designed the legendary *Guglielmo Marconi*, *Galileo Galilei*, *Oceanic* and *Eugenio C.*, all built at Monfalcone. Like the great Italian liners of the period, the *Winston Churchill* had lines at the bow which were like a wineglass – concave at the waterline to cut through the waves efficiently, but convex above to maximise the deck space. The hull was designed to be loaded with cars through both bow and stern, whereas *England* loaded from the side. There were lifting bow and stern visors, designed to continue the shape of the hull so that when they were closed no one could have known that the ship was a car ferry. The hull also had an extra deck so that the car deck could be double-height to carry lorries and buses.

Kay Kørbing recalls the building process: 'DFDS actually ordered a whole series of ships from the Italians – five passenger vessels and two bulk carriers. I was initially only given the job of designing the interiors of the first of these new ships, the *Winston Churchill*. Every three weeks or so, I flew to Milan with Bryan Walker and then drove to Genoa to keep an eye on progress in the office there. The interior design of the *Winston Churchill* was similar to that of the *England*, but slightly more colourful, in line with late-1960s taste. I think the blend of Italian naval architecture and Danish interior design was a great combination and the new ship had immense style.'

The new DFDS flagship was launched as the *Winston Churchill* on the 25th April, 1967 and the company's newsletter, DFDS Express, proclaimed 'A Great Ship Takes To The Sea'. She was indeed a great liner in miniature, being one of the best-appointed of her type. After sea trials, she left Genoa for Esbjerg, then sailed for Harwich from where, after berthing trials, she sailed up the Thames and moored at Greenwich, opposite the Royal Naval College. There, amid great celebrations, she was named by Baroness Spencer-Churchill. When asked by the media about the choice of name, Consul Warrer, the DFDS chairman, explained 'Our wish to name this ship *Winston Churchill* stems from a deep sense of grateful veneration for a man who gave himself to his country and the whole free world.' The Danish Ambassador added, 'No Dane will ever forget what we owe to Winston Churchill. He was a shining light in our darkest years.' There was a bust of Churchill in the lounge and Baroness Spencer-Churchill, his widow, unveiled a plaque. She was presented with a silver tray with an outline of the ship as a souvenir of the happy occasion. The gleaming new *Winston Churchill* then set sail for Harwich and the start of a brilliant career during which she was to sail at different times to most of the important ports in northern Europe.

The second class smoking room, seen here in original condition, also featured a glazed rear bulkhead. This spacious room, one deck above the original night club, later became the new Compass Club, complete with dance floor, in the early 1970s. *Author Collection*

Within, she was similar in layout and decoration to the *England*. Her lounges and restaurants were panelled in palisander, rosewood and African wengé. The first class restaurant, a particularly elegant space, had a large tapestry panel by Urup Jensen. To the stern, its second class equivalent had an abstract photo mural of ripples in water by the distinguished photographer Keld Helmer Petersen. One deck below was the ship's nightclub, located well away from cabins, so as not to disturb sleeping passengers. It was panelled in teak with bright orange and red colours, a copper and aluminium dance floor and a cocktail bar in front of the fully glazed rear bulkhead which gave a fine panoramic view over the stern. Throughout, there were glazed partitions to allow light to flood through the ship by day; and full length curtains which could be drawn at night to make the same spaces cosy and intimate.

From 1967 until 1974, the *England* and *Winston Churchill* sailed mostly on the Esbjerg-Harwich route but, starting in the winter of 1966, the *England* went on cruises to the West Indies and West Africa during the off-peak season. She was fitted with an outdoor swimming pool and carried fewer passengers than when in North Sea service, in one class only. From 1970, DFDS abandoned the class distinctions on all its ships and their facilities became available to everyone.

NEW SHIPS FOR THE OSLO AND AALBORG ROUTES

While the finishing touches were being added to the *Winston Churchill*, two new ships for the Copenhagen-Oslo route – the second *Kong Olav V* and *Prinsesse Margrethe* – were also under construction at Riva Trigoso. They were due for delivery in 1968 and a further, broadly similar pair for the Copenhagen-Aalborg route were to follow in 1969. The new 'Oslo boats' were even more luxurious than their predecessors. With much-needed full-length car decks and more substantial superstructures, they were perhaps slightly too short and too tall to be truly elegant, but within, they were luxuriously appointed.

Kay Kørbing devised vibrant interiors in turquoise, orange and red tones. The first class accommodation was divided into a number of intimate rooms with glass

The second of the two new 'Oslo boats', the *Prinsesse Margrethe*, undergoes trials in the Gulf of Genoa during August 1968 - note that she is flying the Italian flag. *Author Collection*

partitions. The centrepiece was the nightclub with its brass-panelled circular bar and dance floor. A new innovation was the Pop Room, a disco which was located low down in the hull where the noise would not disturb other passengers. As the Oslo service took 16 hours, these ships had extensive restaurants, bars, shops and even a hairdressing salon.

In contrast, the Copenhagen-Aalborg service was a short overnight hop linking the north of Jutland with the Danish capital. It was very popular in the 1960s as passengers could board the ships late in the evening and arrive early the next morning for a full day's business in the city. However, the development of Denmark's motorway system and shorter ferry links further south meant that by the time the first of the new ships, the *Aalborghus*, was delivered, the route was less successful. A strike at the shipyard delayed the delivery of the *Trekroner*, the sister ship, until 1970. By then, DFDS had decided to abandon its domestic routes as it could not compete with the state-

The *Aalborghus* and *Trekroner* undergoing rebuilding into Mediterranean cruise ferries in the drydock at Marseilles. *Author Collection*

The former *Aalborghus*, transformed into the sleek, all-white *Dana Sirena*, is seen shortly after entering Mediterranean service in June 1971. Note the new large windows forward on the saloon deck and the extension of the aft sun deck to form an outdoor lido area. *Author Collection*

subsidised railway-owned DSB ferries and, also, the Swedish authorities were preventing the ships from calling at Helsingborg en-route to enable duty-free shopping onboard. The outcome was that the route was abandoned and a search for a new use for the ships began.

DFDS had observed that tens of thousands of Germans and Scandinavians headed south towards the Mediterranean in their cars each summer, yet the local companies had very few ships with car-carrying capacity. Spotting what appeared to be a good business opportunity, DFDS had the two ships transformed from overnight ferries into sleek, white ferry-cum-cruise liners at the Société des Anciens Établissements Groignard shipyard in Marseilles. Kay Kørbing remembers the conversion:

'As the *Aalborghus* and the *Trekroner* had been designed for a route on which they sailed at 10 p.m. and arrived at six in the morning, they had very few public rooms – a cafeteria and a couple of bars and that was it. Also, they had little deck space, so we dismantled a whole area of cabins to make the Hamlet Lounge on the saloon deck and more to the stern to make a nightclub. We made reclining chair lounges into cabins with private facilities, so we were able to re-use a lot of materials. One of the sundecks was extended out to the stern to make space for an outdoor swimming pool with glass

Both *Dana Sirena* and *Dana Corona* had extensive tiers of teak sun decks aft. Passengers (and some judiciously posed models) relax around the lido as the *Dana Sirena* heads for the holiday resorts of Malaga and Palma de Mallorca.
Author Collection

The *Dana Regina's* design represented a complete break from the evolutionary approach of previous DFDS ships. Her striking, modern profile and all-white livery made her an impressive sight as she powered her way across the North Sea. *Author Collection*

shelter screens. All this was done simultaneously on both ships as they lay in a drydock, one behind the other.'

The two vessels were transformed from black-hulled ferries into the gleaming white 7,672-ton *Dana Sirena* and *Dana Corona*. The new livery, nomenclature and marketing name, DFDS SEAWAYS painted on the hulls in elongated blue letters, soon spread to all of the company's passenger ships.

The two ships sailed for Genoa, where they tied up on either side of the terminal at Porto Calvi. With flags flying and sirens blowing, they sailed on the 25th June, 1971, the *Dana Corona* bound for Tunis and Alicante and the *Dana Sirena* for Malaga and Palma de Mallorca. The new service was a success at first, but gradually locally-owned, state-subsidised companies acquired their own car ferries and the Danish invaders could not compete. A variety of routes were tried but, with a downturn in the late 1970s, the *Dana Sirena* was withdrawn and then led a nomadic life under charter to other shipping lines, mainly in northern Europe. In the autumn of 1979, she was rebuilt by Aalborg Vaerft with a new, tall funnel and extended passenger accommodation for a return to Mediterranean service. At this point, the two ships swapped names and the unrebuilt *Dana Sirena* (ex-*Dana Corona*) was tried on a new service from Genoa to Patras, Heraklion and Alexandria, while the improved *Dana Corona* (ex-*Dana Sirena*) returned to the western Mediterranean. Unfortunately, the financial results were still poor, so the routes were abandoned in November, 1982 and the ships were sold.

The *Dana Sirena* followed a number of other DFDS passenger ships to the Red Sea. She sailed mainly from Suez to Jeddah, carrying huge numbers of pilgrims and migrant workers, mostly unberthed and sleeping on deck – a far cry from her luxurious service for DFDS. Renamed *Al Qamar El Saudi* (the Saudi Moon) and looking the worse for wear, she featured in the 1988 Michael Palin TV series *Around the World in Eighty Days*. She subsequently became *Al Qamar El Saudi El Misri*, owned by Egyptians. Unfortunately, she suffered a massive explosion and was gutted by fire off Sotage in May 1994. An American destroyer rescued 110 pilgrims, who were returning from the Haj, and the former *Dana Sirena* sank.

Earlier, in 1985, the *Dana Corona* had been sold to the Chinese. Until recently, she has sailed as the *Tian E* for the Dalian Steamship Company but is currently laid up. The *Prinsesse Margrethe* and *Kong Olav V*, which had been hideously rebuilt at Aalborg Vaerft in the mid-1970s to increase their capacities, were replaced by larger vessels in 1983 and were also sold to Chinese interests. The former *Kong Olav V* eventually became a Singapore-based casino ship called the *New Orient Princess* but was destroyed by fire in 1993. The *Prinsesse Margrethe* now sails in the Mediterranean as the Cypriot cruise ship *Princesa Cypria*.

DANA REGINA AND DANA ANGLIA

By the early 1970s, growth on the Esbjerg-Harwich route was so great that the company required a further large passenger liner to replace the ten-year old *England*. This time, the order went to a Danish shipyard, the Aalborg Vaerft, and as the hull was too long for their slipway it was launched in August, 1973 without its bow section. This was added later in dry dock. Shipbuilding prices had risen steeply since the *Winston Churchill* was ordered and, at 101 million kroner, the new *Dana Regina*

The *Dana Anglia* represented a further complete change in thinking about North Sea passenger ship design. With her superstructure extending fore and aft and her massive funnel, she nonetheless makes an impressive sight sailing off Felixstowe during a NATO charter in the early 1980s - one of the rare occasions when she strayed from her regular Esbjerg-Harwich service.
Stephen Gooch

cost twice as much. Kay Kørbing was again responsible for the design:

'When my office was developing the *Dana Regina*, we were also working on parts of the *Vistafjord* for Norwegian America Line and, although they were designed for very different purposes, I think that many of the ideas from *Vistafjord* were incorporated in *Dana Regina*. The most obvious influence was in the external profile, which I styled. I think that is where the tall, tapering funnel and the overall shape came from. The new Royal Viking Line cruise ships were another influence, at least in the layout of the public rooms and in the use of large picture windows. There were also the new SOLAS fire regulations to be considered, which prevented us from using wood panelling. Consequently, the *Dana Regina* used a lot of moulded fibreglass and other modern finishes, so that she appeared very bright and spacious.'

The 12,129-ton *Dana Regina* was Denmark's largest passenger ship, finally surpassing the *Frederik VIII* of 1914. As such, she was a showcase for the newest and best in Danish design and technology. Powered by Burmeister & Wain diesel engines, she had a sleek hull with a bulbous bow and was designed for a $21^{1}/_{2}$ knot service speed. She could carry 975 passengers and 250 cars and her bow doors were of a novel design which opened out and to the sides of the hull. One reason for this was that during a storm in 1968, mountainous seas had smashed open the *Winston Churchill*'s lifting bow visor and only the brave action of the crew in tying hawsers round the locking pins had prevented the ship from being lost. With the new design, such an accident would be impossible.

Inside, as all the public rooms served a single class of passengers, Kay Kørbing designed a spacious arcade with lounge chairs and floor-to-ceiling windows along the port side, with kitchens and services to starboard. A cosy bar called the Admiral's Pub, shops, a playroom and conference rooms were located along the arcade. At the forward end of the saloon deck was the Codan Restaurant, which was connected to the circular Mermaid Bar and the adjoining Bellevue Lounge, both on the deck above, by an elegant, open-tread, brass-clad staircase with smoke glass balustrades. Above, there was a golden ceiling dome inset with twinkling lights. Towards the stern of the Saloon Deck was the Scandia Coffee Shop with its cheerful wavy copper ceiling and leather-upholstered aluminium chairs and a mural by Rolf Middleboe which concealed the servery. The Compass Club, the ship's nightclub, was situated at the stern and had floor-to-ceiling windows round three sides, a back-lit ceiling with oblong slits (similar to the Queen's Room on *QE2* which Kørbing had visited in 1968) and low-slung red stools and chairs by Jan Ekselius. One deck below and amidships, was the entrance hall with open staircases and aluminium relief panels on the bulkheads. Outside, there were wide, sweeping sun decks and the lifeboat davits were mounted above the boat deck, as on *Vistafjord*, thus giving uncluttered expanses of teak on which the passengers could promenade. With her many specially commissioned artworks and with such careful attention to every design detail, the *Dana Regina* was the height of 1970s stylishness and it was rumoured that as well as sailing between Harwich and Esbjerg, she might also go cruising.

She was named in Copenhagen by Queen Margrethe on the 1st July, 1974 and, after a visit to the Pool of London (when she became the largest ship ever to sail through Tower Bridge), she entered the Esbjerg-Harwich service on the 8th July alongside the *Winston Churchill*. The older *England* was cascaded to the seasonal Esbjerg-Newcastle route.

A good ship often lures more traffic, and so two years later DFDS ordered another large passenger ship from Aalborg Vaerft for delivery in 1978. By this stage, Bryan Corner-Walker had been promoted and was replaced by a new technical director, John Kristiansen and, consequently, the *Dana Anglia* represented a complete change in style from previous DFDS liners. The ever-growing cost of shipbuilding would have made the construction of a vessel of *Dana Regina*'s quality prohibitively expensive, so the new one was built instead with the high capacity of a modern ferry as the top priority. The *Dana Anglia* was also shorter and broader than the *Dana Regina* and its bluffer hull and superstructure design enabled it to carry a third more cars and passengers than the earlier ship. At 14,399 tons, she took over as

Denmark's largest passenger ship and was certainly impressive, if unconventional, with a vast conical-shaped funnel towards the stern. So tall was it that on a publicity visit to the Pool of London in May, 1978, the exhaust extensions had to be temporarily removed to clear Tower Bridge.

The *Dana Anglia* began her first voyage in regular service on the 13th May, 1978 and has operated on the Esbjerg-Harwich route almost exclusively ever since. Tragically, during the festivities onboard, Knud Lauritzen, the owner of DFDS's parent company, died suddenly. His passing had unfortunate repercussions for the Lauritzen group as a whole and for DFDS in particular. Without the old shipowner's leadership, it suffered from a succession of boardroom changes, was overrun by business advisers and made some almost ruinous investment decisions.

TOR BRITANNIA AND TOR SCANDINAVIA

In the early 1980s, DFDS began a phase of unprecedented expansion. The company snapped up several smaller ferry lines and even entered the American cruise market. Most of the ferry purchases were unwise as the ships were ageing and the routes marginally profitable, but among their many acquisitions, DFDS gained control of the Tor Line from its financially ailing Swedish parent, the Salén group, in 1981. In doing so, they not only acquired a large and successful network of ro-ro freight services, but also two of the largest and most outstanding North Sea passenger liners of their generation, the magnificent 15,650-ton *Tor Britannia* and *Tor Scandinavia*.

Completed by the Flender Werft yard at Lübeck in 1975 and 1976, respectively, these ships had brought never-before-seen luxury to the Tor Line's triangular Felixstowe-Gothenburg-Amsterdam routes. In order to fit through the tidal lock at Amsterdam, their width was restricted to 23.6 metres, and so, to compensate, they were exceptionally long. To cut sailing times significantly, they were also very fast with four powerful Pielstick PC3 engines giving a top speed of over 26 knots. With a sharp clipper bow, a long and low superstructure, a massive streamlined funnel and a sweeping tier of sun decks at the stern, each of the Tor sisters was impressively good-looking.

Designers from Britain and Scandinavia were assembled to produce the interiors of the pair. While first and foremost intended for North Sea routes, the Tor ships were also designed with the possibility in mind of being used as cruise liners. They featured outdoor lido areas with sheltering glass screens on their topmost decks forward of the funnel. The majority of the cabins were located forward, away from the noise of the engine uptakes, and the public rooms were spread over two decks towards the stern. The main deck contained a large café and grill and this was linked to the restaurant by an attractive arcade on the port side. These rooms were all the work of Kay Kørbing and were decorated in the bright colours typical of the period. Kørbing was also responsible for the cabins and the companionways and for co-ordinating the work of the other designers. On the boat deck, the Finnish husband and wife team of Vuokko and Thorsten Laakso boldly decorated the entertainment spaces. Forward, there was a large circular nightclub in orange and red tones and aft was the disco and casino in orange and green with startling psychedelic murals.

As well as being very successful in the North Sea services on various routes, the *Tor Scandinavia* was chartered during successive winters to sail to the Middle- and Far East to promote Dutch goods and trade. Her last such voyage was during the winter of 1982-83. Meanwhile DFDS intended to send *Tor Britannia* to join Scandinavian World Cruises, its American cruising operation, as the *Scandinavian Star* in 1981. The idea was abandoned as the group was plunged into a serious financial crisis. It had expanded too quickly and by 1983 many of its subsidiaries were making considerable losses, especially Scandinavian World Cruises (see below).

Radical action was called for. Under new management, DFDS was re-structured and the troublesome subsidiaries were sold off. Many routes were abandoned and several ships were sold, including *Tor Scandinavia* and *Dana Anglia*, which went to an investment bank, Dansk

The imposing *Tor Britannia* arrives at Felixstowe in 1980, shortly before her acquisition by DFDS. The faint outline of 'Sessan' can still be seen on her blue hull, the result of a short-lived marketing alliance between Sessan Line and Tor Line. Sessan was taken over by its Kattegatt rival, Stena Line, while Tor was absorbed into the burgeoning DFDS empire.
Ambrose Greenway

Investeringsfond. Unlike the rest, these were chartered back and continued in service. The *Dana Regina* and the *Dana Gloria*, a former Finnish ferry which had been bought in 1981, were moved from the North Sea to boost the reliably profitable Copenhagen-Oslo route. It was then that the Tor sisters became a great asset as their speed enabled them to cover an intensive schedule on both the Harwich-Esbjerg and Harwich-Gothenburg routes. They were repainted in the new company livery for passenger ships – white all over with a blue waistband and diagonal 'go faster stripes' in three shades of blue.

In 1991, Blohm & Voss in Hamburg rebuilt the two ships, at which time the Swedish architect Robert Tillberg almost obliterated their original interiors. They were renamed *Prince of Scandinavia* (the former *Tor Britannia*) and *Princess of Scandinavia* (ex-*Tor Scandinavia*). In 1996, the *Prince of Scandinavia* was chartered to the Tunisian company Cotunav to sail in the Mediterranean for one summer season. After further rebuilding work at the Gdansk shipyard in Poland in 1998, during which they were fitted with sponsons to comply with new SOLAS regulations, both ships at present continue in front line North Sea service.

THE REORGANISED FLEET

Of DFDS's other ships, the *England* was laid up at the end of the 1982 summer season and sold the following year to Cunard for service between Cape Town and Port Stanley, carrying workers and equipment involved in building the Falkland Islands airport. Always a 'good sea boat', she coped admirably with the rough conditions she encountered during her long voyages across the South Atlantic. There followed a spell in lay-up at Birkenhead and then, in 1986, she was sold to the Greek oil and property tycoon John S. Latsis who at first used her in the Red Sea as the *America XIII* and, later, as the *Emma*. Latterly laid up at Eleusis, she was totally gutted for conversion into a private yacht, but the project was abandoned. Named *Europe*, but reduced to an empty, rusted shell, she was eventually sold for scrap. En route to the breakers, she sank in the Red Sea in April, 2001.

The *Winston Churchill* was more fortunate and continued in service on various routes between Esbjerg, Newcastle, the Faroe Islands and Gothenburg. While sailing from there to Newcastle in August, 1979, she was nearly lost when she ran aground on Vinga Island and the engine room flooded. Everyone was rescued and the ship was salvaged. It was not until the following summer that repairs, which included the construction of a new bottom, were completed. Later, in 1987, she commenced a series of highly popular spring and autumn cruises to the Norwegian fjords and the Baltic ports. After a sensitive refurbishment at Rendsburg in 1989, she remained in DFDS service until 1996 when she was damaged by an engine room fire while bunkering at Esbjerg. Sold to a Norwegian, Norman Tandberg, for service in the Gulf of Mexico as the *Mayan Express*, she was sent to the Westcon shipyard at Olen in the Alfjord near Stavanger for repair. She has been laid up ever since, caught in a financial dispute between the yard and her owners. As this is written, she has passed into the hands of the shipyard and is being offered for sale.

Unfortunately, by now she is in very poor external condition – but her engines remain sound.

The *Dana Regina* was sold to the Swedish firm Nordström and Thulin in 1989 for further service in the Baltic. Known at different times as *Nord Estonia* and *Thor Heyerdahl*, she is now the *Vana Tallinn*, operating mini-cruises from Helsinki to Tallinn for the Estonian Hansatee Line (which trades as Tallink) and painted in a garish colour scheme of blue and red stripes.

In recent years, DFDS has been much more cautious about ordering new ships and the few passenger vessels it has purchased have all been second-hand. The most impressive recent addition to the fleet is the cruise ferry *Pearl of Scandinavia*. Originally completed in 1988 as the *Athena* for Rederi Slite, the Swedish partner in one of the giants of the Baltic ferry industry, the Viking Line, she later found her way to the Far East. There she operated for Star Cruises as the *Langkapuri Star Aquarius*. Purchased by DFDS in 2001 and extensively refurbished, she now sails between Copenhagen and Oslo. Her diverse career serves to illustrate how close, and at times indistinguishable, contemporary Scandinavian cruise ship and ferry designs have become.

Østasiatiske Kompagni - The East Asiatic Company

Founded in 1897 by the mercurial Danish seaman and entrepreneur Hans Niel Andersen, with the active support of the Danish government and the blessing of the Royal Family, the Østasiatiske Kompagni became one of the largest shipping and trading enterprises in Denmark.

H. N. Andersen was born in 1852 in Nakskov, a shipbuilding town on the island of Lolland. There, he was apprenticed to Hr. Ridersborg, a local shipbuilder, who taught him to become a ship's carpenter. His real ambition, however, was to go to sea and, aged 19, he

The 1890-vintage *Doune Castle* was sold in 1904 to become Det Vestindiske Kompagni's *St. Domingo*. The following year, she was absorbed into the EAC fleet and renamed *Curonia*. *Laurence Dunn Collection*

The revolutionary motor ship *Selandia* introduced a new profile to the East Asiatic Company's fleet by dispensing with a funnel altogether. This set the style for many of the company's subsequent passenger motor vessels. *Laurence Dunn Collection*

joined the crew of the sailing ship *Mars* for a return voyage to South America. Only around 18 months later, in 1873, Andersen signed on for his first voyage to the Far East. The vast potential wealth of the East, particularly Hong Kong, made a deep impression on the young man. In 1884, and by then a master mariner, he founded his own merchant's business, Andersen and Company, in Bangkok. He acquired concessions for the export of teak and for the import of manufactured goods from Europe. A few small vessels were purchased and, with trade flourishing, a branch office was opened in Copenhagen in 1894. Three years later, Andersen founded the Østasiatiske Kompagni, which took over Andersen and Company's interests and began trading officially in March, 1897.

Much of Andersen's success came from his remarkable energy and organising ability. He was politically astute and diplomatic and he became highly influential. Quite apart from his successes in the worlds of shipping and commerce, his influence was felt during the First World War when he visited King George V, the Tsar in Moscow and even the Kaiser in Berlin, in an effort to end the fighting. He remained the East Asiatic Company's chairman and guiding light until his death in 1937, aged 85.

The company's first ship was a small wooden three-masted barquentine called *Ragnhild*. However, it was not long before steamers and, later, motorships joined the burgeoning fleet. In 1905, the firm bought Det Vestindiske Kompagni, also of Copenhagen, which ran a service to the West Indies and whose fleet contained the passenger ship *St. Domingo*, which had started life as the Union-Castle Line's *Doune Castle*. She was soon renamed *Curonia*. Originally designed for the Mauritius trade, she had been built by Barclay, Curle & Co., Ltd. of Glasgow in 1890. Three further ex-Union-Castle liners joined the fleet in 1905 – the *Raglan Castle* (also re-named *St. Domingo*), *Dunolly Castle* (which became *Juliette*) and *Arundel Castle* (which was given the name *Birma*). The first two were also products of Barclay, Curle and dated from 1897, while the *Arundel Castle* had been built by Fairfield, also on the Clyde, in 1894. All measured something over 4,000 gross tons. Meanwhile, a larger number of mainly second-hand cargo vessels were purchased to increase capacity and to improve the frequency of services.

In 1906, the company's interests expanded to encompass the North Atlantic trade through a new subsidiary, the Russian American Line. This transatlantic service was bolstered in 1908 by the addition of a new flagship, the *Russia*, an 8,596-ton twin-funnelled steamship built by Barclay, Curle & Co., Ltd. She was followed in 1910 by the 7,858-ton *Kursk* from the same yard. They were robust, conventional, workaday ships, but the East Asiatic Company's next significant addition was revolutionary – and was to represent an important milestone in the history of ship design.

SELANDIA – THE MOTOR SHIP PIONEER

One of Burmeister & Wain's directors, Ivar Knudsen, had been intrigued by the possibilities of using Rudolph Diesel's oil engine for the propulsion of sea-going ships and had supervised the design and construction of a prototype marine diesel engine as early as 1897. The Italians were producing diesel engines for small ships by

The white-liveried motor passenger-cargo liner *Erria*, built at Nakskov in 1932, was typical of the East Asiatic Company's newbuildings of the inter-war years. *Author Collection*

1906, but it was the Danes and the Dutch who produced the first diesel-powered deep-sea vessels. Knudsen persuaded H. N. Andersen to order a hugely important ship in December, 1910. Designed by the talented naval architects of the Burmeister & Wain shipyard, the 4,964 gross ton *Selandia* was principally a cargo carrier but had accommodation for 28 passengers and her interiors were designed by Carl Brummer. Having previously devised schemes for DFDS's transatlantic liners, Brummer had become perhaps the first architect to specialise in ship interior design and his carefully-controlled neo-classical scheme set the pattern for subsequent East Asiatic passenger-cargo vessels. Externally, the *Selandia*'s distinctive three-masted, funnel-less profile (with slender exhausts attached to the centre mast) attracted much comment.

She ran trials on the 15th February, 1912 and reached 12 knots. Her maiden voyage departed Copenhagen on the 22nd February and members of the Danish Royal Family followed her passage along the Danish coast as far as Elsinore. Arriving on the Thames on the 27th February, she was inspected by leaders of the British shipping industry. Winston Churchill, then First Lord of the Admiralty, was shown over her and made a speech praising this "epochal" advance in the development of shipping. The *Selandia* proved to be highly successful and a succession of further vessels of similar design followed her in the ensuing decades. Her near-sister, *Jutlandia*, a

The handsome twin-funnelled *Europa* is seen on trials in 1931. She was the second of three vessels ordered from Burmeister & Wain for the company's transatlantic service. *Laurence Dunn Collection*

product of the Barclay, Curle yard, was in fact the first British-built motorship.

For fully-fledged passenger vessels, however, the quietness of steam remained preferable to the relatively noisy, vibrating diesel alternative, so in 1912 a further Barclay, Curle-built steamship, the 6,503-ton *Czar*, joined the transatlantic fleet. A handsome vessel, she was followed from the same yard in 1915 by the 6,598-ton *Czaritza*. The Russian Revolution of 1917 brought the Russian American Line to an end but in 1920 the transatlantic ships were placed on the Libau – New York run under the name Baltic American Line. The *Russia* now became the *Latvia* and the *Kursk*, *Czar* and *Czaritza* were renamed *Polonia*, *Estonia* and *Lituania* respectively. A decade later, the Baltic American subsidiary was sold to the Polish government and became the new Gdynia America Line, in which the East Asiatic Company initially retained a financial interest.

In its first years, the East Asiatic Company's services had consisted mainly of sailings to Bangkok from Copenhagen and other European ports, but by 1912 the growth of the fleet had enabled it to maintain five regular routes to the East. Bi-weekly sailings were made to Hong Kong, Shanghai and Japan from Copenhagen, Gothenburg and Antwerp; three-weekly sailings to Bangkok from Copenhagen, Middlesbrough, Antwerp and Genoa via Port Said, Colombo and Singapore; four-weekly to the West Indies; and at longer intervals to South Africa and to the United Sates Pacific coast ports. By the 1920s, eight regular lines were in operation from Danish and other European ports to Japan, Siam, Java, South Africa, Australia, Canada and to Cuba, Mexico and the U.S.A. Further batches of funnel-less motor cargo liners were ordered.

THE INTER-WAR YEARS

While a succession of three- and four-masted passenger-cargo motorships, still without funnels, entered service during the 1920s – such as the *Malaya*, *Java*, *Danmark*, *Lalandia* and *Meonia* – it was not until 1929 that another fully-fledged passenger liner was delivered by Burmeister & Wain. The 10,110-ton *Amerika* was a splendid twin-funnelled (but single screw) motorship. She was the first to be fitted with two examples of a new, more powerful type of Burmeister & Wain engine and reached a speed of 16.55 knots on trials. First class accommodation was provided for 52 passengers, but in the slightly improved sister *Europa* of 1931 this was increased to 56. A similar, but rather larger third sister, the *Canada*, was competed in 1935. All three ships were war casualties, the *Canada* being the first East Asiatic ship to be sunk when she struck a mine in the English Channel on the 3rd November, 1939. She was certainly the largest – but not the most famous – of the company's passenger ships. That honour went to the 8,4457-ton *Jutlandia*, completed in 1934 at H. N. Andersen's hometown of Nakskov. Yet another four-masted funnel-less motorship, her fame came after she was converted in 1950 to a Danish Government hospital ship for the United Nations during the Korean War. Instead of 59 passengers, she could now accommodate 300 patients. She was re-converted and resumed her normal trade from Denmark to the Far East in 1954.

During the Second World War, much of the East Asiatic fleet was scattered and many ships were lost. Fortunately, the company recovered quickly and by the mid-1950s it was stronger than ever. By this stage, its fleet consisted almost entirely of cargo liners, each able to carry only a handful of passengers, and tankers. The last of the graceful, four-masted passenger-cargo liners to enter service was the *Falstria*. Her keel had been laid in Nakskov back in 1940 but completion had been delayed by the War. Finally, on the 30th November, 1945, she entered service, sailing from Copenhagen to New York. During a 19-year career with East Asiatic, she was to sail on most of its principal post-War routes, from Denmark to North and South America and to the Far East. Although she was principally a cargo-carrier, she had comfortable, if traditionally decorated, accommodation for 54 passengers in 22 doubles and 10 singles. Public rooms consisted of a dining room, an impressive hallway with a domed cupola, a smoking room, a lounge-bar and a children's room. There was even a small swimming pool.

Only a few of the pre-War passenger-cargo vessels remained in service until the early 1960s. Latterly, the East Asiatic Company became an operator of container ships. More recently, however, its shipping interests were absorbed into the giant Maersk Line. The East Asiatic Company still exists as a business but is no longer a shipowner.

A pleasing stern quarter view of the second *Jutlandia* – her graceful lines somewhat reminiscent of the age of sailing ships. Uniquely amongst the EAC fleet, she had a Maierform bow. *Author Collection*

2
The Norwegian Liners

Den Norske Amerikalinje - Norwegian America Line

Norway has been a nation of seafarers since Viking times, but her emergence as a major maritime power has been comparatively recent. The repeal by Britain in 1850 of the Navigation Laws, which had until then excluded foreign carriers from trading between Britain and her colonies, paved the way for Norway's participation in international trade on a worldwide scale. Expansion was rapid and by 1880 the country had the third largest merchant fleet in the World, an immense achievement for so small a nation.

The transition from sail to steam was initially a slow one, brought about by the beginning of regular liner services by the shipowners of rival countries and the need to maintain schedules. The first Norwegians to develop steamship services were the merchant families of Bergen, who exported fish and other perishable commodities and for whom speed was essential. The formation of Norway's own transatlantic passenger line, however, was a consequence of the massive emigration from Norway to the New World, an exodus that grew beyond the capabilities of the earlier sailing ships. In 1825, when the first emigrant ship had left Stavanger, the country's population was little over one million, yet within three generations the number of Norwegians who had crossed the Atlantic had reached three-quarters of a million. (In proportion to the nation's population, this migration was exceeded only by the Irish.) In the 1870s, emigration was running at 14,000 a year, yet passengers to Quebec still faced a passage of around eight weeks.

It was against this background that a company was founded in Bergen to run a steamship service to North America, conveying emigrants in summer and cargo in winter. The Norwegian America Steamship Line operated only for a short time before a temporary decline in emigration starting in 1874 forced it to close. In 1879, the Thingvalla Line was formed in Copenhagen and established a regular service between Scandinavia and America, picking up Norwegian emigrants at Kristiania (later renamed Oslo) and Kristiansand. For over 30 years, Thingvalla and its successor, DFDS, carried the bulk of this traffic.

NATIONAL PRIDE AND THE NEW LINE

By the early 1900s, there was again enthusiasm for a Norwegian-flag transatlantic passenger service. The union between Norway and Sweden was dissolved in 1905 and Norway became a fully independent state for the first time. There were many sceptics, but patriotism won through and financial backing for the transatlantic project was secured from prosperous Norwegian descendants in North America. The formation of the Norwegian America Line was strongly contested by DFDS who thought that any new line should be a joint Scandinavian venture, though naturally under Danish management. There was some support for this idea, but the Danes had underestimated the extent of the Norwegians' national feeling and their ability to finance the venture. Besides, Sweden also opposed the Danish plan and the Swedish American Line was formed in 1915.

The Norske-Amerikalinje officially came into being in Kristiania in August, 1910 and the first election to the board of directors took place the following February. Later, in November 1911, the company signed a contract with Cammell Laird & Co., Ltd. of Birkenhead for the construction of a 10,000-ton liner. A sister ship was ordered from the same yard that December. The first-ever Norwegian America liner was named *Kristianiafjord* and on

The first of the Norwegian America liners, the short-lived *Kristianiafjord*, is pictured steaming slowly off Bergen harbour, early in her career.
Ambrose Greenway Collection

A comfortably appointed lounge in first class onboard the *Kristianiafjord*. This was actually atypical of the accommodation on the first generation of Norwegian America liners, which had relatively large capacities for third class emigrants, accommodated amid much more spartan surroundings.
Williamson Art Gallery & Museum, Cammell Laird Archive

the 4th June, 1913 she opened the route from Kristiania to New York with calls en route at Kristiansand, Stavanger and Bergen. His Majesty King Haakon VII and members of the Norwegian Parliament were guests of the company for the coastal voyage to Bergen and the inauguration of the new service was followed with great enthusiasm. In September, 1913 the *Kristianiafjord* was joined by her sister *Bergensfjord* and together they operated a successful two-ship service. Both liners were coal-burners of 10,650 gross tons with a service speed of 15 knots and carried passengers in three classes: 104 first, 232 second and 762 third.

They had not been in service for a year when the First World War broke out. Norway's neutrality ensured the continuation of the service and, ironically, the War helped to strengthen the link from Bergen to New York as it became one of the few vital means of communication between Europe and America. The success of the venture led the Norwegian America Line to plan a three-ship service and a contract was signed with Cammell Laird & Co., Ltd. in January, 1915 for the construction of another liner. However, with the British merchant fleet suffering mounting losses, British shipyards were under increasing strain to make good the shortage of tonnage and the

The *Kristianiafjord's* very masculine smoking room with its buttoned leather chairs.
Williamson Art Gallery & Museum, Cammell Laird Archive

An undated postcard shows the *Bergensfjord* as she appeared in the 1920s.
Ambrose Greenway Collection

Admiralty insisted that ships then under construction for neutral nations should be requisitioned. The contract was accordingly suspended. The ship was not launched until May, 1917 but soon afterwards disaster struck the Norwegian America Line when the *Kristianiafjord* ran aground off Newfoundland and became a total loss. Fortunately, all her passengers and crew were saved. It was imperative that she be replaced and the Norwegians persuaded the British government to permit the newbuilding, which was called *Stavangerfjord*, to be handed over to them. She was delivered in the autumn of 1918. She sailed empty and incomplete to New York, releasing space at the shipyard for British vessels, and was fitted out in the United States.

The *Stavangerfjord*, one of Norwegian America's most successful and enduring liners, is greeted by a large crowd as she arrives at her berth in Oslo harbour in the early 1920s. *Author Collection*

The rather austere third class dining saloon on the *Stavangerfjord* with its long tables, fixed chairs and prominent, exposed ceiling ducting. Spaces such as this were thoroughly rebuilt once emigration to the USA declined in the mid-1920s and a more discerning tourist clientele had to be catered to.
Williamson Art Gallery & Museum, Cammell Laird Archive

THE FAITHFUL STAVANGERFJORD

The *Stavangerfjord* was slightly larger than the earlier pair, with room for 88 first, 318 second and 820 third class passengers. Although small and slow in comparison with the British and German Atlantic record breakers, she was a purposeful-looking ship with a straight stem, a modern cruiser stern and two very tall, almost vertical funnels. She was to become one of the most successful and enduring of all the Atlantic liners. With the *Bergensfjord*, she maintained the Norway-New York service for almost the entire period between the wars and during this time both ships carried well over 400,000 passengers. For a while, emigrants continued to account for many of the westbound passengers, but American restrictions on immigration had largely ended this exodus by the mid-1920s.

During and after the First World War, the Norwegian America Line began to build up its cargo fleet to cater for the growing freight traffic, particularly grain imports from North America to Scandinavia. Calls were also introduced at Canadian ports for both passengers and cargo. In 1921, the company purchased the Scandinavian East Africa Line, which had been formed in 1912 and from then on it also maintained services from Northern Europe to East Africa, Madagascar, Réunion and Mauritius. (This involvement later developed into more extensive services to the African continent.)

In 1920, the *Bergensfjord* was converted to burn oil, which slightly increased her speed, and the *Stavangerfjord* was similarly altered in 1924. The following year, the *Stavangerfjord* operated the line's first cruise to the North Cape and she made several such trips in the late 'twenties and 'thirties. By now, the Norwegian America ships were being somewhat overshadowed by the new Swedish American liners. In 1931-32, therefore, they were sent to the A.G. Weser yard to be upgraded and to have their reciprocating machinery augmented by the installation of low-pressure turbines. This increased their speed to $17^{1}/_{2}$ knots and considerably reduced their fuel consumption. Alterations were made to their passenger accommodation, with the combining of first and second class into a new cabin class and a decrease in the number of third class berths.

As this view shows, the short-lived *Oslofjord* of 1938 was a solid motor ship which must have looked splendid in the Norwegian America Line livery. Note that she has a fully-enclosed wheel house - an unusual feature for a passenger ship of her period. *Ambrose Greenway Collection*

THE ILL-FATED FLAGSHIP

In the mid-1930s, the company decided on the construction of a new, more luxurious liner, suitable both for tourist travel and cruising. Thus in November, 1935, the line's new Technical Director, G. Zetlitz-Nilsson started the design development and bids were received from a number of shipyards. The lowest of these was from the Cantieri Riuniti dell'Adriatico at Monfalcone in Italy. However, the Italian invasion of Abyssinia and the resulting League of Nations sanctions caused the Norwegians to look elsewhere. It was indeed ironic that instead of going to Fascist Italy, the order went to Nazi Germany and the contract was awarded to the Bremen shipyard of Deutsche Schiff- und Maschinenbau A.G. Weser, usually known as Deschimag-Weser.

The new *Oslofjord* entered service on the North Atlantic route in June, 1938. At 18,650 gross tons, she was considerably larger than the company's earlier ships and was also its first oil-engined passenger liner. She could carry 800 passengers in three classes – 150 cabin, 250 tourist and 400 third – with comfortable saloons finished in a variety of Scandinavian timbers. Her interiors, designed by Georg Eliassen, were in the National Romantic idiom, being embellished with ornately carved woodwork and numerous pieces of Norwegian folk art. Interestingly, her most outstanding space was the tourist class Leif Eriksson Hall, panelled in Norwegian pine. Indeed, on the *Oslofjord* and all subsequent Norwegian America passenger ships, tourist class rooms were spacious and of a very high standard.

Prior to entering North Atlantic service, a special maiden 'Jubilee Cruise' was arranged to celebrate the line's 25th anniversary. The new flagship sailed from Oslo on the 21st May to Copenhagen, Ålesund, Hjorundfjord, Andalnes and Bergen. During a banquet held in Oslo on the ship's return, H.M. King Haakon VII bestowed the Order of St. Olav upon Director Henriksen and Captain K. S. Irgens. The *Oslofjord* sailed from Oslo on her first crossing to New York on the 4th June, 1938.

During the winter of 1938-39, she opened a new chapter in the history of the Norwegian America Line when she was chartered to a New York travel agency to make a series of cruises from that port to Havana and Nassau. Except for the cruising yacht *Stella Polaris*, which we shall meet in a later chapter, the *Oslofjord* was the first Norwegian ship to cruise these waters.

The commissioning of the *Oslofjord* enabled the older *Stavangerfjord* to be withdrawn for a thorough modernisation. Her tall, thin funnels were replaced by rather shorter, wider ones, resembling those of the *Oslofjord*. With three passenger liners in service, the company seemed well placed to capture a significant share of the North Atlantic traffic. Its cargo services had also expanded to thirteen ships, but the threat of war in Europe was looming.

In December 1939, the *Stavangerfjord* arrived at Oslo and was laid up. The other two liners remained in service but in March, 1940 the *Bergensfjord* was held up in New York due to the refusal of her master to carry United States mails. He considered this would be putting the vessel at undue risk and was eventually allowed to sail for Norway without the mail. The ship arrived at Oslo at the beginning of April and left again shortly afterwards for New York. A few days later, on the 9th April, Norway was invaded. The *Bergensfjord* thus managed to escape, but had a hazardous crossing, dodging German U-boats. She reached New York on the 15th April. The *Oslofjord*, too, was safely on the other side of the Atlantic and both ships were placed at the service of the Allies. In Norway, the German occupying army, finding the *Stavangerfjord* berthed at Oslo, commandeered her as a troop depot ship and she spent the entire period of the War tied up at her berth.

Following her arrival in New York, the *Bergensfjord* was laid up until November when she was taken over by the British Ministry of War Transport and sailed to Halifax for conversion to a troopship, a rôle in which she operated with distinction throughout the War. At the same time, the *Oslofjord* was ordered to sail to the U.K. for troopship conversion. Regrettably, on the 13th December, having arrived off the Tyne, she was badly damaged by an acoustic mine and, although beached, she became a total loss.

In February 1946, after surviving the War without serious mishap, the *Bergensfjord* became one of the first vessels to be chartered to carry G.I. brides to the United States. After this duty, she was handed back to her owners but, at 33 years old, she was considered unsuitable for her original rôle. She was sold in 1946 to Panamanian Lines, one of the eventual constituents of the Home Lines, and was rebuilt at Genoa and renamed *Argentina* for service between Italy and the River Plate ports. Later, she operated between Italy and Venezuela and on several North Atlantic routes before being sold in 1953 to the Zim Israel Navigation Co. for service between Haifa, Marseilles and New York as the *Jerusalem*. Her final Atlantic crossing was in 1955. She was eventually scrapped in 1959 as the *Aliya* after 46 years of service.

The *Stavangerfjord* had, in contrast, spent a rather sheltered war period in the comparative safety of Oslo harbour. After the War had ended, she served as a repatriation ship before being given an extensive overhaul. In 1946, she made the Norwegian America Line's first post-War sailing to New York. Overall, the company's fleet had suffered heavy losses, the hardest blow being the mining of the *Oslofjord*. This, together with the disposal of the *Bergensfjord*, left the line with only one passenger ship and for nearly four years the *Stavangerfjord* operated the Oslo-Bergen-New York service on her own.

THE POST-WAR OSLOFJORD.

Careful consideration was given to the design of a new *Oslofjord*. Preparatory design work had already been carried out during the War by the company's new Chief Naval Architect, Kaare Haug, who was to be responsible for all subsequent Norwegian America liners. A contract was signed in 1948 with the Nederlandsche Dok en Scheepsbouw company of Amsterdam and the keel was laid in March of that year. Norway's Kronprinsesse Martha performed the launching ceremony on the 2nd April, 1949 and by mid-October, having created something of a record for rapid fitting out, the new liner was ready for service.

The *Oslofjord* was a 16,800-ton motor ship with Stork oil engines, which provided a speed of 20 knots. The hull was mainly of welded construction, with sleek lines to cut through the Atlantic waves with the greatest ease. Within, there were holds for 2,500 tons of cargo, handled by derricks and electric cranes fore and aft, although it was unfortunate that at first there proved to be insufficient demand for so much cargo space. Passenger accommodation was provided for 179 in first class and 467 in tourist class and, although primarily intended as an Atlantic liner, the *Oslofjord* was also designed for the possibility of making winter cruises.

The interiors were the work of Arnstein Arneberg, who had designed Oslo's famous City Hall, and the Dutch architect J. A. Van Tienhoven, later best known for his work on Holland-America's spectacular *Rotterdam*. The *Oslofjord* had highly polished inlaid woodwork throughout,

During the 1950s, the company's brochures boasted that 'Streamlined Beauty and Yachtlike Elegance of design characterize Norwegian America Line ships' - no wonder they were so proud of their new *Oslofjord*, whose aluminium superstructure brought a new and often-imitated, curvaceous profile to transatlantic liners.
Ambrose Greenway Collection

The veteran *Stavangerfjord* was the oldest transatlantic liner in service by the 1960s. Known as 'the dowager of the North Atlantic', she retained a loyal following who appreciated her cosy, ornately carved interiors. She is seen tied up at New York towards the end of her long and distinguished career. *Mick Lindsay Collection*

A commodious lounge onboard the *Oslofjord*, characterised by finely-crafted wood veneers, comfortable armchairs and generous displays of Norwegian folk art. *Author Collection*

The Garden Lounge was a popular look-out which wrapped around the first class lounge and library at the forward end of the *Oslofjord's* superstructure. The architect of this and other first class spaces was Arnstein Arneberg. *Author Collection*

linoleum floors with rugs, bent wood chairs and couches. It was all comfortable, homely but unremarkable – reflecting the austerity and shortages of the early post-War years.

What was innovative for Norwegian America was the idea of designing the *Oslofjord* as a dual-rôle liner and cruise ship. In addition to an indoor swimming pool, an open air lido was installed on the after deck during cruises and a particular feature of the ship was the semi-circular Garden Lounge on the Promenade Deck, looking forward through large windows. The library, behind, had a view forward through the Garden Lounge and was decorated with tapestries depicting Norwegian outdoor life. Moving aft, there was an impressive hallway with a grand staircase; then a lounge with a dance floor and a cocktail bar and ladies' lounge on either side. The remainder of the Promenade Deck was given over to tourist class facilities – a large lounge-cum-ballroom, a writing room and an aft-facing smoking room. The first class smoking room was one deck higher on the Sun Deck, while the dining rooms were low down in the hull on B Deck, where passengers would be less conscious of the ship's motion in rough weather. The *Oslofjord* had a total of nine decks and her superstructure made extensive use of aluminium alloy.

After the successful completion of her trials, the new liner made a cruise from Amsterdam to Oslo, where she arrived amid great celebrations. She then sailed on her maiden transatlantic voyage on the 26th November, 1949, from Oslo to New York via Copenhagen, Kristiansand, Stavanger and Bergen. An attractive, elegant vessel, she was soon a favourite with passengers and operated the North Atlantic service together with the elderly *Stavangerfjord*, as well as performing several Caribbean cruises from New York and longer voyages to the Mediterranean and Pacific areas.

A rather alarming incident occurred to the *Stavangerfjord* in December, 1953. She had left New York with over 600 passengers onboard and encountered strong winds and heavy seas. The weather deteriorated rapidly, with winds approaching gale force, and on the 9th December, some 340 miles north-east of Cape Race, the *Stavangerfjord's* rudder was completely ripped away from her stern. She hove-to and awaited assistance. Fortunately, one of the company's cargo vessels, the *Lyngenfjord*, was in

The Tyne-built *Bergensfjord*, Norwegian America's second post-War liner, had an altogether more massive superstructure with less cargo space. A welcome feature was her glazed promenade deck.
Mick Lindsay Collection

the area and was diverted to the aid of the damaged passenger ship. A line was put aboard and the *Lyngenfjord* attempted to tow her fleetmate, but heavy seas made this impossible and the towline parted. The master of the *Stavangerfjord*, Captain Olaf Bjorenstad, decided to resume the crossing at a speed of 10 knots, attempting to steer by using the ship's twin screws. The *Lyngenfjord* acted as an escort. On the 13th December, about 300 miles north-west of the British Isles, the famous British ocean-going tug *Turmoil* took over escort duties and, six days later, the *Stavangerfjord* arrived safely in Oslo.

A NEW BERGENSFJORD

The success of the post-war passenger service and the growing popularity of cruising encouraged the company to place an order for another liner, slightly larger than the *Oslofjord* and carrying more passengers at the expense of cargo capacity. A contract was signed with Swan, Hunter & Wigham Richardson, Ltd., Wallsend-on-Tyne and the new ship, reviving the name *Bergensfjord*, was launched on the 18th July, 1955 by Princess Astrid of Norway and was delivered one month ahead of the contract date. She left the shipyard on the 14th May, 1956 for Bergen, Stavanger, Kristiansand and Oslo, where she arrived to a festive welcome on the Norwegian National Day, the 17th May.

As with the innovative *Oslofjord*, the new 18,750-ton *Bergensfjord* was designed by Kaare Haug. The most noticeable external difference between the two liners was the *Bergensfjord*'s altogether more massive superstructure, which at the time was claimed to be the largest all-welded aluminium alloy structure yet attempted on any ship. The engines were of the same type as those of the *Oslofjord*, but somewhat more powerful to give a speed in excess of 20 knots. Another innovation to improve comfort and safety in rough weather was the fitting of Denny-Brown stabilisers, which proved their worth early on when on trials the ship ran into a Force 8 gale off Fair Isle and was rolling 16 degrees. This alarming motion was completely

The first class public rooms, designed by Arnstein Arneberg, were spacious and carefully detailed. The grandest space in first class was the hallway, with its open tread spiral staircase and adjacent shopping arcade.
Author Collection

The *Bergensfjord's* colourful tourist class interiors were designed by the Dutch architect J.A. Van Tienhoven and were perhaps a precursor to his highly acclaimed work on the 1959 *Rotterdam*. The impressive dining room was located deep in the hull and had a double-height central section, lined with leather. On the end bulkhead is a mural by Per Krogh depicting a 'Voyage of Dreams'. *Author Collection*

eliminated once the stabilisers were deployed.

The *Bergensfjord* could carry 103 passengers in first class and 775 in tourist class. The interior design was again by Arnstein Arneberg and J. A. Van Tienhoven. Most public rooms for first class passengers were located forward on the promenade deck and included the dining room which had large windows overlooking the sea. The room was entered from a commodious foyer with a grand staircase sweeping down from the first class cabins above. Forward of the foyer was the Garden Lounge while above, on the sun deck, was the first class smoking room. Tourist class rooms, including a large ballroom, occupied the remainder of the promenade deck. The impressive tourist class dinning room on B-deck was two decks high.

Like the *Oslofjord*, the new *Bergensfjord* was designed for transatlantic service in the summer and cruising with a reduced passenger capacity in the winter, when an open swimming pool was installed over one of the cargo hatches. With the *Bergensfjord* in service, the Norwegian America Line again had three passenger liners and the opportunity was taken to withdraw the veteran *Stavangerfjord* for extensive renovation. She was sent to Swan, Hunter in September, 1956 for the improvements to be carried out. There, stabilisers were fitted as these had proven so successful on the new *Bergensfjord*.

The following February, the *Oslofjord* was undergoing routine maintenance at Hoboken, New Jersey. While she was in drydock, the blocks supporting her collapsed, causing damage to the ship and injuries to some of the crew. Fortunately, she was repaired and returned to service.

REPLACING THE STAVANGERFJORD

It was not long before attention was turned towards an eventual replacement for the veteran *Stavangerfjord*. In 1960, the Norwegian America Line directors instructed their technical department to draw up specifications for a luxurious two-class, 800-passenger liner for transatlantic service, which would have a capacity of 450 when cruising. The majority of the cabins were to be outside staterooms and all were to have showers and toilets. All passengers were to sleep in beds, not bunks, and both ballrooms and dining rooms were required to have sufficient capacity to accommodate all cruise passengers at the same time. Air conditioning was to be installed throughout for both passengers and crew, and both were to have their own outside swimming pools, as well as an indoor pool. The new liner's service speed was to be 22 knots and the latest safety regulations were to be exceeded by a wide margin. Like her predecessors, the new ship was to be a twin-screw

Bathed in sunlight, the beautiful *Sagafjord* makes a fine sight in Southampton Docks in August 1972. A Port Line cargo ship is berthed in the background. *Ivor Trevor-Jones*

motor vessel with an all-welded aluminium superstructure and, again, Kaare Haug was in charge of the design.

The specification for the new liner, requiring spacious public rooms and cabins, meant that the dimensions would have to be considerably increased in comparison with those of the *Oslofjord* and the *Bergensfjord*, although her width was restricted to only 80 feet because of the drydocking facilities in Oslo. The same basic hull form as on the earlier ships was chosen and in May, 1962 model tests were carried out at the Norwegian Technical High School in Trondheim. The greater length made the new hull more efficient than that of the *Bergensfjord* and further tests with a bulbous bow showed that fitting such an attachment would make no improvement. It would also, of course, have impaired the ship's ability to sail through ice.

In September, 1962 a contract for the construction of the ship was signed with the French shipbuilders Société des Forges et Chantiers de la Méditerranée of La Seyne, for delivery in 1965. The keel was laid in May, 1963 and later that year it was announced that the new ship was to be named *Sagafjord*.

Meanwhile, the decision had been taken to withdraw the *Stavangerfjord* and on the 3rd December, 1963, aged 45 years, she departed New York on her final transatlantic crossing. No other Atlantic liner had served a single owner for so long and, as she eased away from the pier, some 1,500 people were there to see her off. Her masts were topped with Christmas trees and a 125 feet long pennant fluttered above her superstructure. Despite the festivity, her ensign was flying at half-mast, for America and the World were mourning the late President Kennedy. The *Stavangerfjord* reached Oslo on the 14th December, having completed 770 Atlantic crossings. When Captain Odd Aspelund rang 'Finished With Engines', he was bringing to a close the career of a ship unequalled on the North Atlantic. In her 45 years, she had steamed nearly 2.8 million nautical miles and had carried 403,628 passengers, ranging from emigrants to Norwegian royalty. Shortly afterwards, she left Oslo on the long voyage to Hong Kong for scrap.

THE ELEGANT SAGAFJORD

At the same time, construction of the line's new flagship was continuing in France and on the 13th June, 1964 the *Sagafjord* was launched. She was eventually delivered on the 18th September, 1965, some six months behind schedule, and arrived in Oslo on the 24th. At 24,000 tons, she was considerably larger than the company's earlier ships, although she had the same unmistakable streamlined profile. Her superstructure was higher and longer, however, and she had a single mast. She was undoubtedly one of the most beautiful ocean liners ever built, with long, flowing lines and a remarkable consistency of form and detail. Behind her long, flared bow, the superstructure was piled up in receding tiers with swept-back bridge wings and an imposing tapered funnel, the profile of which matched the sweeping lines of the aft sun decks. Painted in the handsome Norwegian America livery, the *Sagafjord* made a fine, modern impression.

An international team of architects and designers was

Life aboard the *Sagafjord*: Ingrid Guse poses with her travelling companion, Pia, on her left and other friends in the Saga Dining Room. *Ingrid Guse*

responsible for the interior design and decoration under the co-ordination of the Norwegian firm, F. S. Platou. The veranda deck, on which most of the public rooms were situated, was arranged in open plan, giving a splendid impression of spaciousness. The precedent for this arrangement was, of course, the DFDS vessel *England*, completed the previous year with highly praised interiors by Kay Kørbing, who had a significant input in the design of the *Sagafjord*. As on the DFDS vessel, the traditional concept of a wraparound enclosed promenade was abandoned, thus allowing the public rooms to occupy the full width of the ship, with large windows overlooking the sea.

Forward on the veranda deck was the circular Garden Lounge, built on split levels around a dance floor. This handsome space, together with the adjoining library and writing room, was the work of Kay Kørbing. He recalls: 'The *Sagafjord* was among the most beautiful ships I was involved in. On an overnight vessel, every corner of space counts but, as this was a luxury liner, I could afford to be more generous. Compared with what the Italians and the French were building in the 'sixties, though, she was quite a modest ship. The design journals were full of articles about the *France* and the *Leonardo da Vinci* and how wonderful they were, but I think the *Sagafjord's* owners got much better value for money overall and every detail was carefully thought out by the design team. I produced a new version of my lounge chair for the Garden Lounge, with a wicker seat and back to give the feeling of a modern interpretation of the traditional ocean liner winter garden. I was very proud of the *Sagafjord*.'

The French architect Georges Peynet designed the theatre, immediately aft (previously he had planned the theatre of the *S.S. France*). The most spacious room on the ship was the magnificent ballroom, designed by the Norwegian Finn Nilsson. With its high ceiling and a floor area covering 8,000 square feet, a bright red colour scheme and subdued lighting, it was spacious, yet instantly welcoming. From this room, glass doors led out to the lido deck and open-air swimming pool, which had an

Designed by Kay Kørbing, the impressive forward stairway with open treads continued through the full height of the ship. The *Sagafjord's* hallways were characterised by the use of dark wood veneers and soft lighting. *Keld Helmer Petersen*

The *Sagafjord's* magnificent Saga Dining Room glowed as the light reflected in its matt gold walls and immaculate white table linen. Behind the photographer, through a glazed bulkhead, is the grand staircase at its entrance. *Author Collection*

The largest public room on *Sagafjord* was her commodious tourist class ballroom, located aft and with a glazed rear bulkhead. *Author Collection*

illuminated fountain at night. One deck above was the Polaris Nightclub, the work of Han Van Tienhoven, the brother of J. A. Van Tienhoven. He was also responsible for the main entrance hall. The magnificent Saga Dining Room seated 468 and was designed by F. S. Platou and Njål Eide. Its central section was two decks high and, descending a splendid staircase leading down from the deck above, passengers made a grand entrance through doors in a double height fully glazed bulkhead. Behind the staircase, there was a bas relief panel of Viking longboats by the noted Norwegian artist, Carl B. Gunnarson.

Everywhere there was an air of quiet luxury and spaciousness with large cabins (90 per cent of which were outside rooms) and wide, uncluttered corridors. Throughout, the ship was further enhanced by numerous specially commissioned works of art by contemporary Scandinavian artists.

Much thought was given to ways of introducing automation to enhance safety, so there was widespread use of remote control and closed-circuit television in the engine room. Many of these innovations arose from an intensive survey carried out aboard the *Bergensfjord* to assess areas where improvements could be made and the workload of the crew reduced. On the technical side, the *Sagafjord* had two Sulzer diesels and the ship was fitted with a bow thruster unit to make manoeuvring in confined spaces easier.

The *Sagafjord* sailed on her maiden transatlantic voyage from Oslo on the 2nd October, 1965 and on the 16th November she left New York on her first cruise to the West Indies. She soon established herself as one of the finest and most popular cruise ships afloat and spent an increasing part of her time in this rôle. Ingrid Guse remembers an eastbound transatlantic crossing in 1968: 'Like lots of young Danes in the 'sixties, I had ideas about going away to see the World, so I arranged to go over and work in the United States for a year. There I made some Scandinavian friends and we decided to sail home on the *Sagafjord*. We travelled second class, but it was one non-stop party from New York to Oslo. First class passengers who were in their twenties came down to second class and we had some great cabin parties. The men had large, square horn-rimmed sunglasses and suits like the ones Michael Caine or Richard Burton wore and the women had beehive hairdos, miniskirts and fur coats. Everyone felt so hip. I've been to the 'States several times since, but never again sailed across the Atlantic. It was catching the end of an era and I'll never forget that trip.'

The *Vistafjord* leans gently to port as she is swung by tugs to berth at Tilbury in the summer of 1978.
Ambrose Greenway

DEPARTURES FROM THE FLEET

Soon after the introduction of the *Sagafjord*, Norwegian America Line decided to offer their oldest passenger liner, the *Oslofjord*, for sale. Since there were no satisfactory offers for what was first and foremost an Atlantic liner, she was sent instead to Amsterdam for a major three-month refit, beginning in November, 1966. This work involved the re-styling of her accommodation, the extension of the promenade deck aft and the installation of a permanent lido area near the stern of the lengthened sun deck. Following these modifications, the *Oslofjord* returned to the transatlantic service and was again offered for sale or charter. She was subsequently chartered for ten months by the Greek Line to operate a series of cruises from Southampton to Portugal, the Atlantic islands and West Africa. When these voyages were completed, she returned to Norwegian America Line. She later began a further series of cruises from Southampton, but eventually, in the Autumn of 1969, she was chartered to the Costa Line for cruises from San Juan, Puerto Rico, in the winter and from Genoa in the summer. Renamed *Fulvia* and painted in Costa colours, she retained her Norwegian registry and sailed with Norwegian officers. Sadly, one of these voyages proved to be her last.

On the 19th July, 1970, during a cruise from Genoa to the Canaries with 488 passengers onboard, an engine room explosion started a fire which spread rapidly. The order was given to abandon ship and all onboard were evacuated by the lifeboats without loss of life. In response to the *Fulvia's* call for help, the French liner *Ancerville* diverted to the scene and picked up all the survivors. The next day, the *Fulvia*, still burning and now drifting off the island of Tenerife, was taken in tow, but her aluminium superstructure started to collapse and she sank despite all salvage efforts.

Meanwhile, the *Bergensfjord*, after only fifteen years of service with the company, was sold to the French Line as a replacement for their *Antilles* which had sunk after striking a reef and catching fire during a Caribbean cruise. The *Bergensfjord* was renamed *De Grasse* and operated some cruises which even took her back to Norwegian waters. However, faced with increasing costs, the French Line decided to abandon its passenger ship operations and the vessel returned to Norwegian ownership, being sold to Thoresen & Co., who renamed her *Rasa Sayang*.

Her new operations were quite unusual for the time: two week cruises from Singapore to Indonesia. The *Rasa Sayang's* reputation was scarred in June, 1977 when she caught fire and was abandoned by her passengers and crew. Fortunately, the damage was slight and within a year she was sold to Cypriot-flag Greeks who renamed her *Golden Moon*, supposedly for Aegean and Mediterranean cruising. In fact, she never left her moorings at Perama, near Piraeus. In 1979, she was reportedly chartered to a Dutch travel agency but this too came to nothing. A year later, her owners arranged a charter to the Soviet-controlled CTC Lines for cruising out of Sydney. Once again called *Rasa Sayang*, she was undergoing a refit at Perama when, on the 27th August, 1980, she was swept by fire and was towed into a shallow area of the harbour, where she capsized.

The Norse Bar onboard the *Vistafjord* was a popular and elegant venue for cocktails. *World Ship Society*

FINALE – THE VISTAFJORD

By the 1970s, the viability of Atlantic crossings was in terminal decline and Norwegian America Line wisely decided to concentrate on the up-market cruise business. In December, 1969 an order was placed with Swan Hunter Shipbuilders Ltd. on the Tyne for the construction of a further luxury cruise vessel, designed to the same high standard as the *Sagafjord*.

The new ship was launched on the 15th May, 1972 as the *Vistafjord* and was handed over to her owners exactly a year later. As with the *Bergensfjord* some seventeen years previously, the new flagship arrived in Oslo on Norwegian Independence Day, the 17th May, 1973. A great deal of advanced thinking had gone into the new design, yet the *Vistafjord's* external appearance retained the same attractive lines that characterised all of the company's post-War passenger ships. Her superstructure was a deck taller than that of the *Sagafjord* and she had a slightly more severe profile, without the inward curves of the earlier ship's bridge and funnel.

The *Vistafjord* had a gross tonnage of 24,291 grt and could carry 550 passengers in one class, served by 390 crew. Two Sulzer diesel engines gave a maximum speed of $22^{1}/_{2}$ knots. The extra deck reflected the ship's larger cruising capacity and, when she was new, it was claimed that no competitor offered so much space per passenger. Most of the cabins were outside rooms and 164 of them were singles which could be interconnected to become suites.

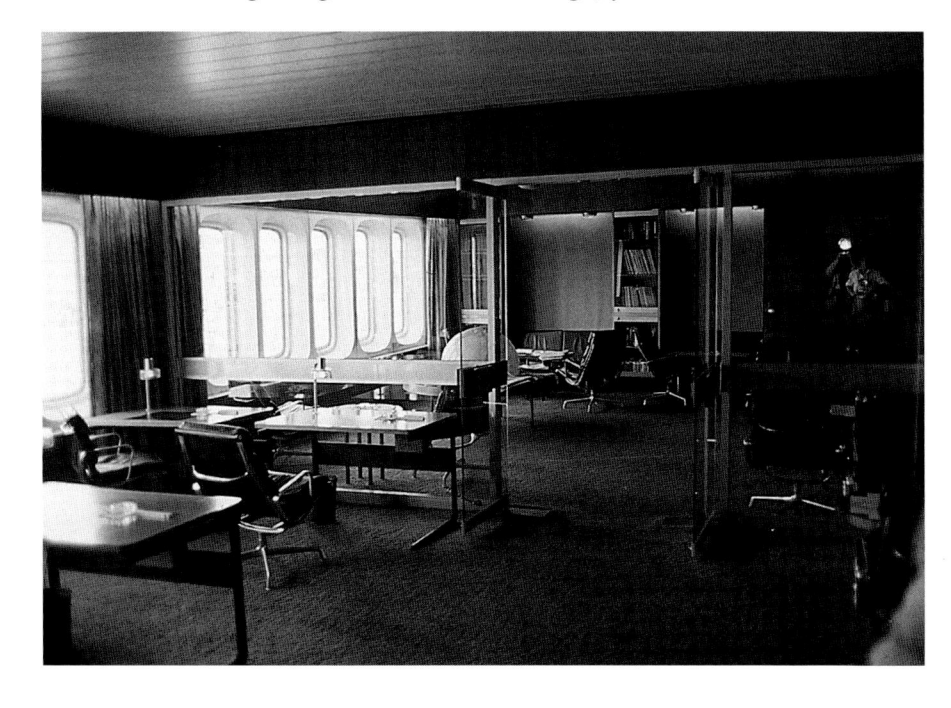

The *Vistafjord's* library was spacious and relaxing - ideal for whiling away the hours on the long cruises for which she was famed. *World Ship Society*

Located on her main deck and, consequently, fitted with large windows, the *Vistafjord's* dining room lacked the grandeur of that on her older sister. With its slightly raised ceiling and cheerful orange tones, it was bright and spacious and perhaps better suited to *Vistafjord's* role as a full-time cruise liner, making only occasional transatlantic positioning voyages. *World Ship Society*

The main public rooms on the Veranda Deck were arranged in a similar pattern to those on the *Sagafjord*. The Grand Ballroom, again the work of Finn Nilsson, was even larger than on the former ship. Forward on this deck were bars, a library, a writing room, an elegant theatre designed by Kaare Haug, and a very popular Garden Lounge by Kay Kørbing. One deck above the Grand Ballroom was the Club Viking, an intimate nightclub designed by Njål Eide, where dancing could continue into the early morning without disturbing anyone. The Vista Dining Room was located below the ballroom, one deck higher than the restaurant on the *Sagafjord*, and could accommodate all the passengers at one sitting with room to spare. Being only a single deck high, it was less impressive than that on the *Sagafjord* but had a feeling of roominess provided by its extra width and by the large windows along each side. Although her hallways were panelled in teak, overall the *Vistafjord* used less woodwork as her designers anticipated the forthcoming SOLAS 1974 fire regulations.

The new ship sailed on her maiden voyage from Oslo to New York on the 22nd May, 1973 and has since been employed cruising from both sides of the Atlantic. Sadly, she proved to be the last Norwegian America liner. Apart from the huge operating expenses of a ship with such a high crew-to-passenger ratio, escalating building costs made it uneconomic for such a vessel to be constructed in the future.

As it was, in the early 1970s, the cost of maintaining ultra de luxe liners with all-Norwegian crews began to outstrip what sufficient numbers of even the most discerning passengers could afford to pay. In 1980, the two ships were sold to a newly-formed company, Norwegian America Cruises. It was 90% owned by Norwegian America Line, with the remaining 10% of shares belonging to Leif Hoegh, another prominent Norwegian shipowner. In March, 1981 Hoegh bought Norwegian America Line and thus gained sole control of the *Sagafjord* and *Vistafjord*.

At that time, Pauline Power joined NAC's marketing department: 'Norwegian America was a very elite, very exclusive company. We truly believed that we had the best cruise ships in the World and our many repeat passengers tended to agree. The ships themselves gradually took on different characters. The *Sagafjord* was the essence of a world cruise liner carrying many Americans – you might say that she was a floating stately home for the old money aristocracy of America. Her cabins had vast closets for all their ballgowns (something the *Vistafjord* lacked) and her interiors were designed on a grand scale. Outside the restaurant, there was an epic staircase which positively invited you to dress up and glide down! On the other hand, the *Vistafjord* was based primarily in Hamburg and attracted many wealthy German passengers. She also had a lot of German crew. Bigger in capacity, she also had smaller cabins and thus was used on long cruises rather than the full world cruises of the *Sagafjord*.'

Even with more international staff and Bahamian registry, Hoegh must have found that a two ship operation had much higher overheads than larger cruise companies, so he started looking for a suitable buyer for his otherwise highly successful liners. The *Sagafjord* and *Vistafjord* would have been prize catches for any fleet and rumours spread that they might join the highly rated Royal Viking Line. Instead, Norwegian America Cruises was sold to Cunard Line in 1983 for $73 million. With very few changes other than the adoption of Cunard's famous funnel colours, they cruised on serenely. Doubtless realising that it would be folly to change a winning formula, Cunard set up a subsidiary, Cunard-Norwegian America, to operate the two ships with Scandinavian officers and they retained their previous image and international clientele.

According to Pauline Power: 'The old NAC staff were at first concerned about Cunard's intentions. Remember that in the early 1980s, Cunard seemed to be moving downmarket with ships like the *Cunard Princess*. However, they made a magnificent job of running the two NAC ships and even made some welcome improvements. They had windows cut in the *Sagafjord's* dining saloon and thus made an already magnificent space into a superlative one. The *Sagafjord* was seen to have a slight edge over her newer and larger sister. She was twice voted Cruise Ship of the Year in Fielding's Worldwide Cruises guide and in 1985 was the only liner in the World to be given a 5 star rating. However, her external appearance had been spoiled for me when in 1980 an extra deck was built above her bridge to house penthouse cabins with private balconies.'

In cruise service, the *Sagafjord* and *Vistafjord* rarely met, as the former tended to be American-based, cruising in the Pacific to the Far East or on summer voyages to Alaska. The *Vistafjord*, meanwhile, developed a peerless reputation for her Europe-based cruises, except in winter when she operated Caribbean itineraries.

Unfortunately, in 1996, while cruising in the South China Sea, the *Sagafjord* suffered a serious engine room fire. She might well have been repaired but the financially-ailing Trafalgar House Group, Cunard's parent company and a firm more interested in the construction industry than in shipping, was taken over by the Norwegian Kvaerner engineering group. Trafalgar House had allowed Cunard to stagnate for years, with no new ships at a time when the rest of the cruise industry was expanding rapidly. Kvaerner wanted to sell Cunard and the *Sagafjord* was set aside while negotiations took place. Fortunately, a charterer was found in the form of the German travel agency, Transocean Tours, who, having failed to secure the *Regent Sea* when her Greek owners went bankrupt and the ship was arrested, instead requested the *Sagafjord*. This was an ironic coincidence as the *Regent Sea* was actually the *Sagafjord's* old rival, the beautiful former Swedish American liner *Gripsholm*. Prior to her arrest, she had already been marketed by the Germans under her original Swedish name. The *Sagafjord* was therefore quickly repaired and was herself renamed *Gripsholm* to fill the gap.

On one of her first cruises from Bremerhaven, on the 4th August, the former *Sagafjord* had more bad luck as she ran aground off the Swedish coast, but thankfully she was easily repaired. After the charter ended, she was put up for sale and was bought by a British company, Saga Holidays, who specialise in vacations for passengers aged over fifty. After a refit, the ship became the *Saga Rose* and now cruises mainly from Dover and Southampton. Over the years, her magnificent interiors have been altered from their elegant Scandinavian modernity to better suit conservative British tastes. However, the *Saga Rose* remains one of the most pristine and elegant liners in service today.

The *Vistafjord*, on the other hand, has continued in the Cunard fleet. In 1995, she too acquired extra superstructure containing penthouse cabins which obscured the funnel. In 1998, Cunard Line was finally sold by Kvaerner to the Carnival Corporation, the World's biggest cruise group, who were anxious to expand further into the de luxe end of the market. Carnival announced plans to consolidate Cunard as a recognisably British brand name and to emphasise the company's history and traditions. Wearing full Cunard livery for the first time, the former *Vistafjord* was renamed *Caronia* in Liverpool during November, 1999. Inside, she is now barely recognisable as the modern Norwegian liner she once was. Indeed, her new décor pastiches earlier styles of shipboard design. Nevertheless, the *Caronia* remains a popular cruise ship and is much admired for her luxury worldwide itineraries. In May 2003, it was announced that *Caronia* would be sold to Saga Cruises and from 2005 would be re-united with her former NAL fleetmate, *Saga Rose* (ex *Sagafjord*).

Det Bergenske Dampskibsselskab (BDS) – The Bergen Line

The Bergenske Dampskibsselskab was formed on the 12th December, 1851, largely as the result of the enterprise of a Bergen businessman, Michael Krohn. At the time, the city's only steamship links were irregular sailings from Kristiania, the Norwegian capital. The new company proposed to operate not only coastal steamers but also services direct to the Continent.

An order was placed with a Newcastle shipbuilder, Thomas Toward, for an iron-hulled paddle steamer, to be called *Bergen* which would carry passengers and mails to and from Hamburg, a convenient entry port to the Continent. Soon, another ship, the Clyde-built *Norge*, was acquired. However, the line had hardly established itself when, in September 1855, the two ships collided outside Kristiansand harbour. The *Norge* was lost and the *Bergen* was badly damaged. The company survived and eventually prospered, although the early years were very difficult. In 1894, it became one of the participants in the recently-established Hurtigrute, the subsidised coastal express service to the far north of Norway.

Meanwhile, on the 2nd June, 1890, the company's *Mercur* arrived in the Tyne from Trondheim and Bergen, marking the start of passenger services between the British

Bergen Line's Swedish-built *Jupiter* of 1916 is seen off the Norwegian coast during the 1930s. Her bridge is open, but with enclosed wings to give some shelter to her navigating officers. *Author Collection*

port and western Norway which have lasted well over a century.

In 1907, an expansion of the continental services began with the acquisition of the Stoomvaart Maatschappij Noorwegen (Norwegian Steamship Company) of Rotterdam, and the Vestlandske Lloyd of Bergen, giving the Bergen Line a foothold in the Netherlands trade and an expanding network of routes to other European ports, as well as to Britain and Iceland. In their smart livery of black hull, white superstructure and black funnel with three narrow white bands, the Bergen ships soon became a familiar sight in North Sea ports.

The important service to Hamburg was suspended during the First World War, as eventually was the Tyne service. Norway remained neutral during the conflict but the steamship *Vega*, built in 1895, was stopped by a German U-boat and sunk as she was carrying machinery to Britain which the Germans regarded as contraband. The passengers and crew took to the lifeboats and were rescued by a Danish vessel.

Services resumed fully in 1919 and two years later the Bergen Line entered a new sphere of operations – cruising – when it purchased the large steam yacht *Meteor*, which had been built in 1904 for the Hamburg Amerika Line.

Bergen Line's pioneering cruise vessel was the yacht-like *Meteor*. Later, when joined by the larger *Stella Polaris* in 1927, the *Meteor* was occasionally used on the company's North Sea services, as shown here during the early-1930s. *Ambrose Greenway Collection*

The *Stella Polaris* arriving at Malaga in September 1966 towards the end of her long career as a luxury cruise ship. *Ambrose Greenway Collection*

Also in 1921, the company transferred its elderly 1,322-ton passenger steamer *Irma* to its cruise operation. The previous year, a fast new turbine steamer, the *Leda*, had been completed by Armstrong, Whitworth to replace the sunken *Vega* on the Tyne route.

THE LUXURIOUS STELLA POLARIS

In 1927, the Bergen Line took delivery of its first purpose-built cruise ship, the 5,200-ton *Stella Polaris*, built by the Götaverken shipyard in Gothenburg. Designed in the classic tradition of the royal yachts and in appearance a much-enlarged version of the *Meteor*, this elegant white motorliner was an outstanding example of Scandinavian craftsmanship and engineering.

With a clipper bow, single yellow funnel, counter stern and luxuriously appointed accommodation for a mere 198 guests, the *Stella Polaris* was soon acclaimed as one of the finest cruise ships ever built. Her interiors, designed by the Gothenburg architect Gustav Alde, were in an ornate modern romantic idiom, with glowing marquetry, exquisite wood carving and grand stairwells with glittering brass balustrades. From a technical standpoint, she was highly advanced. Two Burmeister & Wain-type diesels propelled her at a stately 15 knots. All of the auxiliary and hotel services, including the galleys and the laundry, were electrically operated. And, although not originally air-conditioned, the *Stella Polaris* was one of the first passenger ships to be fitted with forced air heating and ventilation throughout.

She was captured by the Germans in 1940 and used first as a troopship, then as a barracks ship for the relaxation of off-duty U-boat crews and was slightly damaged by air attacks. The *Meteor*, also seized by the Germans in the spring of 1940, was less fortunate, being sunk at Pillau in 1945.

Once returned to the Bergen Line after the War, the *Stella Polaris* was sent back to her builders for a thorough reconditioning before she returned to cruise service. Among the decorative features added during the rebuilding were a series of glass panels in the internal doors, skylights and partitions. According to Røyne Kyllingstad: 'The majority of these windows were produced at the Hadeland Glassworks by my father, Ståle Kyllingstad and by a fellow artist, Sverre Pettersen. After the Germans surrendered, a new wave of national romanticism swept Norway and there was a revived interest in the folk traditions of the fjordlands. Although my father was instinctively forward-looking, he must have felt that the *Stella Polaris* needed to reassert her Norwegian identity.'

In 1951, the *Stella Polaris* even made a round-the-World cruise. In a period of austerity, however, there were few who could afford the exclusive and leisurely voyages she offered. Besides, the Bergen Line faced the more immediate task of replacing its war-damaged fleet. The *Stella Polaris* was therefore sold to a newly-established Swedish company, the Malmö-based Clipper Line, in December 1951 and retained her original name to cruise from New Orleans to the Caribbean in winter, spending spring and autumn in the Mediterranean, with a summer season of Scandinavian cruises.

In 1964, Clipper Line took over the Liberian-flag

A post-War view of a lounge on the *Stella Polaris*. With her worldwide itineraries, the luxurious Bergen Line cruise ship gained a formidable reputation. *Author Collection*

Incres Line and its passenger liner *Victoria*, also an older vessel. Originating in 1936 as the Union-Castle Line's *Dunnottar Castle*, she had been almost completely rebuilt in 1959. Five years later, the company gave thought to building new vessels but, by then, to have constructed a ship in the same style would have been too expensive and nothing came of the project. The *Stella Polaris* was sold to Japanese buyers for use as a country club at Mitohama. Renamed *Scandinavia*, she is still in use there to-day.

CROSSING THE NORTH SEA IN STYLE: THE VENUS AND VEGA

Four years after *Stella Polaris*'s debut, the company took delivery of another significant ship, the *Venus*, which they intended for their regular North Sea service between Bergen and Newcastle. She was a sturdy 6,269-ton motorship completed in May, 1931 by the Helsingør yard in Denmark. When new, she was the largest passenger vessel trading on the North Sea and her two Burmeister & Wain diesels gave her a service speed of 19 knots. With intense competition from Swedish Lloyd's Gothenburg – Tilbury route, speed was very important and the *Venus* was one of the fastest motorships of her time. Her performance reduced the passage time from 27 hours to 21 hours. She was also historically significant as the first passenger ship to be designed by Knud E. Hansen, who then worked in the drawing office at Helsingør.

The North Sea, although fairly shallow, is a treacherous stretch of water and the fine-lined *Venus* soon became known as the 'Vomiting Venus' on account of her uncomfortable motion. However, she was considered something of a heroine in Norway when in January 1937, under the command of Captain Vilhelm Dreyer, she rescued the crew of the steamer *Trym*, which was sinking in a storm.

The success of the *Venus* prompted the Bergen Line to go one better and in 1938 they commissioned the much larger, even faster motorship *Vega*. She was built in Italy by the famous Cantieri Riuniti dell' Adriatico at Trieste and, at 7,300 tons, eclipsed any passenger liner yet seen in North Sea service. She was said to have been paid for in Norwegian codfish. This was almost certainly true as, at that time, Mussolini was attempting to increase Italy's status as a shipbuilding nation. The noted Italian architect Gustavo Pulitzer Finali, who had previously worked on the legendary *Conte di Savoia*, designed the *Vega*'s outstanding

The *Venus*, seen in new condition, sails along the Norwegian coast between Bergen and Stavanger. *Ambrose Greenway Collection*

interiors. Her first class dining saloon was most impressive, with a double-height ceiling and concealed perimeter lighting. Sadly, the *Vega* only saw service for two seasons and was destroyed by Allied bombing during the Second World War.

The *Venus* was seized by the Germans during the occupation of Norway and was taken to Hamburg where the Allies found her in a sunken state, with her bow shattered, in the spring of 1945. She was salvaged and sent back to her builders' yard for a three-year restoration and modernisation. The hull and superstructure were changed considerably and she was fitted with a new, more rakish bow. Such was the shortage of steel in those post-War days, it was necessary to recycle the damaged frames and plates salvaged when the hull was raised. The *Venus* could now accommodate 133 passengers in first and 278 in tourist class on North Sea service. Spacious new interiors were designed by the talented Danish architect Palle Suenson. The design was clearly inspired by Kay Fisker's pre-war work for DFDS – especially the first class saloon and restaurant spaces. Intriguingly, the tourist overnight accommodation consisted both of cabins and of open dormitories, marketed as 'party class', and intended to provide inexpensive travel for scout and other groups travelling to and from Norway. Her new, more extensive superstructure and broader funnels may have accentuated her unsteadiness in rough seas, but after some years she was fitted with fin stabilisers.

In the 1950s, the Bergen Line's directors observed that there was no regular passenger link between Britain and Madeira and, as Norwegian shipping companies had long been engaged in carrying fruit on the route, it seemed

The Bergen Line's handsome but short-lived *Vega* - the largest North Sea passenger liner before the Second World War. *Ambrose Greenway Collection*

57

The forward-located first class lounge on the *Venus* after her protracted post-War rebuilding. The design was by the Danish architect, Palle Suenson, who later produced interiors in a similar style for DFDS's Aalborg-Copenhagen ships, *Jens Bang* and *H.P. Prior*. *Author Collection*

logical that there might also be a market for inexpensive winter cruises from Southampton to the sun. The little *Venus* seemed ideal for the service and, carrying only 259 passengers in one class, she was an immediate success. Her cabins may have been tiny but her public rooms were comfortable and cosy and the catering was excellent – especially the famous Norwegian buffet luncheons. She was now painted white with buff funnels carrying the three white bands – Bergen Line's cruising livery. She continued in service until 1968, by which time she was a venerable thirty-seven years old.

By then, Fred. Olsen had introduced his fine modern *Black Watch* and *Black Prince* on the winter route to the Canary Islands and, later, Madeira. The Bergen Line had a 50% stake in *Black Watch* and was operating her as the *Jupiter* on the North Sea in the summer months. Besides,

The *Venus*, following her radical post-war rebuilding, had an appearance more resembling that of the lost *Vega*. The work involved scrapping the superstructure, before rebuilding the bow and constructing entirely new upper decks. She makes a handsome sight in her cruising white livery, sailing from Southampton, bound for Madeira in October 1966. *Ambrose Greenway Collection*

The new *Leda*, with her imposing funnel, had a solid appearance and looked most handsome in her Bergen Line livery. *Author Collection*

they also had an interest in the new, luxury Royal Viking Line, which was planning a trio of cruise ships to go into service in the early 1970s. The *Venus* was laid up and, although it was rumoured that she might be used for further service, she was sold instead for demolition.

THE ADAPTABLE METEOR

After the Second World War, the Bergen Line, like the other Hurtigrute companies, started rebuilding their fleet of coastal passenger/cargo/mail ships. They ordered several new motor vessels from the Danish builders, the Aalborg Vaerft. One of these was instead completed in 1955 as the new *Meteor*, a small and exclusive cruise ship which could also be used on the Hurtigrute and on the North Sea. She measured only 2,856 tons and as a cruise ship carried just 146 passengers (although this was increased when she was running on the coastal route or across the North Sea). For many years, this small yet sturdy ship cruised the Caribbean from December to March, usually based in San Juan, before crossing the Atlantic to Monte Carlo for early-summer Mediterranean cruises. She spent the late summer in the Norwegian fjords and the Baltic. In the summer of 1970, she was sent to Vancouver for cruises to Alaska. It was during one of these northern voyages, in May 1971, that she caught fire and was badly damaged. 32 members of the crew were trapped and killed. Although declared a total loss, the hulk was sold to the Epirotiki Line of Piraeus and rebuilt for further service among the Greek islands and further afield as the *Neptune*.

After a long career, she was laid up in 1995. I went aboard her in February, 2002 as she lay in Elefsis Bay and found her to be in a very sorry state. Then I watched her being towed away to Aliaga in Turkey for scrapping. As she left Elefsis in pale spring afternoon sunlight, she passed another idle passenger vessel, her former Bergen Line fleetmate the *Jupiter/Black Watch* (see below). It was a sad sight.

LEDA – A NORTH SEA FAVOURITE

Unlike many of the other Bergen Line ships at the end of the Second World War, the *Venus* could at least be repaired. Otherwise, her glamorous new running-mate *Vega* had, as we have already seen, been lost; and the *Leda* of 1920, a fine turbine steamer, had been sunk by Russian shellfire in the Baltic. Fortunately, the 1915-vintage *Jupiter*, a steamer which had been built by Lindholmens Varv. at Gothenburg, survived relatively unscathed and served the Bergen Line until 1955. Clearly, however, a replacement ship was needed.

An order was placed with Swan, Hunter & Wigham Richardson, unusually for a twin-screw turbine steamer rather than a motorship. The new ship, reviving the name *Leda*, was launched from the Wallsend on Tyne yard by Prinsesse Astrid of Norway in September, 1952 and entered service the following April. The new *Leda* was a real beauty with a long, sleek hull and a single large black and white striped funnel. With a service speed of 22 knots, she was also fast and could make the Newcastle-Bergen crossing in an unprecedented nineteen hours. Her passenger accommodation was comfortable, but traditional in styling, although one innovation was her self-service cafeteria in tourist class.

The *Leda* had a big advantage over her predecessors in that she was fully stabilised – the first North Sea passenger ship to be so equipped. Ann Glen remembers a crossing from Bergen to Newcastle in 1965: 'We travelled across Norway by train to Bergen and, when we arrived, the weather was cold, grey and blowing a gale. My travelling companion and I were terrified at the thought of having to sail in those conditions, but the *Leda* proved to be an excellent sea boat. She was strongly built, fast and steady. It was also fortunate that our cabin was amidships and accessed off the promenade deck, so the view was through a window in the cabin door. Fearing the worst, we went straight to bed. The *Leda* sailed out of Bergen taking the waves head-on but we only felt the slightest motion and arrived at Newcastle on schedule.'

The *Leda* could carry 112 passengers in first class and 382 in tourist class with hold space for 65 cars and a

The *Leda's* interiors were robust and comfortable, rather than luxurious. Here we see her first class restaurant and her cosy, wood panelled first class lounge.
Author Collection

The *Leda's* cafeteria, for the use of second class passengers, was the first on a North Sea passenger ship. *Author Collection*

considerable quantity of cargo. A solid, hard-working and popular ship, she gave 21 years of reliable service on the North Sea but, in the end, her lack of drive-through vehicle capacity and her fuel-hungry turbine machinery ended her usefulness as a ferry. She was withdrawn at the end of the 1974 summer season and was laid up in Bergen.

After that, she had a rather chequered career. In 1977, she was in use as an accommodation ship for oilrig workers. Later, she passed to Kuwaiti owners who planned to convert her into a livestock carrier. Fortunately, this proved not to be economically feasible and so, instead, she found further employment as an accommodation ship, this time at a rig-building site in the Hebrides. She was next purchased by Dolphin (Hellas) Cruises of Piraeus and converted into the cruise liner *Albatros*. In 1988, she became the *Betsy Ross* for the Greek-owned American Star Line which aimed to offer American-themed cruises. The venture was a failure and the ship was then chartered to TFC Cruises of South Africa, who found her unsatisfactory. In 1989, she was chartered to the StarLauro Line as the *Amalfi*, but was soon arrested for debt in Venice. In 1990, she was purchased by another Italian-owned concern, Stargas, and renamed yet again, becoming *Star of Venice*. She had a brief stint as a floating hotel but was mostly laid up until being re-activated for Mediterranean cruises in 1998. The season was cut short by mechanical problems but she was towed to Ravenna for further use as a hotel ship. There were reports that she might be re-engined but by then she was becoming very elderly and in 2000 she was towed away to Aliaga for scrapping.

The cruise ship *Meteor* is seen at Oban during a Round Britain cruise during the 1960s. Her small size enabled her to berth in harbours where larger cruise ships had to anchor offshore. *Alastair Paterson Collection*

A saloon on the *Meteor*, designed in a manner similar to that on her near-sisters employed on the Hurtigrute Norwegian coastal express service. *Author Collection*

THE LAST YEARS

The Bergen Line entered the car-ferry age in 1966, when, jointly with Fred. Olsen, it introduced the *Jupiter/Black Watch*. Four years later, it bought a part-share in Olsen's *Black Prince* which assumed the name *Venus* when running under Bergen colours. The unusual story of these two innovative sisters is told in the chapter on Fred. Olsen Line (see below).

By 1984, Det Bergenske Dampskibselskab had sold off many of its shipping interests and had rather lost its way. It became the subject of a fierce battle for control, won by A/S Kosmos, a member of the Jahre group. The Bergen-Newcastle service was transferred to the new Norway Line and before long the famous Bergen Line name disappeared altogether.

Fred. Olsen Line

The foundations of the Olsen family's business were laid in the middle of the 19th century when three Norwegian brothers, all ship's captains, bought their own vessels. Fredrik Christian Olsen acquired his first two sailing ships, the schooners *Johanne Christine* and *Elizabeth*, in 1848, and over the years owned more than 20 ships. Petter Olsen's shipowning career began in 1852 with the brig *Thilda*. In his lifetime he owned a total of 16 sailing ships, besides part-interests in several steamships. Andreas Olsen bought the barque *De Tre Venner* in 1860 and subsequently owned another five sailing ships. Petter's son Fredrik was thus continuing an established family tradition when, in 1886, he took over the management of two of his father's vessels.

The motor ship *Brabant* initially had no funnel, but instead the exhaust was carried up the second of her three masts. Later, she was rebuilt with a more conventional silhouette, as shown in this view, taken in the 1950s. *Author Collection*

62

He had had business training in England and France, had taken his master's ticket at the age of 23 and had commanded several of his father's vessels when he started his career as a shipowner. He well understood the need to switch from sail to steam despite the fact that sailing ships still remained cheaper to operate. In 1896, he ordered his first steamship, the *Bayard*, for service between Fredrikstad and Garston on the River Mersey. She was built by Nylands Verksted (later part of the Aker Group) and was delivered in 1897. A year later, she was followed by the *Bonheur*, built for a service to London.

In 1899, to cope with the increasing work involved in the management of steamships in regular services, Fred. Olsen moved his office from the family's home village of Hvitsten on the Oslofjord to Kristiania (now Oslo). He was so successful that he was approached in 1900 by the Ganger Rolf company, who operated a line between Norway and Rouen but were in difficulties. They asked Fred. Olsen if he would take over the management of the line, which he did with great success. His rapidly growing reputation for dynamism and farsightedness paved the way for his later activities. In 1901, he acquired the Faarder Company's passenger and cargo service to Grangemouth; in 1906 the Østlandske Lloyd's lines to Newcastle and Antwerp; and in 1912 the Norden Shipping Company's route to Holland. These lines formed the basis of the Fred. Olsen North Sea services, although the passenger sailings to Grangemouth were soon switched to Newcastle, which was more conveniently located for goods and passengers bound for both northern and southern Britain.

During the following thirty years, the Fred. Olsen Line expanded in several areas, including the fruit trades from the Mediterranean and the Canary Islands to northern Europe. There were also services to North and South America. Although Norway remained neutral during the First World War, the Olsen fleet suffered several losses. Olsen then went into partnership with another shipowner, Johan Muller, who helped him to rebuild the company.

One of Fred. Olsen's more notable ships was the funnel-less passenger and cargo motorship *Brabant*, delivered by the Akers Mek. Verksted in Oslo in March, 1926. Of 2,300 tons, she entered service on the Oslo-Antwerp route less than seven months after DFDS's *Parkeston*, the first passenger motorship on the North Sea. When Fred. Olsen died in 1933, his sons, Rudolf and Thomas, took over. In 1937, the motorship *Bretagne* was delivered from Akers, also for the Antwerp service. She sailed on a weekly schedule, her single Burmeister & Wain diesel giving a respectable speed of 16 knots. The noted Norwegian architect Arnstein Arneberg was responsible for the design of her interiors. She was sold in 1958 to the Hellenic Mediterranean Lines of Piraeus, becoming their *Massalia* and remaining in service until 1967. Seven years later, she was scrapped at Elefsis.

THE FIRST BLACK PRINCE AND BLACK WATCH

While the Antwerp service received new tonnage, the route to Newcastle was still being operated by the steamer *Bessheim* of 1912 and her more modern sister, the 1923-built *Blenheim*. However, two replacement vessels were eventually ordered from Akers for delivery in 1938. The *Black Prince* was the first to be launched, by Kronprinsesse Martha in December, 1937. Trials in the Oslofjord in May, 1938 were followed by the new ship's maiden

Small but well-designed, the purposeful-looking *Bretagne* sails up the Oslofjord on her regular Oslo-Antwerp service. *Fred. Olsen & Co.*

The elegant *Black Watch* of 1938 leaves her home port of Oslo, bound for Newcastle. Her bow was embellished with a bronze figurehead and her name on the stern was in bronze scrolls with a garland of swans.
Fred. Olsen & Co.

departure for Newcastle via Kristiansand on the 1st July. She was joined by her sister ship *Black Watch* in December, 1938.

At 5,035 gross tons, they were the largest motorships yet built in Norway and were certainly among the most beautiful liners in North Sea service. While they lacked the streamlined modernity of DFDS's *Kronprins Olav*, another regular visitor to Oslo harbour, they were nonetheless very innovative ships. The Olsen brothers aimed to provide their passengers with a taste of Norway from the moment they stepped onboard and once again commissioned Arnstein Arneberg to design the interiors. Accommodating 185 first and 65 second class passengers, they were not only liberally decorated with Norwegian art and craft works but were also particularly inventively planned. For example, the main dining saloon could be split into a series of smaller rooms using retractable bulkheads and the galley was located on the deck below with an interconnecting lift. Power came from Burmeister & Wain diesels giving a speed of 18 knots, as against the 14 knots of their predecessors.

These fine new ships had tragically brief careers with Fred. Olsen. Following the outbreak of the Second World War, they were laid up in the Trondheimsfjorden due to the high cost of war risk insurance. The German Navy seized them in 1940 for use as accommodation ships but both were eventually lost. *Black Prince* was wrecked by Allied bombers at Danzig on the 21st December, 1942 and then burned; while *Black Watch* was sunk off Harstad, also by Allied aircraft, while serving as a submarine depot ship. The wreck of *Black Prince* was salvaged but was considered too badly damaged to make restoration worthwhile. After plans to convert the hull into a cargo vessel had fallen through, the unlucky ship was scrapped at Burcht in 1951. Thus, it was left to the Antwerp ship *Bretagne* to reopen Fred. Olsen's important Oslo-Newcastle service when peace returned.

BLENHEIM AND BRAEMAR – THE STREAMLINED TWINS

New ships were urgently needed and in 1951 Fred. Olsen took delivery of the new *Blenheim*, named in honour of the British wartime leader Winston Churchill, whose birthplace was Blenheim Palace. She was a strikingly streamlined 4,766-ton mini-liner. Two years later, she was joined by the almost identical *Braemar* – her name chosen in recognition of the village close to the Highland home of the British Royal Family, Balmoral Castle. With shipyards struggling to cope with demand to make good the losses of war, the new Olsen sisters had an unusual birth. They could even claim to have had two builders as their hulls were constructed at the John I. Thornycroft shipyard at Southampton, from where they were towed to Norway for the installation of machinery and for fitting out at the Akers Mek. Verksted in Oslo. In some respects, the two ships resembled the then-new Norwegian America liner *Oslofjord*. They had long, fine-lined hulls with built-up bows to cut through the North Sea swells. Their superstructures were streamlined and set well back, but it was their then-unique combined mainmast and funnel arrangement that caught the eye. Their bows were decorated with bronze sculptures, which had become a

The innovative post-War *Braemar* shows her highly curvaceous profile in this view taken towards the end of her career with Fred. Olsen. By this stage, she has lost her bow bronze decorations. *Author Collection*

traditional Olsen embellishment. Fitted with Burmeister & Wain diesel engines, they had a service speed of 16 knots. Within, they were luxurious, with air-conditioning throughout; spacious wood-panelled public rooms which had been designed by Arnstein Arneberg; and even a sauna to while away the hours.

Unfortunately, the *Blenheim* was badly damaged by a fire caused by an electrical fault in the restaurant while she was on passage from the Tyne to Oslo on the 21st May, 1968. It spread quickly to the bridge, which made it impossible to send a mayday message. Fortunately, a Danish fishing vessel spotted the burning ship and sent an alarm. The *Blenheim's* sister, *Braemar*, rescued the passengers and, while the Ellerman Wilson Line ferry *Spero* stood by in case assistance was needed, twelve crew members stayed aboard to fight the flames. Finally, with her superstructure almost entirely burnt out, the *Blenheim* was towed to Kristiansand and laid up. She was sold in 1969 to another Norwegian shipping company, A/S Uglands Rederi, and drastically rebuilt as the car-carrier

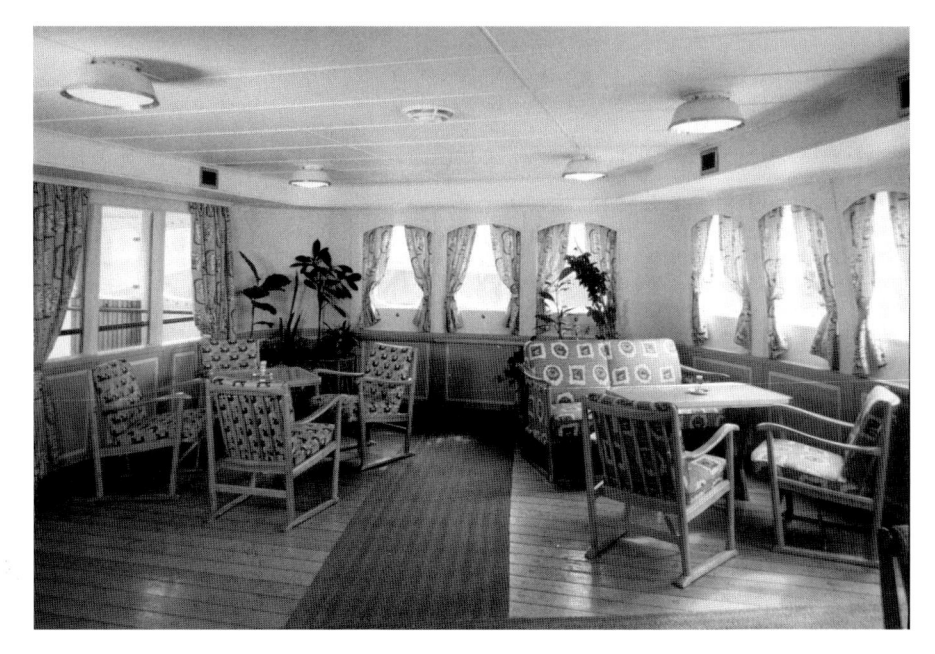

The forward-located observation lounge on the 1951 *Blenheim*, designed by Arnstein Arneberg and using furniture supplied by Heal's of London. *Author Collection*

65

The dining saloon on the *Blenheim* – note the embroidered motifs on the seat backs, part of a wide range of decorations reflecting the arts and crafts traditions of Norway. *Author Collection*

The streamlined *Blenheim* shows her paces in this fine aerial view, probably taken during the mid-1950s. *Author Collection*

The first class entrance hall of the *Blenheim* was amply adorned with Norwegian sculpture and decorative panels. Clearly, Fred. Olsen wanted passengers to feel that they had arrived in Norway the moment they stepped onboard. *Author Collection*

Cilaos. She operated initially between European ports and the Indian Ocean islands and then later on other routes, including voyages between South America and the Caribbean. She was sold for scrapping in Pakistan in 1981.

Meanwhile, the *Braemar* continued in service until the 2nd August, 1975, by which time she was the last traditional non-ro ro passenger ship on the North Sea. She was sold to a London financial house for use as a casino ship in the Philippines. Laid up in 1979, she too went for scrap.

THE VERSATILE NEW BLACK WATCH AND BLACK PRINCE

In 1966, the Fred. Olsen and Bergen Lines together took delivery of two handsome new ships which combined the roles of cruise liner; roll on/roll off passenger and vehicle ferry; and refrigerated cargo vessel. Naval architects can rarely have faced such a seemingly unlikely and unenviable task as preparing designs for a single vessel to fulfil these three very disparate functions. Yet the two sisters proved to be very successful.

The reason why the two companies, rivals for so many years, joined together in this project stemmed from the seasonal natures of their most important trades. In the summer, both Fred. Olsen and the Bergen Line now needed car ferries for British holidaymakers crossing the North Sea to Norway, while Olsen had a long-established winter trade bringing fruit from the Canary Islands to London. Olsen also inherited the popular cruise run to Madeira which Bergen Line had begun with their famous *Venus*, taking British passengers on inexpensive voyages south to the sun, escaping the northern winter for a couple of weeks.

The two ships were designed by the Olsen technical department under their naval architect John Johnsen and were ordered from the Lübecker Flender Werke of Lübeck in Germany in 1964. Measuring 9,500 gross tons, these small but perfectly formed liners were an immediate

The *Black Watch* (otherwise known as *Jupiter*), in her Fred. Olsen livery, departs Tilbury on her winter service to the Canary Islands in 1982. *Ambrose Greenway*

success. The first of the sisters was jointly owned and had two registered names, in accordance with her dual owners' styles of nomenclature – uniquely, she changed her identity from the Fred. Olsen's *Black Watch* to Bergen Line's *Jupiter* each spring. Then, she became an Olsen ship again after completing her summer season on the Bergen-Stavanger-Newcastle route.

She had been launched in March, 1965 by Lady Scott, the wife of the British Ambassador to Norway and had both names and company flags painted on her bow for the occasion. She was completed in time for the Bergen Line's 1966 summer season. The second ship, named *Black Prince* and at first solely owned by Fred. Olsen, followed that autumn and joined her sister in the Madeira and Canaries service. Each summer, she ran, still for Olsen, between Kristiansand and Harwich.

Revolutionary ships at the time, the pair created a bold, modernistic impression with their long, sleek and fine-lined hulls in grey and their low, streamlined superstructures. The bows of both ships were adorned with a figurehead, in *Black Watch/Jupiter's* case a bronze sculpture of a sea nymph, mounted on mosaic wings – an attractive embellishment in the tradition which Olsen had revived in the 1930s.

While other, less enlightened shipping lines might have found such decorations anachronistic by the 1960s, Fred.

Olsen explained its delightful policy in a brochure published in 1968: 'The revival of the old custom of decorating ships with figureheads has occasioned much controversy. "Why bother? They don't earn you any money" some say. "An unnecessary relic of a bygone age," say others. Fred. Olsen and Company does not agree. A ship cannot be compared to a bus or a railway train or any other more or less inanimate object of convenience. A ship is a home for its crew, a ship is in the closest of contact with the elements, a ship is almost a living being. It deserves a little decoration. It deserves care and attention and love, and if it gets these things it will be a happier ship, its crew will be a happier crew, and together they will do a better job.'

Equally distinctive was the shape of the funnel, said to have been inspired by a Viking helmet – an unmistakable design with its boldly chiselled sides tapering to the rear. The ships always wore the basic Fred. Olsen livery, but in summer the *Black Watch/Jupiter's* funnel was decorated by the Bergen Line houseflag. In winter, this was replaced by the Olsen flag. In 1970, Fred. Olsen sold a part-share in *Black Prince* to Bergen Line under a similar arrangement to that by which the two lines already owned her sister and, as the *Venus*, she joined *Black Watch/Jupiter* in the summer service from Bergen to Newcastle.

Later, in October 1975, when Fred. Olsen and Bergen

Line combined their North Sea services, the two sisters wore the full Olsen livery all year round, but with the three famous horizontal white stripes of the Bergen company added in the summer. As ferries, the *Black Watch/Jupiter* and her sister could each carry 587 passengers (some in reclining seats, but most in cabins) and 185 cars; but this number was reduced to 350 berthed passengers when they were employed in the winter service to the Canaries.

In 1982, the North Sea services from Bergen were taken over by DFDS, who thereafter chartered the two sisters each summer. I first met them in 1984 when the *Jupiter* was running for the Danish company on their Newcastle-Esbjerg service. I was thrilled to see her lofty funnel, and that of the *Venus* on the run to Stavanger and Bergen, rising above the terminal at Tyne Commission Quay. As we drove along the quayside to board, it was possible to make out the painted-out silhouette letters of her alter ego *Black Watch* welded into the *Jupiter*'s hull. It suddenly dawned on me that this was the same ship about which my great aunt had enthused. A lover of cruising, she favoured the *Black Watch* over all others, liking her small scale, congenial staff and her cleanliness.

We drove aboard and a group of seamen manhandled the car down a hatch into a cargo hold below the main car deck. We then climbed up to the main foyer, which was carpeted in Black Watch tartan – another reminder of the *Jupiter*'s other role. Despite this dubious choice, the space was very elegant – not in the stripped-back style of the Kay Kørbing-designed DFDS ships, but rather more ornate with carved woodwork and decorative brass balustrades on the two curving staircases, between which hung a fine portrait of King Olav and Queen Maud of Norway. The *Jupiter*'s interiors left one in no doubt that this was a proud Norwegian ship and although space seemed confined in places, little expense had been spared in furnishing it to the highest standards.

Forward of the hallway on the Lounge deck was the Westminster Lounge (originally the First Class Lounge), a beautiful circular room with a centrally-located dance floor and vertically slatted screens to make quiet corners. The combination of wood panelling, indirect lighting and dark green upholstery made a warm and cosy atmosphere. Aft of the hallway was the Dining Saloon, decorated in cream and with attractive moulded glass light fittings set into the ceiling, suffusing the space with a warm glow. It was connected to the former Tourist Class Dining Room (being used as a cafeteria in summer) by an arcade on the starboard side of the galley.

Aft of the restaurants was the duty free shop. This appeared to be merely a counter where drink and cigarettes were sold, but from a design point of view, it was one of the ship's most intriguing features. Directly above, there was an indoor lido area with a glazed roof over the small swimming pool. This space was decked over in summer and became a lounge filled with reclining seats. The pool itself was drained and, once the pool-liner was removed, a door in the side made it into a store room for the duty free shop's goods. Every corner was put to use on these ships.

Towards the stern was the Neptune Lounge with a long bar on the port side and another circular dance floor and bandstand. Initially intended as the Tourist Class Lounge, it became a lively night club when the ship became one-class in the mid-1970s. The deck below (the Upper Deck) and the one above (the Boat Deck) were given over to cabins. These were well-appointed by ferry standards but would have been very squashed for a cruise ship. Outdoors, the *Jupiter* had extensive sun decks – one could even promenade on the top deck around the funnel – but these were green-painted steel rather than teak planking. The decoration of the *Black Prince/Venus* was similar and the only outward difference between the two ships was that the *Black Watch/Jupiter* had her bow bronze mounted on a mosaic shield with shorter, concave wings.

The winter voyages south to the sun were very different in character from the high-density North Sea summer sailings. The Bay of Biscay is notorious for its unpredictability and, although fitted with stabilisers, the sisters soon gained a reputation for giving a lively ride in stormy weather. The possibility of experiencing rough weather, coupled with the reduced passenger numbers, made them popular with dedicated cruise enthusiasts. Indeed, these trips were among the last liner voyages one could take from Britain. The ships loaded cargoes of export vehicles and consumer goods through their side hatches at a new terminal at Millwall Docks, built for Fred. Olsen in 1969 and designed by the young Norman Foster, later to become one of Britain's most successful modern architects. Inward cargoes consisted mainly of pallets of tomatoes and other fruit from the Canary Islands. These were discharged at Millwall with remarkable speed by means of a highly mechanised and innovative system of conveyors, lifts and specially built fork-lift trucks. Also very ingenious was the ease with which much of the summertime car deck space could be converted into cooled chambers for this perishable produce.

THE BIG SISTER, BLENHEIM

The success of the two ships encouraged Fred. Olsen to order a somewhat larger third sister in 1968, the *Blenheim*. John Brown's Clydebank yard, about to become part of the new Upper Clyde Shipbuilders, Ltd., won the contract with the benefit of a government subsidy. This yard had recently completed the magnificent *Kungsholm* (see below) and was working on the *Queen Elizabeth 2* when the order was placed. A consequence of the subsidy was that the *Blenheim* would initially have to fly the British flag, but as she would be sailing from British ports all year round, this seemed like a good idea.

Outwardly resembling the earlier Lübeck-built pair, the *Blenheim* was in fact rather longer (149.38m against their 141.64m) as she was designed to make full use of the new Millwall terminal. There was greater emphasis on the passenger aspect rather than cargo and she could carry 1,107 summer passengers, nearly twice as many as her older sisters. As a result, she had extra lifeboats and a rather more massive superstructure, especially when viewed from the stern. Seen from a distance, the 10,736 ton *Blenheim* was another long and sleek Olsen liner. However, she did not bear as much close inspection as her German-built near-sisters. Her steelwork, for instance, appeared to be somewhat rippled in places. Within, the *Blenheim* had much elegant dark woodwork and was rather more modern in design than her elder sisters. Certainly, she was an outstandingly well-appointed vessel and a most

The third of Fred. Olsen's trio of ferry-liners, the Clyde-built *Blenheim* is pictured on sea trials in the Firth of Clyde. Her larger capacity is reflected in an altogether more massive superstructure than on her earlier and smaller sisters – especially evident when viewed from the stern. *Author Collection*

A corner of the *Blenheim's* Saga Lounge, panelled in dark rosewood with brass inlays. The public rooms on this ship had names similar to those adopted by DFDS at around the same time, such as Tivoli Restaurant and Viking Room – who copied whom? *Fred. Olsen & Co.*

A popular spot on the *Blenheim* was her swimming pool, sheltered in inclement weather by a retractable glazed roof. *Fred. Olsen & Co.*

popular addition to the Olsen fleet.

Unfortunately, she was delivered six months late, missing the lucrative North Sea season. It was not until September, 1970 that, having completed her trials, she sailed to Kristiansand and from there to the Millwall terminal. She now entered the London-Funchal-Santa Cruz de Tenerife-Las Palmas-London service. Her advent enabled the *Black Prince/Venus* to begin a new winter route from Amsterdam to the Canaries. Then, in May, 1971 the *Blenheim* at last began her summer sailings across the North Sea, alternately from Kristiansand to Harwich and to Amsterdam. She had, however, arrived at an unfortunate time: the early 1970s was a bleak period for industrial relations in Britain and the *Blenheim* was endlessly plagued by strikes of dockworkers and of seamen. By 1979, Olsen had become fed up with the delays and cancellations and they announced that she was to be re-registered in Norway with a Norwegian crew. Predictably, the result was a further strike and Olsen agreed to retain the ship's British registry. They had, however, decided to sell her.

She was indirectly replaced on the North Sea routes by the 1973-built car ferry *Bolero*, which had recently returned from a charter to Stena Line. This ship, too, had been designed to combine the roles of ferry and cruise ship. Built for a consortium consisting of a number of Norwegian shipowners – Fred. Olsen, Fearnley & Eger, Ludwig Mowinckels and R.P.Aukner – she had initially sailed under charter in North American waters, making winter cruises from Miami to the Caribbean and to Mexico and in summer serving as a car ferry linking Portland, Maine and Yarmouth, Nova Scotia.

In 1981, the *Blenheim* was purchased by DFDS, which was then attempting to break into the burgeoning American cruise market with services from New York and Florida to the Bahamas, under the Scandinavian World Cruises banner. The ship was sent to Blohm & Voss in Hamburg, emerging as the Bahamian-registered *Scandinavian Sea* (see below).

Black Watch/Jupiter and *Black Prince/Venus* have had much more fortunate careers. In the Autumn of 1984, the Bergen-Newcastle service was taken over by Norway Line,

The jointly owned cruise-ferry *Bolero* makes her one and only appearance in the Port of New York during her delivery voyage in April 1973. The reason for this unusual call was to discharge new German cars being carried to the USA from Bremen.
World Ship Society

71

which proceeded to charter *Venus* for the summer season. Then, in 1986, the agreement by which Fred. Olsen and the Bergen Line had jointly owned the ships expired. *Jupiter* passed into the hands of the Bergen company, who immediately sold her to Norway Line, while *Black Prince* became wholly-owned by Olsen, who had her converted into a full-time cruise ship.

Now painted in Norway Line's all-white livery with red and blue stripes, and without her Olsen figurehead, *Jupiter* remained very popular on the North Sea for a time and even ran some spring and autumn cruises. However, her tortuous loading arrangements for cars and her inability to carry more than a couple of commercial vehicles told against her and in 1989 Norway Line replaced her with the former Stena Line ferry *Scandinavica* which became yet another *Venus*. The redundant *Jupiter* was sold to the Greek-Cypriot ferry operators Marlines and became their flagship, *Crown M*. Now with a dark blue funnel and red and blue hull strips, she was used in the Italy-Greek trade. Offering rather more luxurious standards than was the norm on those frenetic routes, she became popular for a time. Competition increased, however, and Marlines withdrew her in the autumn of 1996 and, renamed *Byblos*, she has been laid up in Elefsis Bay near Piraeus ever since.

BLACK PRINCE TRANSFORMED

Black Prince is thus the only one of the trio which has remained with Fred. Olsen and she is still a successful cruise ship, with a very loyal, almost exclusively British following. To prepare her for her new role, she was given a major rebuild in 1987 at the Wärtsilä yard in Turku, from which she emerged in a strange white, red and blue livery with flags and a vast evocation of the Black Prince painted on her hull. Ornamental sails could be raised on three masts aft of the funnel. Less controversially, the ship was given a new, floating water sports centre, which could be folded out from the stern door of her car deck while she was at anchor, and an outdoor lido and restaurant. She was now registered at Manila and gained unfavourable reviews in British newspapers when she re-entered service, with passengers claiming that they had 'nursed' seasick Filippino staff, some of whom had never been to sea before.

Later, in 1990, Fred. Olsen attempted to use *Black Prince* in a mini-cruise service from Norwegian ports and Gothenburg to Copenhagen. However, the Danish and Swedish trade unions reacted furiously to a Philippines-registered ship, with its lower crew costs, sailing on this route and she faced such vigorous protests that she was withdrawn. However, re-registered at the Olsen family's home port of Hvitsten and painted in a more subdued livery, the *Black Prince* soon regained her old reputation in the British cruise market. She is now Bahamas-registered and remains as popular as ever. Recently, she has occasionally made longer cruises, which have taken her as far afield as Cape Town and even across the Atlantic to Cuba – a remarkable achievement for a vessel initially designed only to undertake short sea voyages.

THE FORGOTTEN KØBENHAVN

In terms of design development, the *København* was one of the most significant passenger ships in which Fred. Olsen had an interest, yet she is also one of the least remembered. She was actually ordered from the Orenstein & Koppel shipyard in Lübeck by another Norwegian shipowner, Sverre Ditlev-Simonsen and was delivered in 1966 to his newly-formed Norske Københavnlinje (Norwegian Copenhagen Line). She was intended for use on a triangular service from Brevik to Gothenburg and Copenhagen.

The *København* was an important ship as she was the first true cruise ferry to be designed by the prolific and highly innovative Danish naval architect Tage Wandborg, of the firm of Knud E. Hansen A/S. Moreover, the Ditlev-Simonsen family was related by marriage to another important Norwegian shipowner, Knut Kloster who shortly afterwards took delivery of the broadly similar *Sunward* – a vessel credited with being the pioneer modern cruise ship (see below). Like the *Sunward*, the *København* was a striking ship with sleek and powerful lines. Set well back above the bridge was an observation lounge, the rear portion of which contained the exhaust uptakes.

While Kloster's *Sunward* eventually became an outstandingly successful cruise ship, Ditlev-Simonsen's *København* had a chequered career. In 1968, Fred. Olsen bought a 60% stake in the ship and she was repainted in

The short-lived but significant *København* during her brief spell in Fred. Olsen colours in the latter 1960s. *Fred. Olsen & Co.*

Alterations to the *Black Prince*'s stern during her conversion to a full-time cruise liner can clearly be seen as she leaves Palma De Mallorca during a Mediterranean cruise in August 1999. *Author*

Olsen's handsome livery. Her route was now Oslo-Horten-Brevik-Copenhagen. Even this revised schedule proved unsuccessful – especially once the effects of the fuel crisis were felt, with bunker prices rising sharply. Thus the ship was chartered out to the Larvik-Frederikshavn Line from 1970 until 1973. Shortly thereafter, she was sold to Chilean owners, initially for civilian service, but from 1977 she was used as a depot ship for Chilean submarines and named *Angamos*. This obscure use continued until 1993, when she was purchased by a Greek shipowner, George Janatos. Most unfortunately, while she was being towed across the Atlantic to Piraeus, a severe fire broke out and the former *København* burned completely. Even so, the wreck was towed to Elefsis in Greece but was declared a total loss and was sold for scrap shortly thereafter.

THE FRED. OLSEN CRUISE FLEET

As we have already seen, with the introduction of the second *Black Watch* and *Black Prince*, Fred. Olsen began marketing their voyages to the Canary Island as cruises,

***Black Prince* has become one of the best-known ships in the British cruise market. Here we see her Royal Garter Restaurant.** *David Trevor-Jones*

Fred. Olsen Cruise Lines' current *Black Watch* catches the sun in Southampton Docks before setting off on another Mediterranean cruise.
John Adams

which became very popular. Eventually, *Black Prince* was converted into a full-time cruise ship and has sailed with great success on more widespread itineraries. In 1996, Fred. Olsen Cruise Lines (as this division of the huge Olsen group had become) bought a second vessel, for which they revived the well-remembered name *Black Watch*. She had been the *Royal Viking Star* of the Royal Viking Line and her design and career are covered in the later chapter which deals with that company (see below).

In 2001, after a long search, Olsen bought a third cruise ship. She was the *Crown Dynasty* of the bankrupt Commodore Cruise Line (see below). An attractive, modern liner of 19,000 tons, completed as recently as 1993, she now revived another traditional Olsen name, *Braemar*. She too is covered in a later chapter of this book.

The latest addition to the Fred. Olsen cruise fleet – the *Braemar* (III), formerly the *Crown Dynasty* – is seen leaving Dover in the early summer of 2002. *Author*

74

The emigrant carrier *Skaugum*: her origin as a cargo ship is most apparent in this aerial view taken in Sydney harbour.
Peter Newall Collection

I.M. Skaugen

This Norwegian shipping company first entered the passenger trades after the Second World War when it operated the *Skaugum* and the *Skaubryn* from Europe to Australia, Canada and South America, carrying refugees and other emigrants. The company's history dates back to 1912, when Captain Isak Martinus Skaugen purchased a four-masted barque, the *Alcides*. He realised that the future lay with steam vessels, however, and so, having sold the *Alcides* in 1916, he bought his first steam cargo ships, paid for with money raised on the Christiania Stock Exchange. In the 1930s, the I.M. Skaugen line matured from operating tramp ships in North Sea and Norwegian coastal waters to international trade. By 1939, all the steam vessels had been sold and the fleet consisted of three motor tankers and one dry bulk vessel.

In 1948, the company purchased its first passenger ship with which it entered the lucrative emigrant trade. The 11,626-ton diesel-electric *Skaugum* had been launched as a Hamburg America Line freighter, the *Ostmark*, at the Germaniawerft yard at Kiel in 1940. Skaugen had the still uncompleted ship converted into a passenger vessel and chartered her to the International Refugee Organisation.

In 1951, the 9,786-ton *Skaubryn* joined the fleet. Unusually at that time, she was a purpose-built emigrant-carrier. She was constructed by the Oresundsvarvet at Landskrona in Sweden but completed at the Howaldtswerke yard in Hamburg, who had been responsible for the conversion of the *Skaugum*. Notwithstanding her relatively small size, she had accommodation of a remarkably high standard in comparison with that on most other emigrant ships. She could carry 1,200 passengers plus their possessions. In the mid-1950s, a one-way ticket to Australia on *Skaubryn* cost between £150 and £250.

In 1957, the *Skaugum* was rebuilt from a passenger vessel into a freighter as this was thought likely to be more lucrative. She was sold in 1964 to Liberian interests and re-named *Ocean Builder*. She was scrapped at Kaohsiung in 1972.

Unfortunately, the newer *Skaubryn* was tragically short-lived, as she was swept by fire in the Indian Ocean in 1958. The blaze began with an explosion in the engine room on the 31st March and after 45 minutes her master,

The purpose-built *Skaubryn* is seen in Cape Town during one of her voyages to Australia.
Author Collection

The elegant *Kronprins Harald* brought a high standard to Jahre Line's Oslo-Kiel service in 1961. At that time, she was among the World's largest and most luxurious car and passsenger liners. *Author Collection*

Captain Alf Fæste, gave the order to abandon ship. Her full complement of passengers and crew was transferred to the lifeboats and was later picked up by the Ellerman Line cargo ship *City of Sydney*, which later transferred them to Flotta Lauro's *Roma*. The *Skaubryn* continued to burn and eventually sank while under tow on the 6th April. Captain Fæste was later honoured with the Order of St. Olav for his courage in overseeing the safe evacuation of his ship. The loss of the *Skaubryn* ended I.M. Skaugen's interest in passenger shipping for the time being and the company went on to develop its bulk carrier and general cargo fleets during the 1960s.

By the end of the decade, however, it had joined forces with other prominent Norwegian shipowners to form Royal Caribbean Cruise Line (see below). Furthermore, it was briefly involved, as a partner with the J. Lauritzen subsidiary Loke Shipping, in Pearl Cruises of Scandinavia. Between 1981 and 1987, this firm operated the converted Baltic ferry *Finlandia* (later *Finnstar*) as *Pearl of Scandinavia* on itineraries based in South East Asia. For a time, Skaugen also had a joint interest in the Seven Seas Cruise Line, which eventually merged into Radisson Seven Seas Cruises.

In October 1990, the Skaugen group became involved in the ferry trades when it gained control of A/S Kosmos, which ran the Jahre Line (see below) and the Norway Line. It combined the two operations into a new company, Color Line. Within three months, Color Line also bought Fred. Olsen's ferry services across the Skagerak. More recently, however, control of the ferry interests has passed to another Norwegian shipowner, Nils Olav Sunde.

Other Scandinavian Emigrant-Carriers

Four other Scandinavian vessels were employed in the emigrant trades in the years following the Second World War. *Nelly* had been laid down in 1939 by the Sun Shipbuilding & Drydock Company of Chester, Pennsylvania as a C3-type cargo liner for Moore McCormack Lines, for whom she was to have been the *Mormacmail*. However, she was completed as an auxiliary aircraft carrier – the *USS Long Island*. Decommissioned in 1947, she was rebuilt as the emigrant carrier *Nelly* two years later for a subsidiary of the Norwegian-owned Gotaas-Larsen group. In 1955, she was sold to the Europe-Canada Line, a jointly-owned German-flag subsidiary of the Holland America and Rotterdam Lloyd lines. After a refit, she continued in the emigrant trade as the *Seven Seas* and remained active until the mid-1960s. She was repaired after an engine room fire in 1965 and returned to service but was soon laid up in Rotterdam as a student hostel and continued in this role until being sold to Belgian shipbreakers in 1977.

Similarly, the Swedish-owned *Anna Salén* had been built for Moore McCormack in 1939 and was also taken over by the United States Navy for conversion to an aircraft carrier. Thereafter, as the *Empire Lagan*, she was

76

sold to the Gothenburg-based shipowner Sven Salén and registered under his subsidiary Rederi A/B Pulp. Rebuilt as a passenger liner in similar style to the *Nelly*, she was used on various transatlantic routes and to Australia until being sold in 1955 to an offshoot of Hellenic Mediterranean Lines. She saw further service as a passenger carrier and then as a freighter for Far Eastern owners until being broken up at New Orleans in 1962.

Two ex-German cargo ships were temporarily converted for the emigrant trade in the late 1940s: J. L. Mowinckel's *Goya* and the Norwegian government's *Svalbard*. All these ships, however, were rather perfunctory conversions whose origins as cargo liners were very obvious indeed. In terms of design, they were a world away from the great Scandinavian liners of the pre- and post-war eras, yet the ability of Swedish and, in particular, Norwegian shipowners to involve themselves in the migrant trades carrying displaced peoples from other European nations to begin new lives in the Americas and Australia was most significant; the same entrepreneurial spirit and ability to spot and exploit new markets informed their involvement in the development of the cruise industry in the 1960s.

Jahre Line

Born in 1881, Anders Jahre was a prominent Norwegian lawyer, shipowner and industrialist. From 1918 onwards, he played a major role in the development of commercial whaling. For example, he was the first entrepreneur to build industrial-scale whaling mother ships. In 1928, he founded the Anders Jahre shipping company, based in Sandefjord. Later, in the 1930s, his industrial interests expanded when he founded the Sandar oil refinery, as well as the Jahre Chemical Company. Consequently, he developed an expanding fleet of oil and chemical tankers.

In the late 1950s. Jahre spotted a potentially lucrative business opportunity to operate a high quality car ferry service between Oslo and Kiel in Germany. The West German economy was expanding rapidly and car ownership was increasing apace. Consequently, an order was placed with the Howaldtswerke Deutsche Werft (HDW) in Kiel for a revolutionary 7,034-ton cruise ferry of a standard which compared with the finest Scandinavian passenger liners of the period. Delivered in May, 1961, the new *Kronprins Harald* was immediately acclaimed for her elegance and fine accommodations. She could carry 577 passengers in two classes and 120 cars,

The near sister ship *Prinsesse Ragnhild* at sea, shortly after her introduction to Jahre Line's service. *Author Collection*

loaded through side hatches.

Eventually, a slightly larger sister ship, the *Prinsesse Ragnhild*, was ordered from the same builder for delivery in 1966. During the winter season, this equally handsome liner was sent on cruises to the Canary Islands and Madeira and the Mediterranean. These relatively long voyages carried mainly German passengers.

As neither ship had significant freight capacity for their summer role as ferries, a new *Kronprins Harald* was ordered, again from HDW, for delivery in 1976. The original ship of that name was then sold to the Vietnam Ocean Shipping Company and headed east for coastal service as *Ha Long*. Later, in 1991, she passed into Greek ownership and was used briefly by Afroessa Lines on routes from Piraeus to Crete and Cyprus as *Panagia*. After her hard service in the Far East, however, she was in poor condition and was laid up in 1994. Later, she was re-named *Al Safa*, suggesting that it was intended that she might become a Red Sea pilgrim ship, but she was moved to an anchorage near to Chalkis, where she remains, now called *Medousa*.

The replacement *Kronprins Harald* was a purposeful-looking 12,752-ton car ferry with bow and stern doors and ample space for 400 cars, or a mixture of cars and lorry trailers. In 1981, she was joined by an even larger *Prinsesse Ragnhild*, yet another HDW product and, at 16,631 gross tons, the biggest Jahre passenger ship yet seen. Consequently, the original *Prinsesse Ragnhild* was also sold, initially to Liberian owners for use as a floating hostel for oil-rig workers in the Gulf of Mexico, and was named *Ametista*. Soon, however, she was re-sold to the Xianmen Shipping Company of Xianmen, China for operation in the Chinese coastal trade as *Jin Jang*. Two years later, she became the *Ji Mei* and she continues to sail regularly from Hong Kong, nowadays on short casino junket cruises. Although she looks her age externally, being covered in layers of peeling paint, her interiors have been completely re-modelled in a peculiarly East Asian hotel æsthetic to appeal to her gambling clientele.

Anders Jahre, who died in 1982, served for many years as chairman of several other Norwegian shipping and industrial concerns. One of these, the Kosmos group, having acquired the Bergen Line, also bought the Norway Line (which operated the services from Newcastle to Stavanger and Bergen using the Fred. Olsen-Bergen Line vessels *Venus* and, later, *Jupiter* – see above). Soon after, both Jahre Line and Norway Line were brought together to form a single ferry company. Meanwhile, a further *Kronprins Harald* was ordered for the Oslo-Kiel service, this time from the Wärtsilä yard in Turku, Finland, for delivery in 1987. In terms of appearance, however, this angular 31,123-ton jumbo ferry was very different from its sleek 1961 namesake.

In October, 1990, the Jahre Line name disappeared from passenger shipping altogether as both the Kosmos ferry companies were bought by the Skaugen group (see above) and combined into a new company, Color Line. However, the Jahre group continues to be associated with oil tanker shipping; indeed, at one time, the firm operated the World's largest tanker – the giant 260,851-ton *Jahre Viking*.

The Oslo-Kiel route continues to go from strength to strength. In December, 2002, Color Line ordered what will be the largest ever new-build passenger vessel to fly the Norwegian flag. This 74,000-ton giant, designed and constructed by Kvaerner-Masa in Finland, will bring many of the facilities of a fully-fledged modern cruise liner to the route and will keep Norway at the forefront of passenger ship technology and modernity for many years to come.

3
The Swedish Liners

Svenska Amerika Linien
Swedish American Line

Although the Swedish American Line was founded in November 1914, its history can be traced back to 1890 when the shipowner Alex Broström formed Angfartygs Tirfing (the Tirfing Steamship Company), of which Swedish American was later to become a subsidiary. Broström had purchased his first ship, the ketch *Mathilda*, in 1865 and he formed the Tirfing concern to operate four small steamers. The fleet quickly grew to thirteen, specialising in the transport of iron ore. Also in 1890, Broström's son Dan, then aged 20, became a clerk in his father's firm. He became a board member only a year later and set the pace for the rapid expansion of the family shipping business. When Axel Broström died in 1905, his son took control and set about even further expansion.

In 1907, Dan Broström was involved in the formation of the Swedish East Asia Company, set up to trade to the Far East. Subsequently, in 1911, the Swedish Levant Line was formed and, in a joint venture with Norwegian shipowners, the Swedish American Mexico Line followed in 1912 to run cargo services to the Gulf of Mexico and also to ports further up the eastern seaboard of the United States. Also, the matter of establishing a transatlantic passenger service was in the minds of several leading Swedish shipowners, who realised that most of their countrymen emigrating to the New World were travelling in Danish and, after 1913, Norwegian ships. After protracted negotiations with the Swedish banks to raise sufficient capital, the Swedish American Line was founded on the 30th November, 1914 and Dan Broström was appointed chairman.

The First World War frustrated the company's plans to order new passenger ships but in 1915 the Holland America Line offered its liner *Potsdam* for sale and Swedish American seized the opportunity to buy her. A steamer of 12,975 tons, built by Blohm & Voss of Hamburg in 1900, she was renamed *Stockholm* and sailed on her first voyage from Gothenburg to New York on the 11th December, 1915. Owing to war conditions, the service was unable to reach its intended frequency and when U-boats began to pose a serious threat even to neutral merchant shipping around Scandinavian waters, it was suspended almost entirely.

At the end of June, 1918, scheduled services resumed and it soon became necessary for Swedish American Line to buy another passenger ship. In the autumn of 1919, the company purchased the 10,757-ton liner *Virginian*. She was a triple-screw turbine steamer built in 1905 by Alexander Stephen & Sons in Glasgow for the Allan Line's services to Canada from Glasgow and Liverpool. She and her sister were notable for being the first turbine-driven ships on the North Atlantic. She could accommodate 1,580 passengers, of whom 818 were third class and so she was well-suited to the emigrant trade. She was renamed *Drottningholm* after the Swedish king's country palace near Stockholm and, after a thorough refit, entered service in the spring of 1920. These first Swedish American liners sailed with black hulls and with yellow funnels with a blue disc on either side, featuring three golden crowns.

THE FIRST GRIPSHOLM AND THE SECOND KUNGSHOLM

The flow of emigrants to America reached its peak in 1923 when 16,000 Swedes passed through Gothenburg en route for a new life overseas. With other traffic, demand was so great that year that the company chartered another Holland America liner, the *Noordam*, a 12,500 ton vessel which had been built by Harland & Wolff of Belfast in 1902. She became the first *Kungsholm*. Her charter was

Shortly before her sale to Swedish American Line, the *Potsdam* is seen with war-time neutrality markings on her hull in 1915. Her enormous funnel, lengthened previously, is particularly evident.
World Ship Society

79

A 1930s view of the *Drottningholm*, looking graceful in her all-white livery. Note that her lifeboats are now double-stacked. *World Ship Society*

only a temporary measure and the company placed an order with Armstrong, Whitworth & Company on the Tyne for its first-ever specially built new passenger liner. This flagship, to be called *Gripsholm*, was, at 18,815 tons, Scandinavia's largest passenger vessel yet. A pioneer in many respects, she was the first motorliner for passenger service on the North Atlantic and, indeed, the largest, most powerful and fastest diesel-driven liner yet in service. She was designed jointly by the respected British naval architects Sir John Biles & Company and Swedish American's own technical director, Filip Lindahl.

By the time the magnificent new *Gripsholm* was delivered in 1925, the company's business had changed dramatically. The flow of emigrants had subsided almost completely due to the stricter American immigration laws, but the number of passengers travelling for business or pleasure was increasing. Americans were tempted to visit Scandinavia as tourists, many being former emigrants with relatives to visit. Later, to offset the effects of the American depression, cruises were introduced in the winter season. Because of the *Gripsholm*'s comparatively large size and her comfortable accommodation, she became a very popular cruise ship. This was hardly surprising since, as her name suggested, she was a late example of a 'floating palace' – a highly ornate essay in the Gustavian manner, with carved woodwork, marble, flock wallpaper, trompe l'oeuil panels in gilded frames and baroque furniture in both first and second class accommodation.

Unfortunately, Dan Broström was killed in a car crash in 1925, but the Tirfing company and its associates continued to grow, with his brother-in-law J. Albinus Janson as the Tirfing chairman. With the prospect of an expanding tourist traffic, Swedish American Line ordered another ship, the 21,250 ton *Kungsholm*, which was built by Blohm & Voss and introduced in 1928. The previous *Kungsholm*, the chartered Holland America vessel, was returned to her owners and when the new ship entered service, the elderly *Stockholm* was sold to Norwegian owners for conversion into a whaling factory ship, the *Solglint*.

The new flagship was another motorliner, but with very graceful lines. Many motorships of the period, such as the Cosulich liners *Saturnia* and *Vulcania* and the White Star *Britannic* and *Georgic*, were rather tubby in appearance, with short, squat flat-topped funnels. The *Kungsholm*, in

The first Swedish American Line newbuilding, the *Gripsholm* of 1925, is seen on the Tyne prior to her trials in the North Sea. Her thin motor ship funnels drew much criticism as passengers expected liners to have vast stacks, towering over the superstructure and symbolising safety and power. *Ambrose Greenway Collection*

The Gustavian elegance of the *Gripsholm's* first class dining saloon was enhanced by its ivory and gold paint scheme and its ceiling dome, adorned with fresco panels. This view shows the musicians' gallery, where a string quartet would serenade diners, reputedly with a mix of light classical music and Swedish folk tunes.
Author Collection

Even second class passengers were treated like royalty on the *Gripsholm*. Her social hall in second class was better than its first class counterpart on many lesser liners and was modelled on the Hall of State at Gripsholm Castle. Flanking the ornately carved marble fireplace were copies of paintings in the castle. *Author Collection*

The *Gripsholm* at anchor, landing passengers by tender, during a cruise in the 1930s. Her moderate size and luxurious appointments for all classes made her an ideal cruise ship, although her lack of air conditioning would have precluded long itineraries to warm climes. *World Ship Society*

The *Kungsholm* of 1928 had loftier funnels than her sister and, consequently, many felt she had a more harmonious appearance. She is seen here when newly delivered to Swedish American Line. *Ambrose Greenway Collection*

contrast, had two tall, well-raked steamship-type stacks and, after being repainted in Swedish American's new all-white livery in 1933, she became the epitome of elegance. All subsequent Swedish American liners were turned out in this manner and they became known as 'The White Viking Fleet'.

Decoratively, the new liner was radically different from previous Scandinavian ships. During the 1920s, Swedish architecture, art and design earned a solid international reputation for craftsmanship and innovation. Carl Bergsten, the architect of the highly-regarded Swedish Pavillion at the 1925 Exposition des Arts Décoratifs et

The *Kungsholm*'s remarkable interior design brought her immediate acclaim. The first class hallway was an astonishing example of Swedish style of the 1920s. The blue, gold, black and red colours were accented by details in silver plate. *Author Collection*

83

The *Kungsholm*'s swimming pool measured 13x6 metres and was adjoined by a well-equipped gymnasium. There were spectator galleries for swimming galas and even a bar at one end. *Author Collection*

A busy 1930s scene in Gothenburg harbour. Despite the caption, this is actually the *Kungsholm* leaving for New York. *Author Collection*

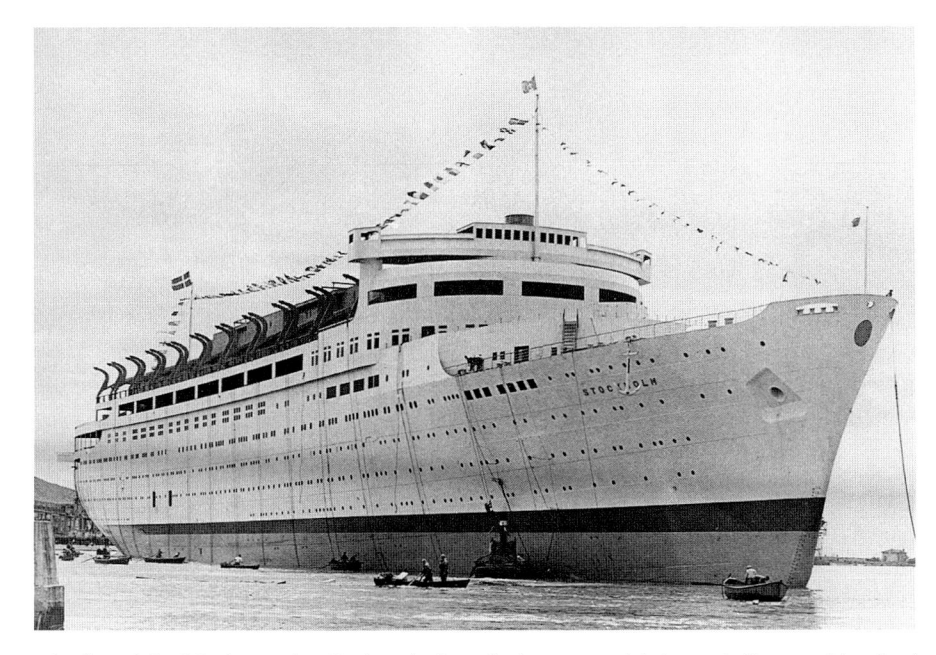

A rare photograph of the unfortunate *Stockholm* taken immediately after her launch. Shortly after, she was destroyed by fire and only her machinery and part of her hull could be recovered for use in her larger replacement. Although the two ships were similar, the first had an outdoor promenade in front of the bridge. *Author Collection*

Industriels Moderne in Paris, designed the new ship's interiors. Her richly coloured modern romantic décor was unmistakably Scandinavian and quite unlike the French Art Deco of the celebrated *Ile de France*. Sailing opposite the *Gripsholm*, the new *Kungsholm* became very popular both as an Atlantic liner and, occasionally, as a cruise ship, with trips to the Norwegian fjords, the Mediterranean and from New York to the Caribbean.

THE UNFORTUNATE PRE-WAR STOCKHOLM

In the late 1930s, the company ordered a further passenger liner, this time from an Italian builder, the Monfalcone yard of the Cantieri Riuniti dell' Adriatico. The new liner was to be a triple-screw motorship with a speed of 19 knots and it was announced that she would be named *Stockholm*. Swedish American Line's brilliant naval architect, Eric Christiansson, designed her. He was heavily influenced by the innovative German KdF liner *Robert Ley* and, indeed, the *Stockholm* was in many ways a two-funnelled version of that ship. Tragically, when nearing completion, she was virtually destroyed by fire at the shipyard and so required a complete rebuild from the waterline up – this time in a slightly enlarged form. She was now 30,390 tons and the biggest Swedish American liner ever.

She ran trials in the Gulf of Trieste in 1941 but, frustratingly for Swedish American, she proved to have serious stability problems and delivery was postponed until she had been fitted with sponsons on either side of the hull below the waterline. Nevertheless, her raked bow, cruiser stern and two well-proportioned ovoid funnels gave a crisp and fashionable appearance.

Most significantly, the *Stockholm* was specifically designed as a dual-role cruise ship and transatlantic liner. She was intended to carry 1,350 passengers in three classes on Atlantic line service between Gothenburg and New

The bulky but impressive 1941 *Stockholm* on trials in the Gulf of Trieste, her hull apparently still painted in light grey undercoat. *Ambrose Greenway Collection*

Internally, the *Stockholm* represented a change of direction for Swedish American Line. Designed by Nils Einar Eriksson, Gustav Alde and Nino Zoncada, her open-plan layout pointed the way to post-War developments. Here we see a lounge and the Showboat Restaurant. *Philip Dawson Collection*

Rebuilt with larger funnels and a more modern-looking bow, the *Gripsholm* sets sail down the Hudson River, passing Manhattan, at the beginning of another transatlantic crossing to Scandinavia in the early 1950s.
Author Collection

York but, when cruising, the first and tourist class accommodations could be amalgamated and the third-class areas closed off entirely, reducing the passenger capacity to a mere 620. Among the special provisions made for the ship's cruising role were an open air swimming pool (most unusual for a Scandinavian transatlantic vessel at that time) and spacious sun decks. All cabins and public rooms to be used in cruise service were completely air conditioned. This, in itself, was noteworthy at a time when many liners designed exclusively for tropical services offered this comfort only in their first-class dining saloons and perhaps one or two other major public rooms.

Within, the *Stockholm* was very progressive. The principal public rooms were the work of Nils Einar Eriksson, one of the architects previously involved in the Stockholm Exhibition and the designer of Gothenburg's famous Concert Hall. He was assisted by Gustav Alde, who had previously designed the interiors of the *Stella Polaris* and the Johnson Line passenger-cargo liners. The detailed execution of their work was supervised at Monfalcone by Nino Zoncada, who also contributed the 'connective spaces', such as staircases and hallways. Even so, as Eriksson, Alde and Zoncada worked in a complementary manner, a high degree of coherence was achieved. As with a number of recent transatlantic liners – most notably the *Normandie* and the *Nieuw Amsterdam* – the exhaust uptakes were split, enabling an open plan central circulation axis on both public room and cabin decks.

The *Stockholm's* accommodation was most notable for the 250 spacious first and tourist-class cabins intended for cruise service. Perhaps the most remarkable feature of the cabin arrangement was that virtually all rooms to be used for cruising were arranged on either side of a single wide central hallway extending the full length of each deck. By developing the traditional 'Bibby' cabin (which gave even inside rooms a narrow space leading to a porthole) into a repeat arrangement of interlocking U-shaped spaces, almost every cabin could be sold as an 'outside'. Furthermore, all were equipped with full-size twin beds, spacious wardrobes and, in most cases, a separate sitting area.

The saloon deck was largely open plan, with lifts and staircases on either beam, creating the same type of centreline circulation axis found on *Bremen, Europa, Normandie* and *Nieuw Amsterdam*, with uninterrupted vistas from space to space. The dining room, located beneath the main lounge, was roughly doughnut-shaped with a central service core from which sliding partitions could be extended to split the room into a series of more intimate spaces. Decoratively, the *Stockholm* represented the very latest in Scandinavian design – and indeed she had a great deal in common with the post-War generation of Atlantic liners. Contemporary Swedish artists decorated the bulkheads with abstract murals. These included, for instance, a charming series of enamel depictions of Mississippi riverboats by Kurt Jungstedt for the Show Boat

Restaurant. The distinguished furniture designer Axel Larsson produced a wide range of modern furnishings, making the *Stockholm's* interiors airy, spacious and far removed from the ornate designs of its predecessors.

Sadly, due to the delay in delivery, Swedish American Line was again thwarted as Italy entered the Second World War on the German side and the fine new flagship remained at her builders' yard. She was sold to the Italian government, who placed her under the management of the Italia Line and had her converted into the troopship *Sabaudia*. In May 1945, she capsized at Trieste following allied aerial bombardment. Yet the *Stockholm* had survived in her pristine glory just long enough to leave a deep and lasting impression for her outstanding design on both her owners and her builders. That influence would be seen in many post-War Scandinavian and Italian liners.

THE NOTORIOUS POST-WAR STOCKHOLM

The Second World War halted the Swedish American Line's transatlantic passenger trade and, by the end of 1941, it had also put a stop to the cruising activities. Although Sweden remained neutral, the Germans refused to guarantee the safety of its merchant ships. The *Kungsholm* was sold at a profit to the United States government, who converted her into the troopship *John Ericsson*. After the War, in 1947, she was bought back by her former owners in a fire-damaged state and was transferred to the South Atlantic Line for the Home Lines service from Genoa to South America as the *Italia*. South Atlantic Line, in which the Broströms had invested money, was one of the constituents of Home Lines and the *Italia* later sailed for them between Genoa and New York. Her greatest success, however, came when she established Home Lines in a regular cruise service between New York and Bermuda. In 1964, she was sold for conversion into a floating hotel at Freeport in the Bahamas.

From 1942, both the *Drottningholm* and the *Gripsholm* were chartered out by the neutral Swedes for the transport of diplomatic personnel and the exchange of prisoners of war. This work intensified as the War drew to a close and the *Drottningholm* became an occasional visitor to Liverpool, where she had once been so well-known as the Allan Line's *Virginian*.

Looking ahead, in 1944 Swedish American Line ordered another *Stockholm*, paid for with the proceeds from the sale of her hapless predecessor to the Italians. Built by the Götaverken shipyard in Gothenburg, she was a much smaller combined passenger and cargo motorship of just 11,893 tons and was launched on the 9th September, 1946. After a protracted outfitting period, since materials were in short supply, she finally entered service in 1948. This *Stockholm* carried a mere 395 passengers in first and tourist class and her Götaverken diesels gave her a speed of 19 knots. The architect Claes Feder, who joined Broströms' technical department in 1952, recalls that 'in the late 1940s, there were not so many passengers travelling between Scandinavia and America, so the post-War *Stockholm* was to have been the first of a series of combination passenger and cargo ships. The design was worked out in rather a hurry and our boss, Eric Christiansson, used to joke that it had been put down on the back of an envelope. Anyway, the *Stockholm* was a terrible sea boat and rolled quite alarmingly. However, she had a small and very exclusive first class section in which many important diplomats travelled between America and Scandinavia. Soon, with demand from passengers returning to pre-War levels, Swedish American required larger passenger liners, so thankfully the directors abandoned plans for further ships of the *Stockholm* type.'

She traded mostly between Gothenburg, Copenhagen and New York, with occasional calls at Århus, Bremerhaven and Halifax (Nova Scotia). She was joined by the rebuilt *Gripsholm* which, following refurbishment in 1949 at the Howaldtswerke shipyard in Kiel, now boasted a modern-looking raked stem and wider funnels. At the same time, the elderly *Drottningholm* was withdrawn. She was sold to the Mediterranean Lines of Panama, another component of Home Lines, and re-named *Brasil* and later *Homeland*. Until February 1955, she traded from Mediterranean ports to both North and South America and between Hamburg and New York. In 1955, after an active career of fifty years, she was broken up at Trieste.

The *Stockholm* became notorious on what should have been an ordinary midsummer Atlantic crossing. She had

Swedish American Line's austerity ship, the *Stockholm* of 1948. In this 1950s photograph, her superstructure has been extended fore and aft, making her look more of a passenger liner than when first completed.
Author Collection

The post-War *Stockholm*'s interiors were altogether more conservative in style than those of her short-lived predecessor. Here we see her first class saloon and her tourist class smoking room. *Author Collection*

The new *Kungsholm* receives final adjustments at the Rotterdam Drydock Company's yard in 1953. *World Ship Society*

left New York on the 25th July, 1956. That night, in dense fog off Nantucket, she rammed the 29,000-ton Italia Line flagship *Andrea Doria*. The larger ship sank and there were 52 fatalities in the tragedy. The *Stockholm* limped back to New York with her bow a crumpled tangle of steelwork. There, she was repaired at the Bethlehem Steel shipyard in Brooklyn. The work took four months.

THE THIRD KUNGSHOLM

In 1953, a further new passenger liner was delivered from De Schelde shipyard at Vlissingen in Holland. This latest *Kungsholm* was a fine twin-screw motorship of 21,165 tons, designed for both the North Atlantic trade and worldwide cruising. Although somewhat smaller than the ill-fated pre-War *Stockholm*, she had a similar appearance with two wide, tapering funnels and a modern, streamlined superstructure. While retaining a traditional elegance, she was also forward-looking as her machinery spaces were placed towards the stern. Unlike the British *Southern Cross*, however, she had a dummy forward stack, which balanced her profile and disguised her innovative layout.

According to Per-Olov Wirén, then Swedish American Line's technical inspector: 'The naval architects had wanted to give the new *Kungsholm* a very up-to-date profile with a single exhaust stack above the engines towards the stern. This would have made good technical sense, but Swedish American was a very traditionally-minded company and its directors insisted that the ship should have a 'normal' profile with two funnels, one in front of the

With floodlit funnels and lightbulbs from stem to stern, the *Kungsholm* makes a fine sight as she lies at her Gothenburg berth. *Ambrose Greenway Collection*

The lofty second class main lounge, panelled in oak, was one of the most successful rooms on the ship. The marquetry panel on its end wall, by Rolf Blomberg, depicted famous characters, events and buildings from Sweden's history. *Ambrose Greenway Collection*

The first class dining saloon on the *Kungsholm* was an odd mix of styles and eras - with modern cove-lit ceilings, a whimsical mural and contrasting Gustavian-style furniture. As with so many liners of the immediate post-War period, the *Kungsholm* was perhaps caught in a phase of stylistic transition. *Ambrose Greenway Collection*

Passengers enjoy tea, sheltered from the sea breezes on the *Kungsholm's* first class verandah.
Ambrose Greenway Collection

other. Whatever we may have felt at the time, there is no doubt that this made our liners exceptionally beautiful and very distinctive – especially once other companies abandoned such traditional profiles.'

The *Kungsholm* could carry around 800 passengers and her interiors had a similar layout to those of the pre-War *Stockholm*, although the new ship, being smaller, had centrally located exhaust uptakes. These saved space but limited the scope for open-plan interior treatments. Claes

Feder remembers: 'In designing *Kungsholm* and her later sister *Gripsholm*, we wanted to create interiors where passengers boarded and immediately felt that they were in a piece of Sweden. Most of her interiors were by an architect from Gothenburg called Per Lindfors who produced elegant, modern designs. Rolf Ahberg and Margaretha Engströmer were responsible for the restaurant while Inge Westim drew the forward lounge. All of these schemes were then co-ordinated by the Dutch

The graceful new *Gripsholm* shows her paces on her trials in the Gulf of Genoa in 1957. As can be seen, the new liner's hull was very similar to that of her contemporary, the *Federico C.* of Costa Line, built at the same shipyard and completed the same year. *Claes Feder Collection*

92

Unlike today's mass-market cruise ships, where every space is used to generate income, liners like the stately *Gripsholm* had numerous quiet areas in which their wealthy clientele could relax and unwind. This is her card room, designed by the Italian architect Nino Zoncada. *Claes Feder Collection*

firm of H. P. Mutters & Zoon, who worked to translate them for the shipyard.'

The *Kungsholm* was beautifully decorated with glowing walnut veneers and marquetry panels on the bulkheads. There were lofty cove-lit ceilings, tapestry and ceramic panels and the finest furniture, which was designed by Axel Larsson. Many of the artworks had been commissioned for the pre-War *Stockholm*. Also, the internal layout with Bibby cabins, but now L-shaped, accessed off central corridors was very similar to her's. Thus, almost all cabins had an outside view. The vast majority also had private facilities. This made the new liner ideally suited for cruising as well as for the established transatlantic liner service.

In 1954, the ageing *Gripsholm* switched to sail for the newly-formed Bremen-America Line, a joint venture between Swedish American and the Norddeutscher Lloyd of Bremen, which was set up to enable Germany to re-enter the transatlantic trade. A year later, she was sold to the German company and rebuilt as the *Berlin*, Germany's first significant Atlantic liner since the War. Meanwhile, Swedish American ordered a new ship to carry the name *Gripsholm*.

THE 1957 GRIPSHOLM

The new 23,190-ton *Gripsholm* was delivered from the Ansaldo shipyard at Genoa in 1957. She was similar in appearance to the *Kungsholm* but her design had been refined by Christiansson and she had more elegantly sweeping lines. According to Per-Olov Wirén: 'I was sent to Ansaldo to supervise the planning and construction. The Italian shipbuilders were great craftsmen and the yards there were then at the peak of their powers. She was very much an improved version of the earlier *Kungsholm*. For example, her bow design was enhanced to make her faster and less prone to pitching than the previous ship had been. Also, the hull plates were riveted to the frames but were welded together to avoid the obvious jointing of the *Kungsholm's* hull and to give her a smoother overall appearance. The *Gripsholm* was a very comfortable ship and many still say that she was our finest-ever liner.'

The *Gripsholm's* saloon deck contained a series of inter-connecting lounges, bars and sitting rooms. Thanks to Nino Zoncada, most of these spaces had a distinctly Mediterranean look – which could only have been advantageous when the ship was increasingly sent cruising to warmer climes. *Author Collection*

Prinsessan Margaretha named her on the 8th April, 1956. The new ship was air-conditioned throughout and, as on the *Kungsholm*, the vast majority of the cabins had outside views and private facilities. She could carry 778 passengers in two classes, first and tourist, on the Atlantic service but she became a one-class ship when cruising. A further innovation was the decision to integrate the promenades within the overall interior design. These spaces became comfortable arcades from which most of the public rooms could be accessed. With her spacious accommodation, the *Gripsholm* became known for her longer de luxe cruises.

Claes Feder remembers: 'Because she was intended to spend a greater proportion of her time on cruises, the *Gripsholm* had a much lighter feeling than our previous ships. Per Lindfors, who had been appointed architectural co-ordinator, again designed many of the public rooms, as did Rolf Ahberg and Margaretha Engströmer, while other spaces, such as corridors and stairwells, were the work of Italian architects. In particular, Nino Zoncada designed the forward lounge/ballroom. Consequently, these spaces resembled those on Italian liners of the period. She was a luxurious ship, renowned for her absolute precision service. Many Hollywood film stars, international business tycoons and minor royals voyaged on her during the 1960s. Sometimes, certain passengers would buy whole suites of cabins to store their furs, ball gowns and even their pet animals, while still having enough space to entertain their friends at private cocktail parties.'

DISPOSALS AND THE FINAL SWITCH TO CRUISING

With the *Gripsholm* in service, the little *Stockholm* was sold in 1959 to the East German government and was renamed *Völkerfreundschaft*, which translates as 'Friendship of the Peoples'. With jet aircraft taking an increasing proportion of the transatlantic passenger trade, Swedish American intended its ships to spend more time in luxury cruising and the *Stockholm* was plainly unsuited for this upmarket role. However, under East German ownership she became the first trade union cruise ship. During the 1970s, she did carry Swedish passengers from time to time when chartered to the Stena Line to make cruises from Gothenburg. Finally retired in the spring of 1985, she was sold to Norwegian owners who re-registered her in Panama. With her name abbreviated to *Volker*, she was first laid up in Southampton, then chartered to the Norwegian government for use as a refugee hostel in Oslo under the name *Fridtjof Nansen*. Her hull remained sturdy and she was later purchased by Nina Compagnia di Navigazione of Genoa for conversion into a modern cruise ship. In 1992, she was taken in hand by a local shipyard for a radical rebuilding programme. (Genoa, ironically, had been the home port of the *Andrea Doria*, the Italian flagship which had sunk after being rammed by the *Stockholm* in 1956.) Work progressed slowly, but in 1994 the old ship emerged as the *Italia Prima*, with new engines, an entirely new superstructure and sponsons added to her

95

The last and finest of the Swedish American Liners - the *Kungsholm* - finally nears completion at the famous John Brown shipyard at Clydebank near Glasgow. *Author Collection*

stern. After a number of seasons cruising quite widely, the *Italia Prima* began sailing on cruises from Havana in Cuba under the name *Valtur Prima*. This venture collapsed and, subsequently, it was rumoured that she might be chartered to Festival Cruises to sail as *Caribe*, once again on the Cuban cruise circuit. Nothing has come of this so far and the now elderly ship remains laid up in Havana.

Reverting now to the 1960s, the number of passengers travelling on Atlantic crossings continued to decline, but at the same time Swedish American's expertly organised luxury cruises became more popular than ever. They tended to operate from New York, carrying many well-off American tourists all over the World. As the 1953 *Kungsholm* was essentially a combined Atlantic liner and cruise ship, the Swedish American directors decided in 1963 to order a larger vessel specifically for cruising. She too was to be called *Kungsholm*.

The existing ship followed the pre-War *Gripsholm* into the Norddeutscher Lloyd fleet. Still a very up-to-date liner, she became the *Europa*, catering for a predominantly German clientele with a combination of Atlantic crossings and luxury cruises. When Norddeutscher Lloyd merged with the Hamburg America Line in 1971 to become Hapag-Lloyd, the *Europa* remained the company flagship.

However, a brand new *Europa* was delivered in 1981 and the previous ship was sold to a subsidiary of the Costa Line of Genoa. They renamed her *Columbus C.*, an unusual name for a Costa liner. It reflected the fact that she was to be chartered for much of her time to German tour operators, including Hapag-Lloyd, and she was given the name *Columbus* in order to revive memories of a popular pre-War German liner. The *Columbus C.* started her new career running between Genoa and South America, then began a series of European cruises. She had an unexpectedly premature end when she struck a breakwater while entering Cadiz harbour on the 29th July, 1984. She was able to dock and disembark her passengers but, severely damaged, she settled to the bottom of the harbour, though remaining upright. Declared a total loss, she was sold to shipbreakers at Barcelona.

THE LAST KUNGSHOLM

The new *Kungsholm*, 26,677 gross tons, was intended to cruise for 80 per cent of the year with only occasional Atlantic crossings. Claes Feder was heavily involved in her design and construction: 'The design concept, including the overall layout and the exterior design, for which I was responsible, was prepared by Swedish American's passenger department. Before we started work, a team of architects sailed on both the existing *Kungsholm* and *Gripsholm*. We looked into every aspect of their operation and interviewed everyone from the captains to the bellboys. As a result of this research, full-scale mock-ups of cabins and parts of the public rooms were built on land next to our office in Gothenburg so that we could make sure that every last detail was in its proper place. Other elements, such as the funnels, were sculpted in wood and tested on models to make sure that they were effective. This work was then approved by Swedish American's management and submitted to the technical department for further development, at first under the guidance of Eric Christiansson, who retired, and then of Gösta Kaudern. Per-Olov Wirén was the Chief Inspector during the construction of the ship.'

Built at the famous Clydebank shipyard of John Brown & Co., the magnificent new *Kungsholm* was due to be delivered in November 1965. Unfortunately, the yard was bedevilled by labour problems during the fitting out stage and delivery was delayed by four months. While this was unfortunate, the £7million ship was described by Axel Bröstrom, the company chairman, as 'one of the finest we have ever received from any shipyard'. However, much of the shipping press focused instead on her late delivery and the penalties to be paid by her builders. In all, John Brown were said to have lost £3 million on the contract. After drydocking in Belfast and trials on the Arran mile in the Firth of Clyde, she sailed to Gothenburg in March, 1966 for the installation of Swedish furniture and artworks. She left on her maiden voyage to New York on the 22nd April.

The latest *Kungsholm* was a very graceful ship both

Many shiplovers thought that the *Kungsholm* represented the epitome of ocean liner perfection and this aerial view certainly shows off her beautiful lines. The ship had a very harmonious design - note how the slant of the forward superstructure is repeated in the rake of the masts and funnels, and how their tapering profiles are carried through in the slanted windows in the superstructure. Notice also the prominent overhanging lido area between the funnels and the large ship-to-shore tenders - evidence of her primary role of cruise liner. Here, the *Kungsholm* makes a magnificent sight as, dressed overall, she passes along the Hudson River.
Ambrose Greenway Collection

from the outside and in her interior. Her classic profile featured two tapering funnels with fins, although the forward of these was a dummy containing generators and water tanks. She had two aluminium masts, a well-raked stem with a bulbous bow and a highly curvaceous stern. As she was designed principally as a cruise ship, there were no general cargo holds. In Atlantic service, she could carry 750 passengers in two classes but, in her more regular cruising role, she usually carried only 450 with 438 officers and crew. Power was provided by a pair of Götaverken diesels which at the time of their construction formed the most powerful twin-screw plant ever built by the Gothenburg-based company and gave the liner a maximum speed of 23 knots. Naturally, the *Kungsholm* was fitted with stabilisers and provision was made for the later fitting of a bow thrust unit.

The passenger accommodation on eight decks was the work of a number of talented British and Swedish designers. According to Claes Feder: 'By the 1960s, Swedish American had developed an interesting management structure. As more and more of its passengers were American, the New York office had expanded and was actually very powerful. The passenger department was always very careful that New York would OK the designs to make sure that everything was suitable for American tastes and we designers, in turn, answered to the passenger department. For the Americans, anything to do with royalty – crowns, pictures of the Swedish Royal Family, Gustavian furniture – was seen as advantageous. Fortunately, it was decided that the *Kungsholm* would be a very modern ship and employing Count Sigvard Bernadotte to create some of the interiors provided the 'royal connection'. I notice that P&O continue this tradition since Viscount Linley, a nephew of the British Queen, has done rooms on the *Oriana* and *Aurora*.'

The lounge and adjacent verandas, at the forward end of the Boat Deck below the bridge, were designed by Count Bernadotte in conjunction with Veit Betlike and

The dining saloon, decorated in shades of blue set against teak panelling, shows the understated elegance for which the *Kungsholm* was famed. Splitting the room into two sections was a partition with four vitrines containing antique porcelain from the East Indies. During the ship's few transatlantic crossings, retractable partitions could be unfolded to make the space two class. Swedish American campaigned vigorously for the abandonment of the class system, imposed by their rivals in the North Atlantic Conference.
Ambrose Greenway Collection

The *Kungsholm*'s main lounge, designed by Robert Tillberg, could accommodate 400 people. The ceramic bas-relief on the end wall, entitled 'Midnight Sun', was by the noted Swedish artist, Carl Harry Stålhane.
Ambrose Greenway Collection

had an intimate atmosphere with dark wood panelling, abstract bas-relief panels and comfortable settees. Glass doors, to enhance the sense of spaciousness, connected all the rooms. The forward section had duplicates of the instruments on the bridge to enable passengers to follow the ship's progress. Behind, there was a rosewood dance floor and a long bar facing forward. Amidships, between the funnels, was a sheltered lido area with a sun deck cantilevered over the ship's sides one deck above. At the forward end of the Veranda Deck was the 307-seat auditorium, designed by British architect Geoffrey Tabb of Tabb & Haselhurst. It served as a cinema, theatre, lecture hall and church. (Tabb & Haselhurst were also employed to supervise the translation of the various designs into the ship while it was under construction.) The library was at the port side and was panelled in yew, with writing desks and settees for relaxed reading.

Perhaps the most impressive room on *Kungsholm* was the main lounge, designed by Robert Tillberg. It was aft of the entrance hall and extended the full width of the ship. Tillberg later became a prolific interior designer for both ferries and cruise ships. In recent years, his work has become notorious for its garish colours, mirrors, brass, marble and glitz – but the *Kungsholm*, one of his early efforts, was much more restrained. The lounge had an impressive cove-lit ceiling with a central dome covered in gold leaf. At its forward end was a stage which could be covered with sliding decorative metal panels when not in use. To the stern was the veranda lounge and smoking room with light grey oak panelling and a raised dance floor. Below, the dining room, on 'A' Deck, was designed by Rolf Ahberg. It filled the entire width of the ship, with raised sections to either side and two ceiling domes with concealed perimeter lighting. A folding partition could divide the room into two classes for Atlantic service. With seating for 500 diners, the *Kungsholm* could easily accommodate all her cruise passengers at one leisurely sitting. On 'D' Deck, lower in the hull, were a heated indoor swimming pool, a fitness centre and, this being a Swedish liner, male and female sauna baths.

The new *Kungsholm* made her maiden arrival in New York on the 2nd May, 1966, receiving an enthusiastic welcome with tugs firing water cannons into the air and sirens and whistles sounding around the harbour. Swedish American was right to believe that the future of passenger shipping lay in the cruise trade as on her maiden crossing the *Kungsholm* carried only 304 passengers. For nine years, the new liner earned an excellent reputation as a luxury cruise ship. While older, fuel-thirsty turbine vessels went to the breakers in large numbers during the fuel crisis in the early 1970s, the efficient *Kungsholm* remained successful.

It was not a lack of customers for her cruises which abruptly ended her career and Swedish American Line's passenger operations, but the demands of the Swedish trade unions. The *Kungsholm* carried nearly as many crew as passengers, and so when the company proposed to re-register its two liners under a flag of convenience, the crews on both ships reluctantly agreed. Unfortunately, the unions in Sweden refused to contemplate any such cost-cutting measures which would have seen Swedes replaced by the cheaper 'international' staffs favoured by a newer generation of rival cruise lines. The result was that in August 1975, Swedish American Line withdrew from passenger shipping completely. Employees in the company's New York office were baffled. After all, they had taken substantial bookings, but their protests to Gothenburg were fruitless. According to Claes Feder: 'For those of us who had worked so hard to build Swedish American Line's following, it was very sad. On the other hand, the Swedish crews had given its ships their unique reputation for excellence. Their immaculate appearance and standard of service were from a different era. Replacing the Swedish staff would have changed the atmosphere of the ships – they would no longer have been Swedish American liners; they would have become less distinctive altogether.'

THE END OF A FAMOUS FLEET

Ironically, the *Kungsholm* was sold to a Norwegian, Øivind Lorentzen, whose company was called Flagship Cruises, and she was placed under the Panamanian flag. On the 6th October 1975, she began cruises out of New York with neither a change of name nor livery (except for the emblem on the funnels). Flagship Cruises had previously built two modern liners in Germany – the *Sea Venture* and the *Island Venture* (see below). Both had been quickly sold to P&O Princess Cruises so it was perhaps not surprising that in 1978 P&O acquired the *Kungsholm* as well. That company had been anxious to find a suitable modern replacement for its ageing *Arcadia*, which was a popular cruise ship sailing from Sydney and carrying mainly Australian passengers.

P&O sent the *Kungsholm* to the Bremer Vulkan shipyard at Bremen for a £3½ million refit which lasted almost four months. When she emerged as the *Sea Princess* in January 1979, her appearance had been radically altered – many thought for the worse – by the removal of the forward funnel and the mainmast; and by the heightening of the aft funnel. As well as modernising the ship's appearance and bringing her profile into line with that of other recent P&O vessels, the taller funnel had the advantage of stopping soot falling onto the after sun decks and so was also practical. Inside, public rooms at the aft end of the veranda deck were replaced with new cabins to increase capacity and profitability.

The *Sea Princess* cruised from Australia for her first three years, before moving to the British market. Then from 1986 to 1991, she was a member of the Princess Cruises fleet, sailing from the West Coast of the United States. In 1991, she was brought back to Britain and cruised the World from Southampton for the next twelve years. Re-named *Victoria* in 1995 in order to distinguish her from P&O's American-based Princess fleet, she remained a highly popular ship and one whose traditional appearance and intimate size attracted a different clientele from today's 'mega-ships'. However, she was on borrowed time. Having been sold by P&O to an investment group, she continued in service until the autumn of 2002, after which she was chartered out by her new owners to a German travel firm, Holiday Kreutzfarten. Re-named *Mona Lisa* and painted in a garish livery (featuring an image of the Mona Lisa on her funnel), she continues in European cruise service despite sustaining bottom damage off Spitsbergen in July, 2003.

Returning to 1975 and the demise of the Swedish American passenger operation, the other ship, *Gripsholm*, was also laid up. She was sold to Mikail Karageorgis, then an important Greek shipowner. He re-named her *Navarino* and used her for two-week cruises in the Mediterranean from Piraeus and Venice, with occasional longer voyages during the winter months. Once again, she developed a high reputation, so it was surprising that a grounding off Patmos resulted in her being sold abruptly to the Finnish company Sally Line in the autumn of 1981. Sally planned to place her on a seven-day Caribbean cruise circuit out of Miami under the auspices of their Commodore Cruise Lines subsidiary. Unfortunately, on the 26th November, just before the sale was completed, she keeled over while in a floating drydock at Skaramanga in Greece.

At first, it was reported that she was a complete loss and would go for scrap. By the following March, however, she had been righted and was re-named *Samantha*. She was eventually rebuilt at La Spezia and fitted out at Piraeus before returning to cruise service in November, 1985 as Regency Cruises' *Regent Sea*. Her fine public rooms remained largely intact – an extraordinary reminder of what was otherwise a long-lost era in ocean liner décor – and the only obvious external change was the fitting of fins to her two funnels. The *Regent Sea* cruised mainly from the western seaboard of the United States, sailing northwards to Alaska in the summer and often via the Panama Canal to South American ports in the winter. Oozing period charm, she became a favourite with passengers who appreciated traditional liners. Her cabins were among the most generous in the cruise business and she gained a reputation for excellent service. Soon, the Regency Cruises fleet expanded to include a handful of other well-known classic liners. Regrettably, in 1997, just as the *Regent Sea* was about to be chartered to a German travel agency, Transocean Tours, who proposed to name her *Gripsholm* again, Regency Cruises went bankrupt.

The *Regent Sea* was sold by auction to an American firm called United States American Cruise Line for conversion to a gambling ship in 1997. Work began and the sun and veranda decks were completely gutted to make way for casinos. Having ripped the best rooms to pieces, the owners ran out of money and abandoned the project. The ship was laid up at Tampa in 1998 with her name abbreviated to *Sea*. With the market becoming ever more crowded with new ships, the once-exquisite liner was never to cruise again and she was sold for scrap in April, 2001. While under tow to the breakers in Alang, she ran into a storm off Cape Recife. Having developed a serious list, she finally sank early in the morning of the 12th July.

Svenska Lloyd - Swedish Lloyd

The Swedish Lloyd passenger service across the North Sea originated as the Thule Line, which had been formed in Gothenburg in 1870. In 1916, the company was taken over by Swedish Lloyd, itself an old-established Gothenburg concern, dating back in fact to 1869. The ships became highly respected on the Gothenburg – London route. Swedish Lloyd freighters also traded to the Mediterranean.

At the time of the takeover, the Thule Line had five passenger/cargo ships on the routes to London and to Granton, near Edinburgh: the *Bele, Thorsten, Thule, Balder* and *Saga*. Except for the *Saga*, they were all ageing, dating from 1879, 1882, 1892 and 1898, respectively. The *Saga* of 1909 was a product of Swan, Hunter & Wigham Richardson, who in later years delivered several more outstanding ships to Swedish Lloyd. In 1919, the Thule Line was fully integrated into the parent company. The striking Thule Line funnel colours, white with a black top and with a blue disc bearing a gold star, were adopted by Swedish Lloyd.

Also in 1919, the company bought the steamer *Western Australia*, which had been built in 1901 by Stabilimento Tecnico of Trieste for the Chinese Eastern Railway and was registered under the Russian flag at Vladivostok. A well-travelled ship, she had been sold to the government of Western Australia in 1910 for coastal service. She now became Swedish Lloyd's first *Patricia* and entered service between Gothenburg and Newcastle, later switching to the important London route. The older ships were sold off during the early 1920s, but the *Balder* was refitted and renamed *Northumbria* in 1930, sailing in the Newcastle service. The Germans seized her during the Second World War as she was lying at Bergen when they invaded Norway; she was later sunk at Gdynia.

Representing the early Swedish Lloyd fleet is this image of the passenger-cargo steamer *Thule*. *Author Collection*

The stately *Suecia* accelerates away from Tynemouth during sea trials in 1929. At this early stage in her career, her forecastle was painted white. *Author Collection*

The dining saloon of the *Britannia* during the 1930s, with 'ladies who lunch' being served by waitresses in well-starched uniforms – all very genteel and elegant. *Author Collection*

The motor ship *Saga*, berthed at the New Fresh Wharf by London Bridge on the Thames at the end of her maiden voyage from Gothenburg on 19 May 1946. *World Ship Society*

TWO FAVOURITE SISTERS, SUECIA AND BRITANNIA, AND THEIR FLEET-MATES

Very importantly, in 1929 Swedish Lloyd took delivery of the beautiful *Suecia* and *Britannia*, fast and sturdy 4,661-ton steam turbine vessels built by Swan, Hunter & Wigham Richardson. Intended for the lengthy Gothenburg to London route, their speed of up to 19½ knots was essential and their sleek hulls with graceful counter sterns, tall slender funnels and lofty well-spaced masts made them two of the most elegant ships on the North Sea. At first, they rolled badly in poor weather, but the fitting of larger bilge keels went some way towards remedying the problem. With their advent, the company sold its first *Patricia* to the British-owned United Baltic Corporation.

In 1935, Swedish Lloyd acquired another Swan, Hunter-built steamer, the *Patris* of the London-based but Greek-owned Byron Steamship Company, for whom she had traded in the Mediterranean. She became the second *Patricia*, sailing between Gothenburg and London. This now became a three-ship service with departures every second day. Unfortunately, in March 1937, while being refitted at the Eriksberg shipyard in Gothenburg, the *Suecia* was seriously damaged in a collision with the hull of a new ship which had just been launched. The *Suecia* sank but was salvaged and repaired.

With the coming of the Second World War, the majority of the Swedish Lloyd fleet was laid up in Gothenburg, since Sweden was officially a neutral country and it became impossible to maintain the routes to Britain. The *Patricia*, however, was chartered, and later sold, to the Swedish Navy for conversion to a submarine depot ship.

Traffic between Gothenburg and London had increased rapidly in the late 1930s and Swedish Lloyd had been so encouraged that before the outbreak of war, it ordered a further, considerably larger vessel for the route. Although the company favoured Tyne-built tonnage, with war looming it was thought more prudent to order the ship from the Götaverken company of Gothenburg who, in fact, sub-contracted the building of the hull to the Lindholmens yard. The 6,458-ton *Saga* was Swedish Lloyd's first motor passenger ship, her four Götaverken diesels giving her a speed of 17 knots. A wide funnel, streamlined superstructure and an all-over white livery gave her a more modern appearance than previous Swedish Lloyd ships. In fact, she resembled a large motor yacht. Within, she was also progressive – at least by Swedish Lloyd's rather conservative standards. One reason for the adoption of sleek glossy veneers and cove-lit ceilings may have been the difficulty of importing the fittings required for a more lavish scheme during Second World War and its immediate aftermath. Even so, expenditure was concentrated where it would have the

The *Saga* was unique amongst Swedish Lloyd ships, which usually tended towards the conservative in their décor, as she was streamlined and largely uncluttered with period ornamentation. Here we see her remarkable first class bar, with its skylights, and the dining saloon. *Author Collection*

The *Patricia* nearing completion at Swan Hunter's Neptune yard on the River Tyne in 1951. She had a robustly built-up forecastle to break the high waves often encountered on the North Sea. *Author Collection*

The turbine-driven *Patricia* at her berth in Gothenburg. *Author Collection*

maximum impact – such as the balustrades of the grand staircase in the first class hallway, which were formed of interlocking bronzed metal leaves.

Because of the war, the *Saga* was laid up at the shipyard and did not enter service until May, 1946. Somewhat slower than the company's earlier turbine steamers, she was withdrawn in 1956 and sold to the French Line to sail between Bordeaux and Casablanca as the *Ville de Bordeaux*. In 1964, she was sold to Bulgaria and, as the *Nessebar*, traded in the Black Sea and eastern Mediterranean until 1975 when she was scrapped in Yugoslavia.

In 1951, Swedish Lloyd returned to Swan, Hunter who delivered the third *Patricia*, a slightly larger near-sister to the *Saga*, but this time a turbine steamer. Stylistically, Swedish Lloyd's ships were rather traditional and the *Patricia's* wooden-panelled interiors were in a variety of styles, none recognisably modern. Her most remarkable feature was a lounge and bar which were described as 'Medieval English' in manner. Resembling a baronial hall, the room was two decks high and complete with stained glasswork and a heavily beamed ceiling. It must have been disconcerting in a North Sea gale! Throughout, the contract department of the famous Stockholm department store Nordiska Kompaniet supplied the furnishings and so the lack of a co-ordinating architect may partly explain the ship's eclectic interiors. There was much fine ornamentation and several striking marquetry panels adorned the hallways, yet there was little sense of overall co-ordination.

The *Patricia* too had a short career with the company, being sold in 1957 to the Hamburg America Line, for whom she was converted into the exclusive and luxurious cruise ship *Ariadne*. Sold four years later to the Eastern Steamship Lines, but keeping the same name, she became one of the first cruise ships to be based at Miami. A chequered career followed. In 1972, she passed to Chandris Cruises, soon becoming the *Freeport II* and, later still, the *Bon Vivant*. After a charter which saw her being used as a floating hotel in Dubai, she returned to cruising as the *Ariane* in 1979, but was shortly laid up in Eleusis Bay. In 1991, by now called *Empress Katerina* and belonging to other owners, she was sent to Vietnam as a film prop in Ho Chi Minh City, then for a similar use in Subic Bay in the Philippines, before her itinerant career ended at a scrap yard at Alang in India in December, 1997.

Meanwhile, the older *Suecia* and *Britannia* continued to give reliable service between Tilbury and Gothenburg until 1966 when the car ferry era arrived. They were then sold to the Hellenic Mediterranean Lines of Piraeus, becoming the Cypriot-registered *Isthmia* and *Cynthia* on HML's route from Marseilles to Beirut by way of Italian, Greek and Egyptian ports. They were scrapped in 1972 and 1973 respectively. They had been among the longest-serving and most successful liners in North Sea service.

THE NEW CAR FERRIES

To respond to the new requirement for car capacity, the three long-established rivals on the England-Sweden routes – Swedish Lloyd, Rederi A/B Svea of Stockholm and the British line, Ellerman's Wilson – collaborated and each ordered a new ship for their respective Tilbury and Hull to Gothenburg routes. The combined service was marketed as the England-Sweden Line. While Ellerman's Wilson ordered the *Spero* from Cammell Laird of Birkenhead, the two Swedish operators ordered similar sister ships from the Lindholmens yard in Gothenburg. In May 1966, Swedish Lloyd took delivery of the *Saga*, a stylish 7,889-ton motor vessel with an imposing streamlined funnel. She had been designed by Knud E. Hansen A/S. Tage Wandborg recalls that Swedish Lloyd was a very traditionally-minded company and specifically asked for a conventional-looking ship. Her hull contained a full-length car deck which loaded through the stern only, with the majority of cabins above and on the main (promenade) deck.

The design of the interior was co-ordinated by the Gothenburg architect Rolf Carlsson. Astrid Sampe of the contract furnishing department of the Nordiska Kompamiet store in Stockholm was responsible for some of the rooms, while others were by Robert Tillberg whose contribution was similar in style to his work on the *Kungsholm*. The ornate smoking saloon, called the Britannia Room, was intended to recall that on the 1929 *Britannia* and contained furniture from that famous ship. Throughout the public rooms there was much polished wooden panelling and a number of specially commissioned artworks. The layout was intriguing. The original intention was that there should be a class division running down the centre line of the ship, with second class to port and first to starboard. In the event, the *Saga* and her running mates operated as one-class ships but still with the two distinct zones, so that the more discerning passengers gravitated to the starboard side where the restaurant was located, while the patrons of the cafeteria occupied the port side. Both these rooms were forward and the lounges aft, with long seating galleries amidships on either side. Servicing and catering was also located amidships. Towards the stern, there was a series of spacious teak sun decks with glazed shelter screens and there was further sheltered deck space between the bridge and the funnel.

The broadly similar sister ship, the *Svea* of the Rederi A/B Svea, followed her into service in October, 1966. She had rather darker interiors with modern furniture in bright

Unlike those on the modernistic *Saga*, the 1951 *Patricia*'s interiors were a throwback to an earlier era of shipboard design. Most remarkable was the Tudor-style smoking saloon in first class. *Author Collection*

Apart from her give-away squared-off stern with a car ramp, the ferry-liner *Saga* had the graceful appearance which typified the Swedish Lloyd fleet. *Alastair Paterson Collection*

contrasting colours, the work of Carlsson and Eva Ralf. Clearly satisfied, Swedish Lloyd had ordered a third example of the type to open a new route from Southampton to Bilbao. She was delivered in March, 1967 as the *Patricia*. At the time, Swedish Lloyd was one of a number of Scandinavian companies attempting to operate car-carrying ferry liners between Southampton and the Continent. The Kloster Rederi of Oslo made an abortive attempt in 1966 to run a Spanish service with the *Sunward* (see below), while Thoresen Car Ferries, another Norwegian concern, operated three ferries between Southampton and Cherbourg. Notwithstanding tensions between Spain's General Franco and the British government over Gibraltar, an oil crisis and British currency problems, plus the antagonism of British seafaring unions, Swedish Lloyd's new route was initially a success.

The liner historian Clive Harvey recalls: 'I made a wonderful mini-cruise to Spain on the *Patricia* when she was a brand new ship. My travelling companion was less keen to sail on what he dismissed as merely a ferry, but when he actually got to the dockside and saw the *Patricia* he changed his mind. She was, after all, a real beauty with interiors designed by some of the same team that had just completed the *Kungsholm*. She was light and airy, with picture windows seemingly everywhere and modern Swedish furnishings. The restaurant had two sections, one for ferry passengers and another for those of us doing the round trip – a substantial proportion, in fact. The cuisine was remarkably good and there was lounge dancing afterwards to a lively band. When they finished their set, they motioned to the passengers that anyone who could play was welcome to take over. A group of our fellow passengers formed a quartet and played for us well into the early hours of the morning as we swayed across the Bay of Biscay.'

As competition intensified on the routes from Britain to Sweden, the Svea Line withdrew from the consortium and Swedish Lloyd purchased the *Svea* in 1968, renaming her *Hispania*. She then joined the *Patricia* on the

Southampton-Bilbao route. However, trade did not justify a second vessel and in 1970 the *Hispania* returned to the Gothenburg-Tilbury route. In the early 1970s, P&O Southern Ferries also entered the UK-Spain trade and the popular Spanish-owned Aznar Line introduced its own car ferries, making life difficult for Swedish Lloyd.

Even on the well-established Gothenburg-London service, competition had become intense. A new Swedish rival, the Tor Line (formed as a joint venture between Trans Oil and Rex Line), had begun operations in 1966 with fast ferries sailing between Felixstowe, Immingham, Gothenburg and Amsterdam. These shorter routes were quicker and more economical, especially during the early 1970s and the era of the fuel crises. Besides, the Swedish Lloyd ships could only manage 18 knots and the company had made a crucial mistake in failing to foresee the growth in lorry traffic across the North Sea. As a result, the ships had been built with insufficient headroom on the car deck. The outcome was that, in 1971, the *Saga* was sold to the Stena Line to sail in the Kattegatt and between Gothenburg and Kiel. The *Hispania* now assumed the name *Saga*. On the 29th December, 1972, 90 miles west of Esbjerg, she collided with the Swedish Orient Line's cargo ship *Sagoland*. Although the latter suffered substantial damage, nobody was hurt in the incident and both ships were repaired.

In 1975, the Tor Line introduced the first of two giant high-speed ferry liners, the *Tor Britannia*, followed into service by the *Tor Scandinavia* (see above). These magnificent vessels proved a knock-out blow for Swedish Lloyd, which suffered a severe financial reverse. Its remaining two passenger ships, the *Patricia* and the *Saga* were laid up in Gothenburg in September, 1977. The *Patricia* was acquired by the Stena Line, becoming its *Stena Oceanica*. She was rebuilt on the Tees in 1979 with a heightened car deck which necessitated a raised superstructure and sponsons. As the *Stena Saga*, she became popular on the Frederikshavn-Oslo route. Subsequently she served on other Stena routes, across the Kattegatt and even between the USA and British Columbia. Today, under other owners, she is based in Singapore as the casino ship *Amusement World*.

The *Saga* (ex-*Hispania*) was sold to Minoan Lines to sail between Piraeus and Crete and from Patras to Ancona as the *Knossos*. In 1984, the previous *Saga*, which had passed through the hands of the Stena Line and then went to Finnish owners, also joined the Minoan Lines fleet as the *Festos*. The two sisters operated in Greek waters until

The ferry-liner *Patricia* sets course through the English Channel, bound for Spain in June 1969.
Alastair Paterson Collection

The first class arcade of the *Captain Zaman II* (ex-*Saga*, ex-*Hispania*, ex-*Svea*) in the Summer of 2002 – showing little change after 36 years of service. *Author*

1998. They were then sold to Turkish owners, Körfez Shipping (which traded as Diler Lines), who at first registered them exotically at Belize City and used them in the Adriatic and the Black Sea. Eventually they were transferred to the Turkish flag. In the summer of 2002, the former *Svea*, *Hispania*, etc. was sailing as the *Captain Zaman II* on the route from Nador to Sete under charter to Comanav, the Moroccan state shipping company. To my surprise, she was in immaculate shape, both externally and internally and most of the elegant décor of her Swedish days was still intact. Since then, she has been sold to SEM Maritime Company, a Croatian concern, who propose to run her between Split and Ancona as the *Ancona*. Her sister, *Sancak 1*, the original *Saga*, ran in the eastern Mediterranean and the Adriatic and she too retained most of her Scandinavian interiors. The two ships, in fact, were the most delightful time capsules of all that is best about Swedish design of the 1960s. Unfortunately, *Sancak 1* was gutted by fire while being overhauled at Tuzla in Turkey in April, 2003.

The dining saloon of the *Captain Zaman II* was last redecorated in 1969, when Swedish Lloyd acquired the vessel from Rederi A/B Svea. At that time, the architects Astrid Sampe and Rolf Carlsson redesigned the space as the 'Restaurant Andalucia' for the Southampton-Bilbao service. *Author*

The dark and atmospheric wood-panelled smoking room, located aft and to starboard, on the *Captain Zaman II*. *Author*

Part of the Wasa Dining Saloon of the *Sancak I* (ex-*Saga*). The iron bas relief was by Bertil Vallien. Sadly, all of this was destroyed when the ship burned out at a shipyard in Tuzla in Turkey not many months after this photograph was taken. *Author*

The first class stairwell on the *Kong Olav V*(II), with Per Arnoldi's mural of rainbows and flowers. *Author Collection*

The circular Mermaid Bar, with its egg-shaped bar stools and brass details, was one of the *Dana Regina's* many elegant design features. *Author Collection*

The first class nightclub on the *Kong Olav V* (II) had a steel and brass dance floor and a circular, copper-panelled bar. The room was separated from the smoking room in front by glazed partitions. *Author Collection*

The *England* arrives at Harwich Parkeston Quay in the late 1960s. Note the frames erected over the aft sun decks for awnings when the ship cruised to the Caribbean and the West Indies during the winter season. *Author Collection*

The 1957 Norwegian America Line brochure unfolds to reveal a narrative about Norway's Viking heritage of seamanship on the one side and about the beauty of its transatlantic liners on the other. *Michael Zell Collection*

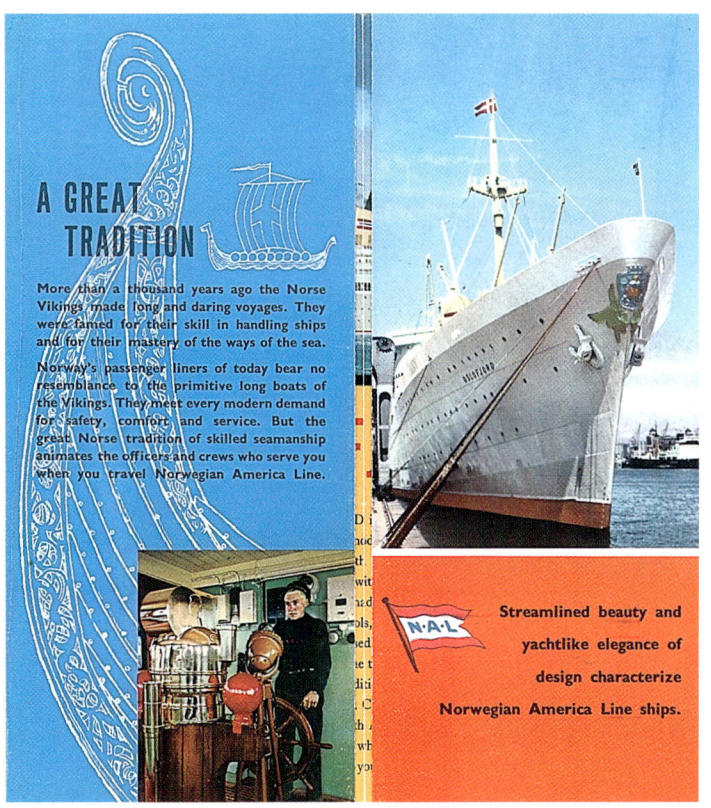

Three Great Ships

M.S. BERGENSFJORD
M.S. OSLOFJORD
S.S. STAVANGERFJORD

Norwegian America Line

A GREAT TRADITION

More than a thousand years ago the Norse Vikings made long and daring voyages. They were famed for their skill in handling ships and for their mastery of the ways of the sea.

Norway's passenger liners of today bear no resemblance to the primitive long boats of the Vikings. They meet every modern demand for safety, comfort and service. But the great Norse tradition of skilled seamanship animates the officers and crews who serve you when you travel Norwegian America Line.

N·A·L

Streamlined beauty and yachtlike elegance of design characterize Norwegian America Line ships.

115

The Garden Lounge on the *Sagafjord* was a masterpiece of shipboard design, being warmly decorated with a raised perimeter area beyond the vertical screens, making it suitable both for daytime relaxation and as an intimate night club venue. *Keld Helmer Petersen*

The *Sagafjord* after being given an additional deck of accommodation over the bridge, is here seen on the St. Lawrence. *Alastair Paterson Collection.*

The interiors of the *Stella Polaris*, seem to be in remarkable condition, as these recent photographs show. She is reputedly in need of a drydocking, however, to repair her hull below the waterline - something which Japanese law forbids as she is now classified as a building. *Peter Knego*

The Gustav Alde designed interiors of the former *Stella Polaris*. *Peter Knego*

The post-War *Leda* had a robust appearance and looked most handsome in her severe Bergen Line livery. Here, she is being manoeuvred in the River Tyne in September 1964. *Ann Glen*

In her Fred. Olsen-Bergen Line livery, the *Jupiter* speeds towards Harwich during her summer North Sea service in 1979. *Stephen Gooch*

The *Black Prince's* **Aquitaine Lounge** (formerly known as the Westminster Lounge) remains an elegant, yet cosy space, with its circular dance floor and slatted screens. *David Trevor-Jones*

The Jahre Line's *Prinsesse Ragnhild* on a Canary Islands cruise in the late-1960s. This handsome vessel was one of many of her generation of ferries to be used as a cruise ship during the slacker winter period. Subsequent ferries have tended to have a far greater emphasis on freight capacity and, therefore, find gainful employment on their regular routes all year round. *Ambrose Greenway Collection*

The graceful *Gripsholm* shows her elegant lines while at anchor on a cruise in this 1970s photograph. Again, we see the similarity of her hull to that of her contemporary, the *Federico C.* of Costa Line, built at the same shipyard and completed in the same year. *Mick Lindsay Collection*

The much-respected *Britannia* of Swedish Lloyd lies at her Tilbury berth during the mid-1960s, towards the end of her lengthy career on the North Sea. *Ambrose Greenway Collection*

Tugs nose Hellenic Mediterranean Line's *Cynthia* (ex-*Britannia*) away from her berth in Naples harbour in July 1967. *Ivor Trevor-Jones*

The *Starward*, seen in her later NCL livery in 1993, towards the end of her period with the company. By this stage, her car deck had been filled with cabins and a sponson had been added to her stern to provide buoyancy to compensate for this extra weight. *Peter Knego*

The new flagship, *Royal Viking Sun* in the Thames at Greenwich during a promotional visit shortly after delivery from Wärtsilä. Although her hull was similar to those of the original Royal Viking trio, her superstructure contained many more cabins, several of which had private verandahs. *Ambrose Greenway*

Norwegian Caribbean Line's pioneering *Sunward* brought a slick new profile to the world of passenger shipping. She is obviously a development of the many Knud E. Hansen-designed ferries then entering service with Scandinavian owners. In this remarkable photograph, taken during the 1966 British Seamens' Strike, she is seen making her maiden call at Southampton with some of Britain's most famous liners – including *Reina del Mar* and *Queen Mary* – strikebound in the berths behind. *Tage Wandborg Collection*

The fabulous *Norway* makes her maiden call at Southampton following her transformation from the *France* in 1980. *Author Collection*

A cabin inside the *Freeport* of 1968, shows the relatively cramped conditions often found on 'first generation' purpose-built Caribbean cruise ships – and also the fashionable psychedelic fabric applied to the end wall. The *Freeport*'s interiors were the work of French designers, Pierre and François Lalonde. *Tage Wandborg Collection*

The spectacular interiors of the *Voyager of the Seas* brought 'mega ship' cruising to a new level. Her restaurant is tiered and fills three storeys, linked by grand staircases, all supposedly reminiscent of the great liners of the Edwardian era – but actually rather more redolent of modern day Las Vegas. *Kvaerner Masa Yards*

The giant *Voyager of the Seas* anchored off Labadee - a private Caribbean island for the exclusive use of RCCI passengers. *Kvaerner Masa Yards*

4
The Sun Vikings

The New Generation Cruise Ships: The Sun Vikings

The influence of Scandinavian shipowners has been far-reaching but can often be almost undetectable to the casual observer. The Scandinavian lines have always been clever at finding new, under-exploited markets, then targeting them by providing often highly-specialised ships to make the most of these niche opportunities. In the 1960s, a number of Norwegian shipping lines observed the growing affluence of the United States and the lack of affordable cruises from American ports. If even a small proportion of the country's population could be persuaded to take cruises, there would be vast business potential. Their hunch was correct. The growth of the Caribbean as a cruise destination in the following decades has been unprecedented and, more than any others, Norwegian shipping lines made cruising available to the masses with their fleets of slick, modern white liners. The challenge for these firms was to attract the people of so-called Middle America, most of whom had never before seen an ocean-going ship, let alone travelled on one – or had even seen the sea. They were, however, experienced consumers and looked for value for money and a shipboard experience not too alien from what they were used to at home.

While previous generations of ocean liners had been floating expressions of national identity, the new generation was very international in its design and operation. The owners may have been Norwegian, but their ships were very much geared to American taste, with hotel-like interiors, international cuisine in the restaurants, often Bahamian or Liberian registry and crews drawn from many nations. These measures also cut costs and helped to make cruising an affordable choice for many people for the first time.

The first such Norwegian liner in the post-War American cruise trade was the 12,800-ton motor ship *Viking Princess*, which was introduced by the Norwegian tanker owner Berge Sigval Bergesen of Oslo, who placed her in cruise service from New York and Miami under the name Sigline A/S in 1964. The *Viking Princess* had been built in 1950 by the Ateliers & Chantiers de la Loire at St. Nazaire for Chargeurs Réunis' service from Le Havre to Latin American ports, carrying 324 passengers. She was sold to Italian owners in 1961 and extensively rebuilt as the 600-passenger cruise ship *Riviera Prima*, but the company went bankrupt and she passed into Bergesen's ownership. Alas, the *Viking Princess*, as she was now called, had a very brief career for on the 8th April, 1966 during a voyage from Miami to Curaçao, she was swept by fire while off the Cuban coast. Two passengers died of heart attacks and the blistered, blackened wreck was taken to a Jamaican port where it was declared a total loss. The remains of the *Viking Princess* were later towed across the Atlantic to shipbreakers at Bilbao in Spain. Berge Sigval Bergesen ceased to be involved in the cruise business.

Norwegian Caribbean Lines

In the same year, 1966, another enterprising Norwegian firm entered the Caribbean cruise trade and this time the venture was to be one of the outstanding success stories in the history of Scandinavian shipping. Knut Kloster, was a director of the Lauritz Kloster Rederi of Oslo, which had been founded in 1906 and had long been involved in the bulk cargo and tanker trades. In the early 1960s, he believed he had spotted a gap in the British ferry market and decided to start a service from Southampton to Vigo, Lisbon and Gibraltar, carrying British holidaymakers and their cars south to the sun. A new ferry, the 8,666-ton *Sunward*, was ordered from the Bergens Mekaniske Verksteder for delivery in 1966.

The ill-fated *Viking Princess* of Sigline A/S was the first of many Scandinavian cruise liners permanently sailing from US ports. *Ambrose Greenway Collection*

The *Sunward* is seen here sailing down the Solent in 1966, during her brief spell in service between Southampton, Vigo, Lisbon and Gibraltar. *Ambrose Greenway Collection*

SUNWARD, THE PIONEER

The *Sunward* was designed by Tage Wandborg of the firm of Knud E. Hansen A/S. Perhaps more than anyone else, Wandborg developed the modern cruise liner from car ferry precedents into the large and glamorous floating resorts enjoyed by so many today. The *Sunward* was a key ship in this development, being essentially an enlarged version of the Hansen firm's typical car ferry design, for which Wandborg had been largely responsible. Dozens of smaller examples of the type had entered service on short Scandinavian crossings in the 1960s. These ships all had uninterrupted full-width car decks with exhaust stacks on either beam and highly flared bows with pronounced knuckle joints at car deck height. The *Sunward* was similarly arranged, but with significant overnight cabin capacity to either side of the vehicle deck and with her public rooms at boat deck level. A streamlined deckhouse above the bridge contained an observation lounge.

The ship's interior design was the work of Mogens Hammer and was bright and airy. The main lounge forward gave a fine view over the bow and the dining room was located aft. In between these principal rooms there was an arcade, on the starboard side of which a small grill room was accessed, while the galley space was adjacent on the port side. Since the *Sunward* had the squared-off lines of a car ferry, it was possible to standardise the layout of the cabins to an unprecedented extent and they were entered directly from corridors running the full length of the ship.

Tage Wandborg recalls that when, in June 1966, the *Sunward* made her first arrival in Southampton, she berthed close to the strike-bound *Queen Mary* – 'providing one of the ultimate contrasts in passenger ship design between the mighty Cunarder and this futuristic little white ship which looked as if it had just come from outer space'. Unfortunately, British government restrictions on currency for foreign travel and the growing diplomatic tension with Spain over Gibraltar made Kloster's service a failure. Meanwhile in Miami, Ted Arison, an Israeli entrepreneur, was marketing two Israeli-owned ferries, the *Nili* and the *Bilu* on short cruises to the Bahamas. The bankruptcy of their owners left Arison with plenty of potential passengers but no ship. When he found that the *Sunward* was available, he contacted the Klosters and persuaded them to place the ship in service out of Miami with his company as sales agents. She was marketed under the name Norwegian Caribbean Lines (often abbreviated as NCL).

THE WHITE SHIPS: STARWARD, SKYWARD, SOUTHWARD AND SUNWARD II

Carrying both passengers and trailer traffic from Miami to Nassau in the Bahamas and sometimes to Jamaican ports, the *Sunward* was an immediate success. A second vessel was quickly ordered, this time from the Weser shipyard at Bremerhaven. Also designed by Wandborg, it represented a further development of the *Sunward*. The building process was somewhat unusual as the ship was constructed in two halves which were joined together in dry dock, and she was completed in only twelve months. Called *Starward* and of 12,940 gross tons, she was delivered in the autumn of 1968, while a further vessel, the *Skyward*, came into service the following year.

According to Wandborg, 'The *Starward* was really a cruise-ferry hybrid with the vehicle deck accessed through

The *Sunward's* interiors, designed by Mogens Hammer, were typical of 1960s Scandinavian car ferries. The furniture, however, is by Kay Kørbing, whose modern designs were used in many 1960s ship interiors. Here we see the main entrance hall and the forward lounge. Today, the former is little altered after nearly forty years of use. *Peter Newall Collection*

Ted Arison, Tage Wandborg, a representative of the shipyard and the interior architect, Mogens Hammer, pose with a model of the forthcoming *Starward* in 1967.
Tage Wandborg Collection

a stern door. This was concealed by a visor, which curved to follow the line of the remainder of the hull. This ship was, in fact, a further key stage in the design evolution from car ferry to proper cruise ship. In addition, she was very well built. It was always a pleasure to work with German shipyards because everything was done to schedule and the precise specified tolerances. Getting a good quality of workmanship at a reasonable price and with a guaranteed delivery schedule was vital for Knut Kloster, who was determined to expand the cruise business from Miami and was able to fill the ships without too much difficulty.'

Initially the *Starward* could carry 540 passengers and the *Skyward* 750. They had a distinctive appearance, with an all-white colour scheme with blue accents and with streamlined funnels, located towards the stern. Forward, there was a sheltered lido area with a two-storey glazed sun lounge above the bridge. The arrangement was very successful and gave the ships a large area of sheltered deck space for sunbathing. The ferry origins of the design showed in the very cramped cabins in which the berths could be turned into settees for daytime use. The staterooms on South Africa's famous Blue Train reputedly inspired their layout.

The *Starward*'s sleek lines were developed from those of the earlier *Sunward*. Here she is seen early in her career when she was a stern-loading car ferry – a fact ingeniously disguised by her shapely stern visor. *Tage Wandborg Collection*

The striking lines of the *Southward* represented new-generation 1970s cruise ship design at its best.
Alastair Paterson Collection

The entry into service of the third ship, *Skyward*, brought Kloster's investment in the Miami cruise business to over $100 million. She received a tumultuous welcome and was feted by the Miami Chamber of Commerce, which was delighted by the tourist wealth Kloster's operation was bringing to the city. Unlike the *Starward*, the *Skyward* was a pure passenger ship without a car deck. Later, in the mid-1970s, the *Starward* was stripped of her vehicle-carrying capacity and the space was used for further cabins and for a theatre. The work was done gradually, while the ship was still in service.

Meanwhile, an additional pair of 16,600-ton cruise ships, to be named *Southward* and *Seaward*, had been ordered from an Italian shipyard, Cantieri Navali del Tirreno e Riuniti of Riva Trigoso, near Genoa. These were Norwegian Caribbean Lines' first fully-fledged cruise liners. Tage Wandborg worked closely with the technical staff at the yard. Knut Kloster had proposed a pair of ships identical to the *Skyward* but in the meantime Wandborg's ideas had developed and he persuaded Kloster to allow him to re-work the earlier design. By then, he had already arrived in Italy and there was very little time before

Water sloshes around in the swimming pool as passengers try to enjoy *Southward*'s transatlantic delivery voyage. Note the very careful attention to the visual coherence of design details – the way that the pool surround is combined with the air conditioning plant to form an 'island' and the way in which the funnels are gently tapered and angled outwards – as with the *Eugenio C.*, which was designed by Tage Wandborg's hero, Nicolò Costanzi.
Tage Wandborg Collection

Rebuilt from the *Cunard Adventurer*, the *Sunward II* completed NCL's four ship 'White Fleet'.
Alastair Paterson Collection

construction was due to begin. 'I worked in my hotel room, which had a balcony overlooking the Ligurian coast. I bought rolls of paper and spread them out on the floor. My patio door was opened and the warm sunshine and sea air filled the room. It was the most inspiring setting one could imagine in which to design ships. Within hours, I had developed the forms of the new ships. I have a great love of Italy and much respect for Italian design. As a young man, I regarded Nicolò Costanzi as my great hero. He not only revolutionised hull design and hydrodynamics through his rigorous research, but he was also an artist and a great aesthete. He was, in fact, a father figure and an architect whose sculptural methods, innovation and aesthetic judgement I admired. His most outstanding ship, in my opinion, was the *Oceanic* of 1965 – a big, powerful hull upon which there sat a low, streamlined superstructure. There was a wrap-around promenade at main deck level with the lifeboats recessed above it. With the machinery located aft, this layout meant that the top of the superstructure could be entirely given over to sun deck space, with several swimming pools and glazed screens on either side, making a spacious, sheltered sun trap. It was the ideal model for a modern cruise ship.'

Wandborg followed Costanzi's example, stowing the lifeboats at main deck level. The tapering line of the glass screens, which sheltered the sun deck, was continued in the shape of the after decks, making a bold yet harmonious composition. The Riva Trigoso yard had just completed five passenger ships for DFDS, designed by the their technical staff and Kay Kørbing. According to Wandborg, 'These DFDS ships were modern in the architectural rather than in the technical sense. They used a lot of woodwork because Kay Kørbing liked that kind of finish and thought it highly appropriate for ship interiors. Being perhaps more technically minded, I was anxious to use all of the latest synthetic materials as they were cheaper, faster

A remarkable period piece: the night club on the *Sunward II*, photographed during her inaugural cruise for NCL. No doubt, the white Eero Saarinen 'tulip' chairs would be highly collectable nowadays. *Tage Wandborg Collection*

to use and appeared to offer greater fire protection.' Clearly, there was an ideological gulf between Kørbing's architectural modernism (following the precedent of Kay Fisker) and Wandborg's desire for technical modernity.

At Riva Trigoso, ships were usually launched in a nearly completed state but, because the yard was busy, the *Southward* took to the water somewhat earlier and was completed at a wharf in Genoa. She entered service in December, 1971 but work on the *Seaward* was abandoned when industrial unrest at the shipyard increased her price by more than 50 per cent. By the time the Italian government intervened by nationalising the yard, NCL had lost interest. Instead, the unfinished hull was sold to P & O and completed as the *Spirit of London*. Around this time, relations between Ted Arison and the Kloster family deteriorated and he left NCL in 1971 to begin his own rival operation – the Carnival Cruise Line.

In 1973, Norwegian Caribbean Lines sold the original *Sunward* to the French government-controlled Compagnie Générale Transméditerranéenne, who renamed her *Ile de Beauté*. She later found her way to the Red Sea, becoming the pilgrim ship *Saudi Moon 1*, before returning unsuccessfully to cruise service as the *Ocean Spirit* in 1989. After that, she became the *Scandinavian Song*, sailing on gambling cruises from Florida ports for SeaEscape. In 1991, she was chartered to Danish Cruise Line, which SeaEscape was operating jointly with the Danish ferry operator Nordisk Faergefart, but this proved equally fruitless. In 1993 she was briefly the *Santiago De Cuba*, operating short cruises from Havana, but soon became *The Empress*, a casino ship based in the Far East, where she is now laid up.

Her replacement in the NCL fleet was the former *Cunard Adventurer*. One of two cruise ships intended for a joint venture between the Cunard Line and Overseas National Airways (the other was the *Cunard Ambassador*), she was built by the Rotterdam Drydock Company (Rotterdamsche Droogdok) and completed in 1971. However, these 'hotel-class' ships fitted badly with Cunard's image as a de luxe cruise line and the company felt compelled to order a larger and improved pair. In the meantime, the *Cunard Ambassador* was damaged by fire and was sold for conversion into a sheep carrier. The *Cunard Adventurer* was also disposed of, going to NCL. They sent her to Bremerhaven for a radical refit which transformed her into the elegant *Sunward II*, used for three and four day trips from Miami to the Bahamas.

THE NORWAY: THE 'NEW' GIANT OF THE CRUISE FLEET

In the 1970s, the NCL 'White Fleet' became known for its popular, modern 'fun' ships, although they were all of modest size compared with the company's next vessel. In the late 1970s, Knut Kloster believed there was potential for a very large ship to sail from Miami – one spacious enough to be a kind of floating resort. Consideration was given to building anew, but a number of laid up ocean liners were carefully examined also. The Italian *Michelangelo* was inspected, but she and her sister had been notorious for their heavy fuel consumption and too few of their cabins had private facilities. To rival cruise lines, the Klosters' final choice – the glorious French Line flagship *France* – must have seemed equally unlikely, especially as she had already been sold to Arab interests for conversion into a hotel at Daytona Beach, Florida. Fortunately, she was resold to Kloster for $18million and towed to the Hapag Lloyd shipyard at Bremerhaven to undergo one of the most complex, yet successful transformations in ocean liner history.

Built with the help of a massive government subsidy in the early 1960s, the *France* had been solidly constructed by the Chantiers de l'Atlantique at St. Nazaire as a glittering showcase of all that was best in French technology, design and decoration. At 1,035 feet, she was the longest liner in the World and she had a dramatic, tapering whaleback bow and two massive funnels, topped with giant wings to throw smoke away from the ship's sides. However, she consumed huge amounts of fuel, was unwieldy when in port and, being primarily an Atlantic liner, had rather formal interiors while lacking sufficient outside deck space for the Caribbean. With expertise from Tage Wandborg, Knut Kloster devised an ingenious plan. The forward engine room would be closed altogether and the two outer propeller shafts would be removed, transforming the ship from a fast quadruple-screw liner into a sedate twin-screw cruise ship. The fitting of three side-thrust propellers at the bow and two more near the stern would make her easily manoeuvrable without the need for tugs.

For Wandborg, the conversion of the *France* into the *Norway* represented a considerable challenge. 'She was a dream-ship, a floating work of art. Did you know that below the waterline her hull has practically no straight lines? No expense had been spared in her construction. For a ship of her size and with such a great draft (eleven metres), she had a remarkable hydrodynamic efficiency. She also had the reputation for giving the most comfortable ride in rough weather, so in that respect she was an excellent choice to become a cruise ship. On the other hand, as with most transatlantic liners, she was very fuel-hungry and her passenger accommodation was quite unsuitable for tropical cruising. The conversion was therefore a great challenge, but it was also one of the most rewarding projects of my entire career. Apart from the joy and professional pride of having returned one of the great liners of all time to profitable service, it cemented my friendship with Knut Kloster and its successful outcome freed up our imaginations. In terms of cruise ship design, there was a significant paradigm shift. After designing ferry-derived vessels of up to 16,000 tons, we suddenly felt, with the *Norway* about to enter service, that anything might be possible.' Inside, the décor was the work of an American designer, Angelo Donglia. Many of the public rooms were re-done in festive colours and pastel tones. On top, vast new expanses of teak sun deck were added, with swimming pools, jacuzzis, outdoor buffets and countless other facilities. The 1,100-strong French Line staff was replaced by an international crew of 800, with Norwegian officers but no less than 25 other nationalities represented. All these changes were to transform the ship's fortunes and make the once-unprofitable *France* a great dollar-earner for the Norwegians. According to her owners, the $130 million cost of her purchase and conversion was only 50 per cent of the price of a new liner half her size.

Turned out with a dark blue hull and NCL funnel colours, the *Norway* made a triumphal visit to Oslo in June 1980, showing the Norwegian people their new national

Impressive interiors on NCL's *Norway* include the Club Internationale, the Leeward Dining Room and, grandest of all, the Windward Dining Room (above). Once the exquisite Chambord Room on the *France*, it retains its striking 1960s modernity.
All David Trevor-Jones

The *Seaward* at Miami in March 1995. Externally, she was clean-lined, but her bland pastel-shaded interiors dated quickly. Note too that none of her cabins has a balcony - now considered to be essential amenities by cruise line marketing departments. *Peter Knego*

flagship. She then set course for Miami and the start of her second illustrious career, sailing to St. Maarten and the Bahamas.

Her mainly American passengers were used to constant entertainment whilst on vacation; and, sailing from Florida ports, they would be familiar with such theme parks as Disneyland at Orlando. Because the earlier NCL ships were relatively small, they had offered a limited choice of entertainment, but now the sheer size of the *Norway* opened up a world of new possibilities. She was a floating resort with a theatre big enough to stage Broadway musicals and she had a vast range of sports facilities. Earlier liners had shuffleboard and tennis courts, but she had basketball and volleyball courts as well as a golf driving range. The entertainment staff organised as many as five or six different activities for the passengers to choose between at any one time. For instance, there were make-up demonstrations, foreign language classes, ballroom dancing lessons, exercise classes, cocktail hours, chess tournaments and trivia quizzes. At the suggestion of a youthful marketing manager, Bruce Nierenberg, NCL leased an island in the Bahamas for the exclusive use of its passengers, which extended the leisure possibilities of cruising even further. There, the *Norway's* guests could participate in scuba diving, barbecues, sports tournaments or simply relax in a hammock tied between palm trees. Across expanses of white sand beach and turquoise water, the great ship made an impressive sight as she rode at anchor.

In 1987, the rival Royal Caribbean Lines introduced the vast new *Sovereign of the Seas* (see below) and, temporarily, the *Norway* was knocked from her top spot as the World's biggest liner. However, in 1991 she returned to Germany, to the Lloyd Werft at Bremerhaven, for a massive refit during which two extra decks were added to her accommodation. These spoiled her sleek lines as a former 'Atlantic greyhound' but, for the time being, made her the World's biggest once again at 76,049 gross tons, as well as making her even more profitable. Since then, she has paid several more visits to Europe, cruising around Britain, to the Norwegian fjords and to the Mediterranean. Alongside the ever-popular *Queen Elizabeth 2*, the *Norway* is one of the World's most famous liners and the sight of both ships docked together at Southampton was a memorable one.

RESHAPING THE FLEET

After the *Norway's* triumphant entry into service, the enterprising Klosters began a phase of expansion by acquiring existing cruise businesses. In 1984, they took over the up-market Royal Viking Line (see below) and its three ships, although they kept it a separate company from NCL. Five years later, they bought the select Royal Cruise Line from the Greek Panagopoulos family. Again, they retained it as a separate brand. Plans were also unveiled for a 200,000 ton mega-liner which was to have been known as the *Phoenix World City*. However, the project never came to fruition and by the late 1980s, NCL had lost its earlier momentum. Rival companies were building bigger and better ships, which made NCL's 'White Fleet' seem insignificant, however frequently they were refurbished. Only the *Norway* really stood out, until the summer of 1986 when the company placed an order with the Wärtsilä yard in Turku for one 42,300 ton vessel, the *Seaward*.

On 26 May, 1988, the new ship made a spectacular maiden arrival at New York in brilliant spring sunshine, with tugs firing water cannons into the air. Thereafter, she sailed for Miami and began seven day cruises to the

The 1992-built *Windward* at Los Angeles before she was lengthened. *Peter Knego*

Cayman Islands. Outwardly, the *Seaward* was sleek and attractive, with low-slung lifeboats reducing the apparent bulk of her superstructure, but her interiors were in the undistinguished pastel-shaded hotel manner of most 1980s cruise liners. In 1990, Kloster became anxious to expand the NCL brand into new areas, so the name Norwegian Caribbean Lines was changed to Norwegian Cruise Line, still with the initials NCL.

The line then ordered two 41,000 ton liners from Chantiers de l'Atlantique. The first of these, named *Dreamward*, paid a visit to Greenwich on the Thames in November, 1992 to show the flag in Britain before she sailed across the Atlantic to Boston. However, by the time the second ship was ready for builder's trials in the spring of 1993, the Kloster group was in financial crisis brought about by its nearly $800 million debt burden. In a dramatic eleventh hour deal following the sale of $300 million in high interest bonds, NCL was able to take delivery of the ship at sea on 12 May and she was subsequently named *Windward* in Los Angeles by the former First Lady of the United States, Barbara Bush.

Petter Yran and Björn Storbraaten had designed the new sisters, giving them an impressive, smooth-sided and streamlined appearance, although initially they seemed rather too tall for their length. Internally, floors were terraced to optimise the views through the many windows. Particularly effective were the two dining rooms, both located aft with one directly above the other, overlooking the stern. Each of these open-plan spaces was arranged on three levels, the lower of which directly accessed the outside sun decks and stern lido areas, making an integrated dining and leisure environment which was ideal for tropical conditions. No doubt realising what a significant earner conference traffic was on the ferry routes within Scandinavia, the designers fitted the *Dreamward* and *Windward* with extensive conference facilities. Even the ships' show lounges, located forward, and observation lounges above the bridges could be converted to suites of conference and meeting rooms by closing retractable partitions.

When the two ships were first built, Norwegian Cruise Line had clearly been stretching its financial resources to the limit and, had money allowed, they would probably have been much larger. In 1997-98, however, the duo was sent to the Lloyd Werft at Bremerhaven to be cut vertically and have new mid-body sections inserted, increasing their size to 50,764 gross tons. At the same time, they were renamed *Norwegian Dream* and *Norwegian Wind*. In 1997, a new livery with all-blue funnels and a gold NCL logo was applied to the entire fleet. All the ships except *Norway* were then renamed with Norwegian prefixes – an attempt to strengthen the firm's corporate identity.

The lengthened *Norwegian Wind* (ex-*Windward*) in her present Norwegian Cruise Line livery. *Peter Knego*

Meanwhile, the original NCL 'white fleet' was sold off. First, Epirotiki Line bought the *Sunward II* in 1991, renaming her *Triton* for Mediterranean cruises. Next, an Indonesian firm acquired the *Skyward* in 1993 for gambling cruises in the Far East as the *Shangri-La World*. (She has since traded as the *Fantasy World* and, most recently, *Continental World*.) The *Southward* was taken over by the British travel firm Airtours in January, 1995, becoming their *Seawing*, based in Palma de Mallorca to carry British passengers on Mediterranean fly-cruises. Lastly, in July, 1995, the *Starward* became the *Bolero* of Festival Cruises and has also mainly been stationed in the Mediterranean.

ADDITION BY ACQUISITION

A number of medium-sized acquisitions boosted the NCL fleet around this time. The *Leeward* had previously been the *Sally Albatross*, a Baltic cruise ship which had been rebuilt from a fire-ravaged ferry in 1992. Having subsequently run aground on rocks outside Helsinki, the hapless vessel had been laid up in a damaged condition until chartered to NCL. She was towed through the Kiel Canal and round to La Spezia for further rebuilding as a Caribbean cruise ship, entering service in November, 1995.

The *Norwegian Majesty*, acquired in November, 1997, had been intended as another Baltic cruise ship. She had been ordered by the Birka Line from Finnyards at Rauma and was due to be delivered in 1992. Birka proposed to run her on short cruises to the Åland Islands but the recession of the early 1990s caused them to cancel the order. The ship was sold to Majesty Cruise Line, becoming their *Royal Majesty*, but eventually passed to NCL. Designed for the Baltic market, she had less outdoor space than is the norm on Caribbean cruise ships, although a 33 metre lengthening carried out in the Spring of 1999 marginally improved matters. In summer she now sails mainly from Boston on cruises along the New

The *Norwegian Majesty*, pictured in 2000 at Miami, was originally intended for Baltic cruise service and was lengthened by NCL to sail in warmer climes. *Peter Knego*

139

NCL's distinctively shaped *Leeward* at Miami. The former Baltic ferry and cruise ship *Sally Albatross* could give a notoriously lively ride in tropical storms in the Caribbean. *Peter Knego*

England coast. Another acquisition, the *Norwegian Dynasty*, had been built by the Union Naval yard in Valencia and completed in 1993 as the *Crown Dynasty* for Crown Cruise Lines (see below).

The *Norwegian Sky* was the result of a troubled building process. She was to have been the *Costa Olympia*, the second of two sisters being built at the Bremer Vulkan shipyard at Vegesack for the famous Costa Line of Genoa. The hull was floated out, but in July 1996, before it could be completed, the Vulkan Group collapsed and work was suspended. The partially-built liner lay at the shipyard until 1998 when the legal wrangles were at last resolved and she was sold to NCL and towed to the Lloyd Werft in Bremerhaven for completion. Costa's plans for the interior were drastically re-worked by NCL's team of designers and a significant number of private balconies (by then considered essential in the American cruise market) were attached to the exterior of the existing shell. While Costa had intended the ship to have two tubular funnels grouped together towards the stern, NCL opted for a much larger and more angular unit. The front profile was also improved with the bridge at a lower level, lessening the bulk of the superstructure and creating glazed screens surrounding the lido decks above.

Within, the *Norwegian Sky* has impressive facilities, which include no less than eight restaurants, ranging from a Mexican tapas bar and a Japanese sushi bar (claimed to be the first afloat) to the more traditional 'Four Seasons' and 'Seven Seas' dining rooms. The show lounge can seat 1,000 passengers and its advanced backstage facilities enable it to present slightly scaled down versions of popular blockbuster musicals. The *Norwegian Sky* sailed from Dover on the 9th August, 1999 bound for New York and an inaugural season of cruises on the New England coast. A near sister ship, *Norwegian Sun*, was ordered from Lloyd Werft for delivery in September, 2001.

Meanwhile, in December, 1997, Kloster made a further, rather unlikely acquisition, the German-operated 'club ship', *Aida*, which had been built by Kvaerner-Masa (formerly Wärtsilä) and was designed to appeal to a younger, German clientele. A handsome, modern ship, the *Aida* is distinguished by giant red kissing lips on her stem and mascara-highlighted brown eyes on either side of her hull – a treatment thought up by the German artist Feliks Büttner. However, Kloster sold the ship back to her previous German owners after only 11 months of operation.

On the 23rd August, 1999, a serious accident brought NCL unwelcome publicity. While returning to Dover from a Baltic cruise on the 23rd August, 1999, the *Norwegian Dream* collided with an Evergreen container ship in the English Channel. The NCL ship's bow was badly crumpled and there were long gashes in the superstructure. Fire broke out on the container ship and the unfortunate *Norwegian Dream* was towed first to Dover, then to Bremerhaven for repairs at the Lloyd Werft, which included the fitting of an entirely new bow unit. It says a great deal for the efficiency of the shipyard that she was able to re-enter service on the 11th October with a Mediterranean cruise from Civitavecchia.

In 1998, yet another acquisition brought a radically different new profile into the Kloster fleet when they bought the Orient Line and its ship *Marco Polo*. She had been the veteran Soviet liner *Alexandr Pushkin*, one of five sisters built by the Mathias Thesen shipyard at Wismar in Eastern Germany in the mid-'sixties. In 1991, she was bought in poor condition by the Orient Line which had recently been founded by a British businessman, Gerry Herrod. As the *Marco Polo*, she sails well away from the established cruising areas, instead taking passengers on explorations of the South Atlantic islands, or north of the Arctic Circle or to remote islands in the Pacific. At 20,502 gross tons, she is rather larger than most of the other expedition ships with which she competes in this limited but growing market. As the more conventional cruise itineraries have become ever more crowded, increasing numbers of passengers have begun to look out for a 'different' cruise experience and Klosters doubtless felt that the *Marco Polo* was ideal to cater to this trend. Such is the popularity of these tours off the beaten track that in the year 2000, the *Norwegian Crown* reverted to her former name, *Crown Odyssey* (see below in the Royal Cruise Line section) and became a companion to the *Marco Polo*. She returned to Norwegian Cruise Line late in 2003, however.

Klosters were struggling to keep pace by the late 1990s, faced with increasing competition and pressure to build ever-larger ships to keep abreast of their rivals, Carnival Corporation, P&O and Royal Caribbean International. In an effort to raise capital, NCL was floated on the New York Stock Exchange in July 1999 but within a few months the company was faced with a joint take-over bid from Carnival Corporation and Star Cruises, a recently-established Singaporean firm which has quickly become the market leader in Far East cruising. Uninterested in being merely a minority shareholder, Carnival withdrew and Star Cruises took over the Kloster organisation and its Norwegian Cruise Line and Orient Line fleets in April, 2000.

Royal Viking Line

Three old-established Norwegian shipowners formed the Royal Viking Line. The Bergen Line and Nordenfjeldske Dampskibsselskab had long co-operated in the Hurtigrute service, an essential local lifeline to the isolated communities along Norway's west coast, but the firm of A.F.Klaveness was new to the passenger market and later withdrew from the consortium. Royal Viking Line was an ambitious venture into luxury world cruising, with each partner contributing one ship.

Three exceptional new liners, each of 21,847 gross tons, were ordered from the Wärtsilä yard in Helsinki, which was then becoming a leading force in the construction of passenger ships. The initial design was made by Tage Wandborg and colleagues at Knud E. Hansen A/S and this represented a significant advance over his earlier ferry-inspired work for NCL. The first of the trio, the *Royal Viking Star*, was delivered to the Bergen Line in June, 1972. The remaining ships arrived in 1973, the *Royal Viking Sky* being introduced in July by the Nordenfjeldske company and the *Royal Viking Sea* entering service in December for A.F.Klaveness.

The three partners had examined a number of recently-built Scandinavian liners for inspiration but, for any company wishing to build innovative de luxe passenger ships, Cunard's *Queen Elizabeth 2* was an obvious precedent to follow. Indeed, both in their interior layout and in their external appearance, the Royal Viking ships seemed indebted to the famous Cunarder. The majority of the interior design work was carried out by Finn Nilsson in conjunction with the Oslo-based architect F.S. Platou. This team was already well-respected for its outstanding work on Norwegian America Line's *Sagafjord*. The decoration of the Royal Viking Line ships, however, was very much a Norwegian interpretation of the *QE2* look, with much use of moulded fibreglass, laminate surfaces, smoke-tinted glass balustrades and partitions and ceilings with oblong slits, obviously derived from the Cunarder's Queen's Room. Nevertheless, the overall ambience was Scandinavian, with many specially commissioned artworks

The brand new *Royal Viking Star* in Southampton in the late summer of 1972. The pronounced flare of her bow, particularly evident in the shadow, looked elegant, but often meant that she had to sail slowly in rough weather to prevent structural damage.
Ivor Trevor-Jones

The lengthened *Royal Viking Sea* at Helsinki in August 1984 during a Scandinavian capitals cruise.
Alastair Paterson Collection

and the Norwegian national colours – red, white and blue – being used throughout, and also in the ships' external livery. The company proudly emphasised both its Norwegian heritage and the Scandinavian hospitality to be enjoyed by its passengers.

As the Royal Viking fleet was designed for long cruises, cabins were large and many had their own sitting areas. A total capacity of only 559 passengers also helped to establish for Royal Viking Line an elite position in the cruise market. The Royal Viking ships were a successful blend of traditional grace and cutting-edge design. They had long, rakish bows flaring up from their otherwise straight hull lines. As in many liners built in those years, the machinery spaces and funnel were located aft, thereby opening up a vast expanse of recreational space on the top deck, sheltered by glass screens, and an observation lounge above the bridge.

David Trevor-Jones, a regular visitor to Southampton docks in the 1970s, remembers his first impression of the *Royal Viking Star*: 'The sight of this brand new piece of Norwegian exotica was very intriguing. The commentary on the harbour excursion boat emphasised that she was a floating luxury hotel for the very wealthy. Certainly, she was a very different kind of cruise ship from the Southampton regulars at that time – the 1950s-built liners of P&O, the *Reina del Mar*, the *Northern Star* and the rather spartan Soviets. This ship was purpose-built and, furthermore, had private facilities in every cabin – something almost unheard of at that time. We thought her a strange beast – rather beautiful despite her straight lines, but different from most of the ships we were used to, except the much larger *QE2*.'

The Royal Viking sisters were promptly acclaimed for their modernity and perfectionist on-board style and service. They soon began to gather a loyal following of passengers who cruised with them voyage after voyage. In fact, so lengthy and diverse were their itineraries that the company brochure was aptly called 'The Atlas'. Royal Viking itineraries included almost every imaginable cruise area – from Alaska and the Amazon to the Black Sea, the Chinese coast and the islands of the Indian Ocean. When A.F.Klaveness withdrew from the consortium in 1975, it seemed at first that its contribution, the *Royal Viking Sea*, might be sold on the open market but she was instead purchased jointly by the Bergenske and Nordenfjeldske companies.

Such was the popularity of the Royal Viking fleet among discerning travellers that between 1981 and 1983 the three ships were stretched to increase their capacity. They were sent in turn to the Hapag Lloyd shipyard at Bremerhaven and sliced in two in front of the funnel. A new prefabricated midships section was then floated into place before the three sections were welded together in dry dock. The ships' gross tonnage increased to 28,221 and their range of amenities also expanded.

Inevitably, some passengers felt that the increase in size and capacity to 758 had spoilt their exclusive, club-like ambience and made them feel more like mass-market ships. Furthermore, in 1984, the two remaining Royal Viking Line partners sold the company to the Kloster group, the owners of Norwegian Caribbean Line. Klosters had no history of operating de luxe ships on the worldwide itineraries offered by Royal Viking but, nevertheless, it seemed that the new acquisition would ideally expand their existing portfolio. At the same time, however, a new generation of smaller, luxury cruise ships – the so-called 'super yachts' – was entering service. These more exclusive vessels, such as the *Sea Goddess* ships, eventually operated by Cunard, creamed away much of Royal Viking's wealthier clientele and suddenly the 'stretched' early-1970s liners seemed outmoded, at least when competing at the top end of the cruise market.

Royal Viking Line fought back and regained its reputation for excellence when it commissioned the *Royal Viking Sun* in 1988. With the wealthiest passengers now demanding cabins with private balconies, the new ship had a very different profile from her predecessors. Similar in some ways to P&O's innovative *Royal Princess*, also designed and built by Wärtsilä, she had her public rooms in the hull and in the lower decks of the superstructure. Lifeboats nestled at main deck level and three decks of cabins with overhanging balconies were located above. The new ship's passenger accommodation was of a very high standard with much use of fine wood veneers and marble, the work of the Norwegian designer Njål Eide, who had previously contributed to *Sagafjord* and *Vistafjord*. Royal Viking Line was delighted when Fielding's respected cruise guide named *Royal Viking Sun* the most luxurious liner afloat in 1989-90.

Emboldened by its rediscovered success, Royal Viking saw an opportunity to emulate its rivals Cunard and Seabourn Cruise Line by acquiring a luxurious 'super yacht'. The 9,975 gross ton vessel had actually been ordered by Seabourn and was under construction at Schichau Seebeckwerft when Seabourn ran into financial difficulties, enabling Royal Viking to take over the contract. Now called *Royal Viking Queen*, she entered service in 1992 and the company was now able to offer even more exclusive itineraries for a mere 200 passengers. However, the 'super yacht' market is a difficult one to conquer, with many ships chasing a select group of passengers. Besides, the recession of the early-1990s was beginning to bite and market conditions were awkward. Kloster, meanwhile, was experiencing cash-flow problems as it struggled to keep pace with the expansion of rivals to its Norwegian Caribbean Line operation. The outcome was that it decided to abandon its Royal Viking brand.

The original 1970s fleet was scattered. In 1991-2, the *Royal Viking Star* and *Royal Viking Sky* were transferred to the Norwegian Cruise Line fleet as the *Westward* and *Sunward*, respectively. Tim Dacey sampled the *Westward* for a trip to Bermuda. 'The deluxe image of the Royal Viking ships had to a large degree been due to their staff and the superlative service. On a previous trip on the *Royal Viking Star*, I remember a fellow passenger ordering lamb chops for breakfast and he got them. A silly detail, perhaps, but it illustrates that nothing was too much trouble. There was only one sitting for dinner, which was leisurely and gave ample time to enjoy the fine cuisine. But by the time the ship had become the *Westward*, a large

The *Royal Viking Queen*, Royal Viking's half-hearted attempt to enter the exclusive yacht cruise ship market, was nearly identical to the ships of the rival Seabourn Cruise Line, in whose fleet the ship now successfully operates as *Seabourn Legend*. *Alastair Paterson Collection*

portion of the dining room had been removed to create a fun room and dining became a two-sitting affair. With an NCL crew, the ship was much the poorer. In any case, she did not fit the market for 3-4 day jaunts from Florida. She was spacious and meant for long voyages and her elegant public rooms looked tatty when lined with slot machines.' The *Westward*, in fact, failed to find a niche in the NCL fleet and was given a cursory refurbishment before joining Kloster's recently-acquired Royal Cruise Line subsidiary as the *Star Odyssey* (see below). The *Royal Viking Sea* was also transferred to Royal Cruise Line as the *Royal Odyssey* (see below).

The *Sunward* (ex-*Royal Viking Sky*) was quickly sold to the Birka Line for Baltic cruising but was then chartered instead to the P&O subsidiary Princess Cruises in April, 1993, becoming the *Golden Princess*. By 1996, she had been disposed of to Star Cruises and sailed to her new Far East base as the *Superstar Capricorn*. Two years later she passed to the shipping arm of the Hyundai Corporation, the vast Korean conglomerate, as the *Hyundai Kumgang* but is now back with Star Cruises as the *Superstar Capricorn*, operating out of Laem Chabaeng in Thailand. The former *Royal Viking Sea* is now the *Crown*, owned by a Norwegian company called Actinor which specialises in ship chartering. After a failed charter to Chinese interests for casino cruises, she was laid up in Shanghai, but eventually found another charterer – Spanish Cruise Line – who have had her refurbished to undertake week-long circuits of the Mediterranean, based in Valencia. (Interestingly, her SCL fleetmate is the *Bolero*, originally Norwegian Caribbean Lines' *Starward*.) As we have seen, the former *Royal Viking* Star now sails as Fred. Olsen's successful *Black Watch*.

The prestigious Royal Viking Line name and the flagship *Royal Viking Sun* were sold to Cunard Line in June, 1994. Within four years, Cunard itself was taken over by Carnival Corporation, by now parent company to many of the World's most famous cruise lines and acknowledged as the industry's market leader. Incidentally, Cunard's parent company, Trafalgar House, had in the interim been owned by Norwegians – the engineering group Kvaerner. Carnival was left to reshuffle its fleets and the *Royal Viking Sun* was sent to its Seabourn Cruise Line in 1999, becoming *Seabourn Sun*. Ironically, Seabourn, which by now also owned the former *Royal Viking Queen*, had once been an upstart rival to the Royal Viking Line.

Royal Cruise Line

In 1989, during a phase of mergers and consolidation in the cruise industry, Kloster acquired the highly respected Greek-owned Royal Cruise Line, a company with an enviable reputation for upmarket European and American itineraries. Its two highly-rated modern ships were the *Golden Odyssey*, a beautiful 10,757 gross tons liner designed by Tage Wandborg and built by Helsingør Skibsvaerft at Elsinore in Denmark in 1974; and the 34,312 gross tons *Crown Odyssey*, then practically brand new, having been built by Meyer Werft in Germany in 1988.

As the *Golden Odyssey* could only carry a single jumbo jet-load of passengers, Kloster thought that she was uneconomic and sold her to East German owners as the *Astra*. She was replaced with the *Royal Viking Sea* which they renamed *Royal Odyssey* and the *Westward* (formerly *Royal Viking Star*) which briefly became the *Star Odyssey*. Kloster attempted to widen Royal Cruise Line's market by introducing world cruises with these larger ships and by introducing the smaller *Royal Viking Queen* as the *Queen Odyssey*, hoping to attract a more exclusive clientele.

However, in an act of desperation to stave off a serious financial crisis and to cut its $1 billion debt, Kloster suddenly closed Royal Cruise Line in January, 1996 and sold its fleet. The *Star Odyssey* went to a firm acting on behalf of Fred. Olsen Lines. It was rumoured that the Klosters were none too pleased when they learned that one of their ships would be re-entering cruise service as Olsen's *Black Watch*, as the two firms were long-standing rivals. The *Royal Odyssey* was transferred to a new NCL venture, Norwegian Capricorn Line as *Norwegian Star*, but was eventually resold and is now laid up in the Far East. The more recently-built *Crown Odyssey* became a luxurious addition to Kloster's NCL's own fleet as the *Norwegian Crown*.

5
Effjohn International Companies

Effjohn International took its name from the merger of two long-established Scandinavian shipping companies, the Johnson Line of Stockholm and the Finland Steamship Company of Helsinki, known as EFFOA – hence Effjohn. The firms had already collaborated through their joint ownership of the Baltic ferry owner, Silja Line. In addition, however, both had at different times been involved in the American cruise business through a number of interesting subsidiaries.

The Johnson Line, for example, was a partner with the American entrepreneur Stan McDonald in Sundance Cruises which from 1983 operated the *Sundancer*, converted from the 1975-built Silja Line ferry *Svea Corona*, on cruises from Alaska. Previously, Mr. McDonald had been one of the founders of Princess Cruises. The *Sundancer* ran aground in 1985 and was declared a constructive total loss by insurers. She was replaced by the *Stardancer*, which had started life as the *Scandinavia* of DFDS and has since become Royal Caribbean International's *Viking Serenade* (see below).

EFFOA became involved in the cruise industry when it took over the ailing Sally Line in 1987, a shipping company based in the Åland Islands. Sally had been a prime-mover in Viking Line, a rival partnership which competed with Silja Line for dominance on the mid-Baltic ferry routes. In the early 1980s, Sally had placed three large ferries on Viking Line's principal Helsinki – Stockholm and Turku – Mariehamn – Stockholm routes. It had also extended its ferry interests with a service across the English Channel from Ramsgate to Dunkerque; and in 1981 had entered the cruise business by purchasing the Commodore Cruise Line.

COMMODORE CRUISE LINE

Commodore had been founded in 1966 by a Miami hotelier called Sanford Chobol. Initially, it operated chartered ships but in 1968 it went into partnership with Sweden's Wallenius Line. Wallenius had just taken delivery of a 7,056 gross ton ferry from the Wärtsilä yard in Helsinki, which it had intended for a cross-Baltic route. When that project was abandoned, it decided to follow the example of Kloster's Norwegian Caribbean Line by entering the cruise business between Miami and the Bahamas. The new ferry was adapted for this new service during the final stages of construction and now had an outdoor lido deck at the stern. She entered service as the *Boheme*. (Mr. Wallenius was in the habit of giving his ships operatic names.)

Captain Rolf Bassenberg has fond memories of the *Boheme*: 'She was the friendliest ship in the Caribbean – at least, we officers and crew liked to think so. Even though she was small, she was known as a 'happy ship' and developed a loyal following. I joined Wallenius Line in 1976 and became the first mate under Captain Jack Hunter, who taught me a great deal about managing passenger ships. I soon became Staff Captain, before moving to the *Caribe 1*. I was delighted to return to the *Boheme* in 1985 in overall command. By that time, the little converted ferry had been dwarfed by the new Royal Caribbean and Carnival ships at Miami, but she found a niche sailing from St. Petersburg (Florida). On the first sailing from there, she ran aground but she was such a strong and easily manoeuvrable ship that I was able to get her off and away.'

During winter seasons from 1973 to 75, Commodore gained extra capacity by chartering the Fred. Olsen-owned

The *Boheme*, in her original Wallenius Lines livery, sails from Miami in the late-1960s.
Ian Shiffman/Table Bay Underway Shipping Collection

A Scandinavian-designed cruise ferry dating from 1968, the *Freeport*, later *Caribe*, was distinguished by her remarkable funnel with a 'flying saucer'-shaped smoke deflector perched at a jaunty angle near its summit. The hull and superstructure had a family resemblance to NCL's *Starward* and *Skyward*. All had, in fact, been designed by Tage Wandborg. *Author Collection*

cruise ferry *Bolero* (see above) to sail in partnership with the *Boheme*. Thereafter, when Olsen recalled the ship to Europe for North Sea service, another vessel was chartered instead. This was the *Caribe*, which had been built in 1968 as the *Freeport* of Freeport Cruise Line to run between Miami and Freeport. (Freeport Cruise Line was the forerunner of the Bahama Cruise Line, which later became a subsidiary of the British company Common Bros.) The *Freeport* had been designed by Tage Wandborg and in 1968 was a smart, modern entrant to the fledgling Miami cruise industry, introducing new standards of excellence with accommodation for 812 passengers and 144 cars. During a nomadic career, during which she seemed neither to fit as a cruise liner nor as a ferry, she transferred to the Baltic in 1973 and sailed between Stockholm and Helsinki for the Ålands-based Baltic Star Line, a Birka Line subsidiary. That autumn, she was sold to the Svea Line for its short-lived Helsingborg-Travemunde (Trave Line) ferry service as *Svea Star*. In 1976, she passed to German owners, Bremer Schiffahrts, who chartered her to Commodore Cruise Lines, at first as the *Caribe* and then, in her final year before sale to DFDS in 1982, as the *Caribe Bremen*.

Four years later, in 1986, the *Boheme* also left Commodore's service, being sold to Majestic Cruises, actually a front for the International Association of Scientologists, who renamed her *Freewinds*. Now based in the Netherlands Antilles, she serves an exclusively Scientologist clientele. She has been fitted with extensive facilities for lectures and shows and, as she is effectively a floating club, even the locks have been removed from the cabin doors.

When Sally acquired the Commodore Cruise Line in 1981, it immediately began looking for a larger ship more suited to cruising, either to accompany or to replace the *Boheme*. The Greek-owned *Navarino*, once Swedish America Line's beautiful *Gripsholm*, would have been ideal but just before the sale arrangements were completed she keeled over while in a floating dry dock at Skaramanga. Sally decided to look elsewhere. In nearby Eleusis, they found the former Greek Line flagship *Olympia* in long-term lay up. Clyde-built by Alexander Stephen & Sons of Linthouse in 1953, this sturdy 22,979 gross ton steam turbine liner had been the fastest in the Greek merchant fleet and had been used for transatlantic service. She had also been popular as a New York-based cruise ship but her career with Greek Line had ended with that company's bankruptcy in 1974.

Captain Bassenberg was sent to Greece to oversee the handover and the subsequent rebuilding: 'The *Olympia* may have looked decayed on the outside and there was a lot of growth on her hull below the waterline, but she had been looked after inside by a pretty thorough maintenance crew who kept the propeller shafts well greased. They were so thorough that between Commodore signing the purchase agreement and the handover, all the Greek Line china and many other fittings were spirited away! We spent three months in a Greek shipyard before we were towed round to Hamburg for rebuilding. The trip to Hamburg was hair-raising. In the English Channel, one of the propeller shafts broke loose and the aft compartments began to flood. Luckily, we made it to Germany. There, the inefficient turbines were taken out and replaced by four Humboldt-Deutz diesels. As a further economy, the owners wanted to reduce the draft of the hull, so the crumbling old funnel was removed to save weight and replaced by a series of bare exhaust pipes – hardly attractive or ornamental. Otherwise, the ship was tidied up and we entered service in August 1983 as the *Caribe 1*.'

In 1988, the appearance of the *Caribe 1* was greatly improved when a new aluminium funnel was placed over the diesel exhaust stacks. She was sold in 1992 to Regal

Cruises and renamed *Regal Empress*. Cabins on the promenade deck were fitted with balconies but otherwise she retained her vintage 'ocean liner' appeal. Cruising in summer from New York, she was kept in immaculate condition and still sported burled wood veneers in her lobbies and in many of her public rooms. Her beautiful wood-lined library and large dining room were delightful with their brass inlays and etched glass panels, while the bridge, in terms of equipment and layout, was of museum quality. Unfortunately, Regal Cruises failed to survive the downturn in the cruise market in the early years of the new century and ceased operations in April, 2003. *Regal Empress* was sold to Imperial Majesty Cruise Line, for whom she operates short cruises to the Bahamas

TWO MORE VETERAN LINERS JOIN THE FLEET

In 1989, the Effjohn group purchased the Bermuda Star Line (formerly the Bahama Cruise Line) and soon merged it into the Commodore Cruise Line. Bermuda Star were then operating three ships and two of these were included in the deal. They were a notable pair of sisters, much-travelled and frequently rebuilt and renamed, and they had begun their careers with the Moore-McCormack Line in 1958 as the *Argentina* and *Brasil*. They too had been sturdily built, by the Ingalls Shipbuilding Corporation of Pascagoula, Mississippi, and they had been styled by the noted American industrial designer Raymond Loewy. At first, they were used on Moore-McCormack's de luxe service from New York to ports on the east coast of South America and, later, they sailed on more diverse cruises. Faced with the joint rises in fuel prices and American labour rates, they were laid up in 1969. Congress eventually permitted their sale in 1972 to Holland America Cruises, for whom they became the *Veendam* and the *Volendam*, respectively.

Always expensive ships to run, due to their heavy hull construction and deep draughts, they were sold in 1983 and went through a succession of name changes before becoming Commodore's *Enchanted Isle* and *Enchanted Seas* in 1990. Three years later, the *Enchanted Isle* was sent to Russia to act as a hotel ship in St. Petersburg in order to encourage passengers to visit that city via the Baltic Line ferries, then being marketed in Sweden and Finland by Commodore's parent company Effjohn. As St. Petersburg was being over-run by a crime wave, the hotel was not a success, becoming a respectable meeting place for criminal gangs to do business. Effjohn withdrew from the Baltic Line project, which subsequently collapsed, and the *Enchanted Isle* returned to a New Orleans-based cruise service.

In 1996, the *Enchanted Seas* became a floating university ship administered by the University of

Commodore Cruise Line's *Caribe 1*, ingeniously converted from the abandoned former Greek Line flagship *Olympia*. Her present funnel, shown here, is placed just aft of the location of the original, which was removed in 1983 during her conversion from steam to motor propulsion. *Peter Knego*

Her immaculate appearance belying her 41 years of service, the *Universe Explorer* sails from Vancouver in August 1999.
Peter Knego

Pittsburgh's Institute of Shipboard Education. As the *Universe Explorer*, she carried students on semester-long worldwide itineraries, studying as they sailed. During the summer vacations, she offered cultural cruises to Alaska to the general public. Both ships were reportedly in better condition than they had been for many years. Their thick hull plating was free of blemishes and they looked well in Commodore's livery. In 1995, Effjohn sold Commodore to JeMJ Financial Services of Miami. More ships were introduced – including the *Enchanted Capri* (originally the Soviet *Azerbaydzhan*) and the *Crown Dynasty* (see below). However, in December 2001, the company filed for bankruptcy, citing high mortgage payments on its expanded fleet as the main reason.

SALLY CRUISES

Built by Wärtsilä in 1980, the car ferry *Viking Saga* formed part of Sally Line's contribution to the Viking Line consortium, sailing on its prestigious Stockholm – Helsinki route. When she was replaced in 1986 by larger ferries, which had been ordered by the other members of the consortium, Sally Line renamed her *Sally Albatross* and used her on short cruises from Helsinki. Her ugly, angular appearance was improved in 1988 by a rebuild at Seebeckwerft in Bremerhaven when she was given a new, streamlined profile. This phase was only a brief interlude, however, for two years later she was largely destroyed by a fire while undergoing repairs at the Finnboda shipyard in Stockholm.

As temporary replacements, Sally Cruises chartered two small cruise ships which had become available owing to the bankruptcy of their Finnish owners. The *Columbus Caravelle* had been built in 1990 for Delfin Cruises, who soon ceased business. She temporarily became the *Sally Caravelle*, while her near-sister, the *Delfin Clipper*, became the *Sally Clipper*. Meanwhile, the gutted and distorted superstructure of the *Sally Albatross* was scrapped but, as the ship remained largely intact below the car deck, this section was rescued and towed to Finnyards to form the basis of a 'new' ship, also to be called *Sally Albatross*. What emerged was quite different from the original vessel – she now had the streamlined, sculptural lines of a modern motor yacht. Much use was made of glazing to protect passengers on the outside decks from the harsh Baltic weather. The resurrected ship entered service in 1992 – but, after the briefest career, she ran aground outside Helsinki on 4 March, 1994 and was badly holed below the waterline. Because the 1980s boom, which had made short cruises popular, had been overtaken by a crippling recession and passenger numbers were declining, Effjohn decided against repairing the damaged ship, which instead was laid up until a charterer could be found. In 1995, she was taken over by Norwegian Cruise Line, towed to La Spezia and rebuilt as the Caribbean cruise ship *Leeward* (see above).

CROWN CRUISE LINE

Another company which became part of the Effjohn group was the Crown Cruise Line, which had been founded in 1984 by Grunstad Maritime Overseas. As its first vessel, it bought the small cruise ship *Ilmatar* from the Vesterålens Dampskibsselskab, a company best known for its fleet of smart motor ships engaged in the Norwegian coastal Hurtigrute service. The *Ilmatar* had been built in 1964 for the Finland Steamship Company's Stockholm – Helsinki service. Only able to carry 50 cars, loaded through side ports, she was the last of her type before the new, bigger ferries took over. She was, though, a very modern-looking ship as her machinery space was towards the stern and so smoke was dispersed through her goalpost rear mast, rather than through a conventional funnel. Her owners' colours were displayed on the rear of the bridge structure, which also served as an observation platform. In 1973, the *Ilmatar* was lengthened by Howaldtswerke-Deutsche Werft in Hamburg and given extra engines. She was now a 7,155 gross tons Baltic cruise vessel capable of carrying 470 berthed passengers between Helsinki, Copenhagen and Travemünde. In 1980, she was sold to Vesterålens for a more wide-ranging cruise venture, which proved unsuccessful.

After her purchase by Crown Cruise Line, she sailed as

After some rebuilding work, the *Ilmatar* moved to Florida as the *Viking Princess*, operating short cruises from Palm Beach, where she is seen laid up in March 1996.
Peter Knego

the *Viking Princess* on short cruises out of San Diego in California, but was soon transferred to Palm Beach in Florida. When, some years later, Crown Cruise Line received the first of its newly-built, more up-market ships, they decided to distance the *Viking Princess* from her superior fleetmates and henceforth operated her under the name Palm Beach Cruises.

In 1986, another ex-ferry was purchased. The *Crown del Mar* had been Spanish *Las Palmas de Gran Canaria* of the Trasmediterranea company. Crown Cruise Line had her converted into a cruise ship and she entered service in 1988, but was unsuccessful and was soon laid up, being eventually sold to become the *D. Juan*. Her career came to an abrupt halt in 2000 when, owing to the debts of her charterers, she was arrested in Tahiti during a world cruise.

Crown Cruise Line had great ambitions and in December, 1987 they ordered a new ship from the Union Naval de Levante shipyard at Valencia in Spain. While the 15,271 ton *Crown Monarch* was under construction, Effjohn had, on behalf of its Commodore subsidiary, placed an order for two 19,200 ton liners with the same shipyard. It then acquired a 50 per cent interest in Crown Cruise Line and decided to market all three new ships under that name. The first of the trio, Grunstad's original *Crown Monarch*, was delivered behind schedule in 1991. The reason she was late was that she was found to have stability problems and had to be fitted with a stern-mounted sponson before entering service.

The two larger ships, named *Crown Jewel* and *Crown Dynasty*, followed in 1992 and 1993. Captain Bo Lewenhagen, who then worked for Effjohn, was sent to oversee the completion and delivery of the *Crown Jewel*: 'Crown Cruise Line had secured a fairly prestigious

A busy scene at Nassau in March 1992, with the *Crown Monarch* showing her boxy stern and sponsons. Also present are the *Costa Riviera* and *Westerdam*.
Peter Knego

149

The *Crown Jewel* in her initial Crown Cruise Line livery in December 1992. *Peter Knego*

charter for this stylish new Spanish-built liner. Sailing direct from the shipyard, she was to be used as a floating luxury hotel to accommodate distinguished guests visiting the 1992 Olympic Games at Barcelona. Unfortunately, the building contract was running way behind schedule and when we should have had a complete ship, what we actually sailed to Barcelona was a just two-thirds finished shell with a great deal of fitting out yet to be done. Gleaming and white on the exterior, within she was a construction site with wires dangling in unfinished rooms. We were instructed to sail to Barcelona anyway and, while we were able to accommodate some guests in tolerable conditions, we spent that initial summer tied up at the quayside fitting out. One compensation was that the crew and the shipyard workers had an outstanding view of the Olympic marathon runners as they raced past the docks.'

Once completed and in service, the three Crown ships were an up-to-date interpretation of the earlier generation of more intimate purpose-built cruise ships introduced in the early 1970s. The *Crown Jewel* and *Crown Dynasty* were particularly attractive, with exaggerated yacht-like lines and sweeping curves of steel work and glass around their promenade and topmost lido decks. Unfortunately, the ships were not a commercial success and were soon chartered to Cunard. However, as Cunard's financially troubled parent, Trafalgar House, sought to divest itself of the shipping line, the Crown ships' charters were not renewed and the three returned to their owner, Effjohn. The *Crown Jewel* soon joined the procession of Scandinavian ships operating for Star Cruises of Singapore, becoming their *Superstar Gemini* in 1995. The *Crown Monarch* is also Singapore-based, being used for short gambling cruises as the *Walrus*. The *Crown Dynasty* was chartered to Norwegian Cruise Line (see above) as *Norwegian Dynasty*, but later reverted to her original name to sail for Commodore Cruise Line from New Orleans. Following Commodore's bankruptcy in 2001, she was sold to Fred. Olsen Cruise Lines, becoming their *Braemar* (see above).

Reflecting the greater integration of its core Silja Line Baltic ferry interest, Effjohn was restyled Neptune Marine in 1996. Two years later, a majority shareholding in the company was bought by James Sherwood's Sea Containers group, based in London and Bermuda. In addition to the Silja ferries, Sea Containers is well-known in transport circles for its freight container business, its fleet of Sea Cat fast ferries and for its Orient Express luxury trains.

6
The Smaller Cruise Lines

Pearl Cruises of Scandinavia

In June, 1982, Pearl Cruises began a year-round operation in the Far East, becoming a pioneer of Chinese- and Japanese-based cruising for western passengers. It was a joint venture between, on the one hand, the Norwegian shipowner I. M. Skaugen; and, on the other, Loke Shipping, a subsidiary of the Copenhagen-based Lauritzen group. Lauritzen were then best known for their freight services between Denmark and Greenland, their fleet of red-hulled polar expedition vessels and reefers and their shareholding in DFDS. (Through another distinguished shipping line, the East Asiatic Company, the Danes already had long-standing trade connections with the Far East.)

With headquarters in San Francisco, Pearl Cruises was specially created to operate one ship, the 12,456-ton *Pearl of Scandinavia*. Originally built by Wärtsilä in 1967 as the Finland Steamship Company's handsome car ferry *Finlandia* for the Helsinki-Travemünde route, she was later sold to Finnlines, which belonged to the Finnish industrialist Enso Gutzeit. Her previously graceful appearance was ruined, however, in 1978-79 when she was transformed to become the *Finnstar*, sailing on warm weather trips to the Mediterranean, the Canaries and West Africa. To enable extra cabins to be built, her funnel was removed and was replaced by a set of bare exhaust pipes. A further rebuild in 1981 brought her up to a higher standard and, as the *Pearl of Scandinavia*, she headed out East.

In 1987, Lauritzen sold the Pearl Cruises business to Ocean Cruise Lines, a Swiss-British-Greek concern. After a further reconstruction the following year, the ship became the altogether more attractive *Ocean Pearl* with a longer clipper bow and an improved funnel design, but her popular itineraries remained largely unchanged. Ocean was itself the subject of a take-over in 1990 when the historic French concern Paquet Line acquired its small fleet. Two engine room fires in February, 1992 and July, 1993 marred the *Ocean Pearl's* otherwise flawless reputation but she continued to cruise out east until Paquet too was taken over, this time by Italy's famous Costa Line. She was sent to the Mariotti yard at Genoa to be rebuilt yet again, as the *Costa Playa* – a trial cruise ship to test new markets for Costa. On the 12th November 1995, she left Genoa for her maiden transatlantic crossing to Puerto Plata in the Dominican Republic. There, she commenced a weekly schedule of cruises to Cuba. The following year, Costa itself was the subject of a take-over, being absorbed into the vast American-Israeli controlled Carnival Corporation. American sanctions against Cuba were restricting the number of passengers taking the *Costa Playa's* cruises and so she was sold to Far Eastern interests and again named *Ocean Pearl*, becoming a casino ship based in Hong Kong. She has since traded as the *Joy Wave* and is now the *New Orient Princess*.

Scandinavian World Cruises

In 1979, the expansionist Danish line DFDS announced that it was setting up a new American subsidiary called Scandinavian World Cruises to operate cruise ferry services from both New York and Florida ports to the Bahamas. The Floridan cruise entrepreneur Bruce Nierenberg had persuaded Lauritzen and DFDS to back the new company. Following his advice, and that of American market consultants, Scandinavian World Cruises believed it could persuade American motorists to

The sleek Finnish car ferry *Finlandia* enters Travemünde harbour shortly after her debut on the Finland Steamship Company's long route from Helsinki. *World Ship Society*

The newly-converted *Pearl of Scandinavia* (ex-*Finlandia*) at Valletta on her delivery voyage to the Far East. In place of her dummy funnel, a new block of cabins has been built aft of her bridge and a large sponson has been added to her stern to support the extra weight.
World Ship Society

park their cars on its ships while it took them south to the sun in luxury. A new 26,748-ton cruise ferry, the *Scandinavia*, was ordered from the Dubigeon Normandie shipyard at Nantes in France for delivery in 1981.

Ominously, DFDS's Annual Report to its shareholders in 1980 confessed to 'butterflies in the stomach' over the boldness of the project. Indeed, DFDS had been badly advised about the Scandinavian World Cruises concept. For what was essentially a ferry route to the Bahamas, even the name was misleading. Flying the Bahamian flag in order to keep costs under control, the Scandinavian World Cruises ships were only allowed to pick up passengers at one US port. This frustrated the concept since they could not make an intermediate call at a Floridan or other American port while en route from New York to the Bahamas. (It has been suggested that Bruce Nierenberg believed that the anachronistic Jones Act, which prevents non-US flag ships from sailing in American domestic service, could have been repealed.) As the *Scandinavia* had to run directly to the Bahamas, two smaller ships were purchased to shuttle from Jacksonville and Port Canaveral in Florida to Freeport in the Bahamas.

The *Scandinavian Sea* had been the 1970-built *Blenheim* of Fred. Olsen Lines (see above), while the

The *Scandinavia* is pictured at sea at the beginning of her short and unsuccessful spell sailing from New York to the Bahamas. Her bluff bow design (somewhat elongated in this close-quarters image taken with a wide-angle lens) was soon damaged in the stormy seas around Cape Hatteras. *Author Collection*

The *Scandinavian Sea* (ex-*Blenheim*) in her Scandinavian World Cruises livery in 1982. Both of the line's smaller ships ended up sailing for Discovery Cruises. Firstly, the fire-damaged *Scandinavian Sea* re-entered service as the *Discovery 1*. After another fire, her eventual replacement was none other than her former SWC fleetmate, *Scandinavian Sun*, which became the *Discovery Sun*. *Author Collection*

Scandinavian Sun was originally the Freeport Cruise Line's 1968-built *Freeport*. She had most recently been on charter from her previous German owner to Commodore Cruise Line as the *Caribe Bremen* (see above). These costly acquisitions were sent to Blohm & Voss in Hamburg for internal rebuilding which transformed them from overnight vessels into day cruise ships. They then entered service in the new Scandinavian World Cruises colours of white with a blue waistband and diagonal stripes in three shades of blue on both the hull and the funnel.

The *Scandinavia*, meanwhile, was delayed at the shipyard and did not enter service between New York and Freeport until the summer of 1982. When she finally arrived in New York, with fire-fighting tugs sending welcoming jets of water into the air, she ranked as the largest cruise ferry yet built. Designed by Knud E. Hansen A/S, with interiors by Robert Tillberg, she had a range of facilities which made her an impressive addition to the DFDS fleet. Internally, she was the prototype for Tillberg's later work on the large Baltic ferries of Viking Line, introduced from the mid-1980s onwards.

During her inaugural season, the *Scandinavia* encountered some ferocious storms out from New York, which scared passengers, while the resulting bad publicity put off others who might have been tempted to make the trip. According to Ted Scull, the distinguished New York travel writer and liner historian: 'Driving from the Northeast to Florida takes two long days and is exceedingly monotonous, so enter DFDS with *Scandinavia*. DFDS and its American partners knew there was a vast driving market with seemingly huge year-round potential and with the bonus of seasonal and holiday peaks. Unfortunately, the ship had no reserve power and was often delayed by bad weather. Departures scheduled for 11pm from New York might be delayed to 4am or 6am (as was my case) and motorists would have to sit in their cars near the docks or go to a hotel – the last thing they wanted to do. They wanted to drive straight onto the ship, have a relaxing short cruise and get off in Florida without delays or other inconveniences. In fact, after two days at sea, passengers for Florida had to change ships at Freeport, making the journey far too long. In terms of comfort, the *Scandinavia* was undoubtedly a very nice ship but transfer to the two day ferries with deck seating, gamblers, party people and steel bands was a real downer.'

Worse still, the feeder service between Port Canaveral and Freeport was troubled by hair-raising safety problems. First, there was an engine room blaze onboard the *Scandinavian Sun*. during which a crew member and a passenger were suffocated by smoke. Then, during a cruise on the 9th March, 1984, a fire broke out onboard the *Scandinavian Sea* and spread with alarming speed. The ship returned to Port Canaveral where all 946 passengers were evacuated. She continued to burn at her berth and it was not until two days later that the fire was eventually extinguished. Reduced to a blackened hulk, the ship was declared a constructive total loss. While laid up at Port Canaveral, she passed through a number of hands before being towed to Valencia as the *Venus Venturer* and rebuilt for further cruise service. Outfitting took place at Barcelona and she was sold once more, this time to Bajamar Shipping, a Panamanian-flagged concern who renamed her *Discovery 1*. In November, 1986 she re-entered cruise service, this time from Port Everglades, mainly running at a sedate 12 knots on 'cruises to nowhere'. In May, 1996 the ill-fated *Discovery 1* suffered

A rare image of the completed *Copenhagen*, on the River Tyne in the livery of K/S Nordline. Shortly after, she was sold to the Soviets and entered service as the Black Sea Steamship Company's *Odessa*.
Mick Lindsay Collection

yet another fire, this time confined to her engine room. As a result she was deemed to be too degraded to be worth further repair and, after a couple of months in lay-up, she was sold to Indian breakers and towed for scrapping at Alang.

The Scandinavian World Cruises fiasco nearly ruined DFDS and many of the existing directors were replaced. The *Scandinavia* was recalled to Denmark and gave a welcome boost when she was introduced on DFDS's well-established Copenhagen-Oslo route in December, 1983. However, she remained a burden to the financially troubled company and so was sold in 1985 to Sundance Cruises as the *Stardancer*. Nevertheless, her livery must have been thought successful as a brand image as it was then applied to all of DFDS's passenger ships.

The remaining Scandinavian World Cruises vessel, the *Scandinavian Sun*, was sold to a new company called SeaEscape in which DFDS at first retained a minority shareholding. SeaEscape then purchased a number of similar former European ferries for day cruises from Port Canaveral. DFDS finally sold its shares in the company in 1987 but its earlier involvement was to come back to haunt it. Like the ships of Scandinavian World Cruises, those of SeaEscape had an abysmal safety record. The *Scandinavian Star*, formerly the *Massalia* of Paquet Line, suffered a number of serious fires. Finally, while she was sailing between Oslo and Frederikshavn on charter to the Da-No Line, an arsonist set light to the panelling in a cabin. The ship was engulfed in acrid smoke and many passengers were killed. DFDS was horrified to see that she was still painted in their livery, although they no longer had any connection with SeaEscape. To enable the Danish police to carry out a criminal investigation, the wreck was brought to Copenhagen and DFDS pleaded with the authorities to have the distinctive hull stripes painted out before the livery could cause further embarrassment.

Nordline

The 13,750 gross ton *Copenhagen* was the last passenger ship to be built at the long-established British shipyard of Vickers at Barrow-in-Furness. Ordered by a new Danish concern, K/S Nordline A/S, she was intended for European cruising based on the Danish capital. Nordline actually consisted of 850 investors who, encouraged by a tax break, intended to enter the cruise business with no less than four newly-built ships. Early publicity material suggested that the first of these would be named *Prins Henrik af Danmark* in honour of the Danish Prince Consort but this idea was later abandoned.

Now called *Copenhagen*, she was a handsome vessel designed, like so many others in this book, by Tage Wandborg of Knud E. Hansen A/S and somewhat resembling his earlier *Freeport* (see above). Sadly, before she could be completed, her owners got into a dispute with the shipyard similar to that between Kloster and the Italian builder of his *Southward* and the cancelled *Seaward*. Again, escalating costs led to the cancellation of the contract and after some time the partially completed vessel was towed to Newcastle to be fitted out by Swan, Hunter which had recently completed the *Vistafjord* and was doubtless anxious to find similar outfitting work to keep its skilled workers in employment. Having been fully completed, the ship returned to Barrow, where she was laid up in full Nordline livery. Eventually, she was sold to Soviet owners, the Black Sea Steamship Company, finally entering service in 1975 as the *Odessa*. As a newly-built ship, she was one of the most luxurious members of the Soviet cruising fleet and she became favoured for her cruises out of New York, New Orleans and Vancouver and, later, in the Mediterranean, the Black Sea and the Baltic. For some years, she also made an annual long-distance winter cruise, including several round-the-World voyages. Following the collapse of the Soviet Union, the Black Sea company suffered financial problems and the *Odessa* was arrested at Naples in 1995. Sadly, this fine ship was laid up in the port's outer harbour until 2002, when an anonymous owner bought her at auction with the apparent intention of returning her to cruise service.

Flagship Cruises

The handsome sister ships *Sea Venture* and *Island Venture* were built by the Rheinstahl Nordseewerke shipyard at Emden, Germany for another joint venture into cruising by enterprising Norwegian shipowners. Øivind Lorentzen and Fearnley & Eger joined forces to develop a Bermuda-based subsidiary, Flagship Cruises, to operate the ships. Designed by the ever-resourceful Tage

The *Sea Venture* looked smart in her original Flagship Cruises livery of dark turquoise-blue and white. *Peter Newall Collection*

Wandborg, the two 19,300-ton liners were delivered in 1971 and were among the most popular cruise ships of the 1970s. The *Sea Venture*, incidentally, took its name from the British naval flagship commanded by Sir George Somers, the Admiral of Virginia, which was wrecked on a Bermudan reef in 1609.

The intention was to use the two sisters on cruises based in New York in summer, with Caribbean and Mexican itineraries in the winter months. Consequently, they would need extensive lido areas for sunbathing, but also sheltered outdoor space for Atlantic weather conditions. The ingenious solution was to place a retractable glazed roof over the lido so that it could be fully enclosed in inclement weather. (This was no doubt inspired by the success of a similar feature on Home Lines' *Oceanic* of 1966 – one of New York's most popular cruise ships.) Forward of the lido, there was an observation lounge and cocktail bar above the bridge. All the other entertainment spaces were arranged in open plan on a single deck with large picture windows, while the dining room was lower in the hull – perhaps another concession to the possibility of encountering rough Atlantic weather. Cabins were compact, resembling those of contemporary Scandinavian car ferries, but the theory was that passengers would spend most of their time enjoying the ships' public spaces.

Interior design was co-ordinated by Finn Nilsson and Robert Tillberg and used the vibrant colours fashionable at the time. Tillberg's more refined treatment of the dining room, with its curved ceiling recesses between the ship's frames, was outstanding and of similar quality to his earlier work on *Kungsholm*. In contrast, Mildred Masters brought American swagger to the Bermuda Lounge, which she gave a gold-panelled ceiling and showy carpets. The most impressive space, though, was the double-height entrance hall. Its dramatic centrepiece was a wrap-around white marble panel, weighing seven tons, adorned by an abstract metal artwork made be students of the Oslo College of Art.

In 1974, Flagship Cruises sold the *Sea Venture* and *Island Venture* to P&O to boost its newly-acquired Princess Cruises fleet. Princess had been created in the mid-1960s to promote cruises from Los Angeles to the Mexican Riviera. It initially relied on chartered tonnage, taking its name from the Canadian *Princess Patricia*, its first ship. Under P&O ownership, the *Sea Venture* became the *Pacific Princess*, while the *Island Venture* was re-styled *Island Princess*. They were joined by another liner designed in the Knud E. Hansen office, *Spirit of London*, which became *Sun Princess*.

In a stroke of marketing genius, Princess permitted the television series *The Love Boat*, which had been conceived aboard their chartered liner *Princess Carla*, to use *Island Princess*, and later *Pacific Princess*, as a setting. The resulting publicity for cruising in general, and for the Princess fleet in particular, was enormous. The series, which reached tens of millions of Americans, promoted a fashionable, youthful and glamorous image – cruising was now perceived as fun and available to everyone, not just

The *Kungsholm* is seen in the Thames at Tilbury during her brief spell with Flagship Cruises. *Ambrose Greenway*

155

older and richer holidaymakers. Within five years, *The Love Boat* was being cited as one of the three prime factors influencing the growth of the cruise industry. The second was air-sea package arrangements, which widened the sphere of influence of Caribbean itineraries by allowing passengers to fly to their ship's port of departure for an inclusive fare. The third was the advent of theme cruises, which were promoted by niche marketing. These allowed passengers to indulge their hobbies, be they golf, professional football, bridge or big band jazz.

With P&O/Princess, the *Pacific Princess* and the *Island Princess* had a formidable reputation and usually sailed full. In the late 1980s, Princess began an expansion programme with a succession of new liners, making it among the most powerful companies in the American market. Its earlier ships were sent off to develop new markets in Europe and South America. In 1999, the *Island Princess* was sold to the cruise subsidiary of the Hyundai group of South Korea for service in the Far East as the *Hyundai Pungak-Ho*. This service was unsuccessful, however, and the ship was resold to the British entrepreneur Gerry Herrod, who had previously founded the Ocean Cruise Line and Orient Lines (see above). He renamed her *Platinum* and, later, *Discovery* for a charter to a British travel agency called Voyages of Discovery for whom she makes mainly British-based cruises. Her sister, *Pacific Princess*, meanwhile, has been sold to an Italian investment group, although for a time she remained under charter to Princess and continued to make a valuable contribution to their American operation, sailing in summer from New York to Bermuda. Recently, she has been chartered to a Spanish package tour operator, Pullmantur, for Caribbean itineraries.

In August, 1975, Flagship Cruises briefly returned to the fray when Øivind Lorentzen purchased Swedish American Line's highly respected *Kungsholm*, which was placed under the Panamanian flag. On the 6th October, the *Kungsholm* began cruises out of New York with neither a change of name nor of livery and trading heavily on her former reputation. Two years later, P&O acquired her as well and Flagship Cruises was then wound up. Thereafter, Øivind Lorentzen concentrated on the development of his bulk shipping businesses and on the NOSAC (Norwegian Specialised Auto Carriers) car-transporting business. Norwegian America Line absorbed his company in 1987-8 as it too had decided to concentrate on expanding its fleet of car carriers.

Cruising Yachts and Expedition Ships

A further example of Scandinavian shipping enterprise was the development by Norwegian owners of a new market for 'cruising yachts' in the 1980s. Precedents for these vessels could be found in the Bergen Line's *Meteor* and *Stella Polaris* in the 1920s and, at a larger scale, in the exceptionally high standards of service and appointments of 1960s ocean liners such as *Sagafjord* and *Kungsholm*.

In the early 1980s, the Finnish Wärtsilä shipyard built new royal yachts for Saudi Arabia and Iraq, the *Abdul Aziz* and the *Al Mansur*. The latter was designed by Knud E. Hansen A/S and had some similarities to the Royal Cruise Line's *Golden Odyssey* of 1974. Both yachts informed the design of a succession of Norwegian-owned de luxe 'yacht' cruise ships. The first of these, a 4,253-ton pair named *Sea Goddess I* and *Sea Goddess II*, were ordered from Wärtsilä in 1982 by Norsk Cruise A/S, which traded as Sea Goddess Cruises. They entered service in 1984 and were immediately acclaimed for their exclusivity – they each had just 59 luxurious suites – and for their distinctive cruise itineraries, taking in smaller ports. They could, for instance, anchor in fashionable yacht harbours and resort towns.

Petter Yran of Yran & Storbraaten of Oslo, who had been responsible for both the exterior and interior styling of the Sea Goddess twins, also styled the next generation of yacht cruise ships. These were nearly twice as big at around 10,000 gross tons and included the *Seabourn Pride* and *Seabourn Spirit* of Atle Brunstad's Seabourn Cruise Line and their sister, the *Royal Viking Queen* (see above). At about the same time, the long-established Norwegian firm of Fearnley & Eger invested in no less than eight similar, 4,000-ton cruise ships, built in Italy and named *Renaissance One* to *Renaissance Eight*. They promoted them as the Renaissance Cruise Line.

One problem with all these ships, however, was that their relatively small passenger numbers and more exclusive and discerning clientele made them especially vulnerable to changing global economics and to newer (and consequently more desirable) competition. The recession of the early-'nineties was a cruel blow to the 'yacht' cruise ship industry. The Sea Goddess ships passed under Cunard management; the Seabourn Cruise Line was partially absorbed by the Holland America Line and is now part of the Carnival empire; and the Renaissance ships were dispersed, one of them eventually becoming the British-owned *Hebridean Spirit*. Subsequent generations of luxury cruise ships have been somewhat larger, in the 30-40,000 gross ton range, and have a wider appeal. Nevertheless, these 1980s experiments proved yet again that Norwegian entrepreneurship was willing to back new initiatives in passenger shipping at all scales – from micro to macro.

The same can be said of the expedition cruise ship market. In 1969, a company called K/S A/S Explorer & Co., managed by Lars Usterud-Svendsen of Oslo, took delivery of a striking little 2,481-ton vessel with a red, ice-strengthened hull. Called *Lindblad Explorer*, she was chartered to an American Swede, Lars-Eric Lindblad, who was one of the pioneers of modern tourism to remote areas such as Antarctica. The subsequent history of this pioneer vessel, which has suffered several near-lethal groundings and has passed through various ownerships, including an associate of the Swedish American Line, illustrates that expedition cruising is a high-risk business. Nevertheless, other Scandinavian owners have been involved in further ventures in this field, which have included *Lindblad Polaris* (a conversion of a Swedish ferry); *North Star* (which became better known as the *Caledonian Star* and was an ingenious transformation of a former German trawler); the 3,000-ton Danish *Discoverer* (which, after many financial tribulations, eventually entered service as the German-owned *World Discoverer*); and the *Song of Flower* (another conversion, this time from a small ro-ro freighter).

7
Royal Caribbean Cruise Line

Targeting the same Caribbean cruise market as Kloster's Norwegian Caribbean Line was another Norwegian group, the Royal Caribbean Line. Again, this was a venture involving long-established family shipping interests. Realising the potential of the Caribbean as a cruise destination, an American hotel owner called Edwin Stephan, based in Wisconsin, had contacted three Norwegian shipowners – I.M.Skaugen A/S, Anders Wilhelmsen and the Gotaas-Larsen group – through the Fearnley & Eger ship brokerage in Oslo.

The shipping activities of these firms were widespread and diverse. For example, Skaugen was principally a cargo shipper which had begun its activities with sailing ships in the nineteenth century and had been briefly involved in the emigrant passenger trade after the Second World War (see above). Wilhelmsen also operated cargo liners but was diversifying as an operator of roll-on/roll-off and container ships, as well as support services for the developing North Sea oil and gas industries. Gotaas-Larsen, primarily a tanker operator, had also been active in the emigrant trade and had for some time been represented in the Miami cruise business through its Eastern Steamship Lines operation. Eastern ran the small cruise ships *New Bahama Star*, formerly the *Jerusalem* of Zim Lines, and between 1961 and 1972, the *Ariadne*, originally Swedish Lloyd's *Patricia* (see above). Later, it operated a former World War II-built American troopship, the *General W. P. Richardson*, as the much-rebuilt *Emerald Seas* on short cruises to the Bahamas. In the course of its varied career, this frequently re-named ship had been American President Lines' transpacific liner *President Roosevelt* and, briefly, the Chandris cruise ship *Atlantis*.

THE SONG OF NORWAY CLASS

Royal Caribbean was formed in 1968 with the three Norwegian firms as partners. Gotaas-Larsen, with its expertise in cruise shipping, assumed overall responsibility for the development of the new fleet of three purpose-built vessels, exclusively for Caribbean cruising. The order went to Wärtsilä in Helsinki, which was becoming the leading builder of the new generation of cruise ships. As with the rival Norwegian Caribbean 'White Fleet', initial design work was entrusted to Tage Wandborg and his colleagues at Knud E. Hansen A/S. Technical design was by Martin Hallen, the chief naval architect of I.M.Skaugen who worked in close co-operation with the Wärtsilä drawing office. The interiors, however, were by the Danish designer Mogens Hammer, who had previously worked on the original Norwegian Caribbean fleet, and, most distinctively, the external silhouettes were styled by the Norwegian architect Gier Grung. Wandborg recalls that 'Grung was a technically adventurous architect who was obsessed with glass. He was known to have designed a number of extraordinary glass villas around Oslo and his office had a plate glass floor which I was at first afraid to stand on. To demonstrate how strong it actually was, he began jumping on it and this show of confidence immediately endeared him to me.'

The most striking and apparent innovation was the funnel design, which incorporated a circular cocktail bar, protruding high above the sun decks over the stern. This 'Viking Crown Lounge' was to become a Royal Caribbean trademark, included, in modified form, in all its subsequent ships. Along with all other structural elements, it was carefully 'sculpted' by Grung into a singular and cohesive composition.

The much-travelled, much-altered *Emerald Seas* in the livery of Royal Admiral Cruises in 1991. *Peter Knego*

157

Displaced by a new generation of mega-liners, Royal Caribbean's *Sun Viking* is seen far from traditional home territory, cruising in the Hardangerfjord in August 1993. *Peter Knego*

The first of the Royal Caribbean fleet, the *Song of Norway*, was delivered by Wärtsilä in October, 1970. The *Nordic Prince* and *Sun Viking* followed, the latter distinguished from her otherwise identical sisters by her bow plating which, at Wandborg's suggestion, was carried up an extra deck, thus giving a more imposing forward profile. The 18,500-ton sisters could each carry 870 passengers on week-long circuits from Miami. They were unashamedly designed to appeal to Middle America, with bright and airy hotel-like interiors and large expanses of varnished teak sun decks. Spacious lido areas extended over the sides between the funnel and the mast.

American passengers responded well to the informal atmosphere on these white cruise ships, which was quite different from that of the traditional vessels. Entertainment was slick, with Las Vegas-style revues, discos and casinos, while the ambience was jovial, with steel bands playing on deck and waiters balancing trays of exotic cocktails on their heads. Increasing numbers of Europeans were also attracted by fly-cruise packages. Clearly, Royal Caribbean had found a winning formula. Such was the ships' popularity that in 1978 *Song of Norway* was returned to her builders to be 'stretched'. A new 27 metre long midship section contained 400 additional cabin berths, new public rooms and enlarged sun decks. To enable the ship to fit back into Wärtsilä's enclosed building shed, the top of the funnel was temporarily removed. The *Nordic Prince* was similarly enlarged in 1980 but the *Sun Viking* remained unaltered throughout her Royal Caribbean career.

SONG OF AMERICA AND SOVEREIGN OF THE SEAS

Kloster meanwhile retaliated with the giant *Norway*, transformed from the famous transatlantic liner *France*. Royal Caribbean did not contemplate a similar rebuilding of an existing ship. In their view, with the market for cruises continuing to grow, the solution was to build anew. A great deal of research therefore went into what would turn out to be the first of a 'new generation' of Royal Caribbean ships for the 1980s. The design process began in 1978 for a larger but more economical version of the well-proven *Song of Norway* class.

As with recent Wärtsilä-built cruise ferries for Scandinavian services, the new Royal Caribbean ship would have the then fashionable cabins forward, public rooms aft superstructure layout with an atrium containing the main circulation space in between. A further aft stair tower led to the Viking Crown Lounge, which was developed into an extruded pod, fully encircling the funnel and giving a 360 degree view. Indeed, the design of the new *Song of America* showed a significant advance over the earlier *Song of Norway* class. Gier Grung and Mogens Hammer were again brought together to style the new ship as part of an expanded team which included the experienced Norwegian cruise ship designers Finn Nilsson and Njål Eide. The apparent bulk of the altogether more massive superstructure was lessened by a series of tiered observation decks at the front and by painting the surrounds of the windows to the public rooms with a broad, dark blue band.

Although the work of Scandinavian designers, the *Song*

The lengthened *Song of Norway* manoeuvres in Los Angeles harbour in April 1996. *Peter Knego*

of America was, as its name suggested, more American than Norwegian in tone. Its interiors were in the anonymous, glitzy, pastel-shaded style of contemporary American roadside hotel design. For its mass-market clientele, the ubiquitous Holiday Inn and Marriott brands were the standards by which cruise ship accommodation was judged. Even the names of the public rooms were calculated to appeal to this market, following the Royal Caribbean tradition of calling them after musicals – hence the Can Can Show Lounge, the Oklahoma Lounge and the Guys and Dolls night club.

The *Song of America* entered service from Miami in November, 1982, operating an intensive seven day schedule to the Bahamas with only eight hours turnaround time in Miami. Externally, she was among the most impressive vessels to sail regularly from the port but Royal Caribbean's directors remained envious of Kloster and his massive *Norway*. Continued strong growth brought about by the mid-1980s economic boom enabled them to trump Kloster by developing their own giant, but purpose-built ship. With technical assistance from Wärtsilä's design team, Skaugen's naval architect Martin Hallen developed the *Song of America* design into a huge 73,192-ton, 2,600 passenger super ship. At the time, Wärtsilä had a full order book and hence, the building contract was placed with Chantiers de l'Atlantique for delivery in December, 1987. (Incidentally, this yard had built the rival *Norway* as the *France* twenty-seven years previously.)

The new Royal Caribbean flagship was appropriately named *Sovereign of the Seas*. Everything about her was conceived on a grand scale. The dining rooms, for instance, would have to be able to feed 1,300 passengers at each of two sittings. In order to predict the movement of passengers, the use of space on the *Song of America* was closely scrutinised and an open plan layout was chosen, with all the major attractions accessed off a giant Hyatt

In March 1999, the *Song of America* makes her final departure from Miami before joining the Airtours fleet as *Sunbird*. *Peter Knego*

159

Monstrously rebuilt from the already visually challenging *Stardancer*, Royal Caribbean's *Viking Serenade* shows off her new bow and shortened funnel in Los Angeles harbour. *Peter Knego*

Regency hotel-style central atrium. This both maximised the feeling of scale and grandeur possible in such a big vessel and made a focal point to enable passengers to find their way around and to meet up. Wide, curving sweeps of stairs and glazed elevators eased the flow of passengers from deck to deck and the majority of the public rooms were located aft of the atrium in the upper decks of the hull. On top of the superstructure was a wide expanse of sun deck with several swimming pools, water slides and groups of jacuzzis. There were games courts and many other amenities.

Sovereign of the Seas arrived at Miami in December, 1987, the biggest, whitest, glitziest cruise ship yet seen. Notwithstanding her great bulk, she was a remarkably elegant vessel with flowing hull lines and a stern reminiscent of that of the great French liner *Normandie*. As well as beating the *Norway* in terms of size, Royal Caribbean also copied another Kloster innovation by leasing a Bahamian island for the exclusive use of its passengers.

THE ADMIRAL CRUISES SHIPS

Meanwhile, the Gotaas-Larsen-owned Eastern Steamship Lines, which continued to offer cheap short trips to the Bahamas using its veteran *Emerald Seas* (see above), merged with two other companies – the associated Western Steamship Lines, which operated another old-timer, the *Azure Seas* (ex-*Southern Cross*), and Sundance Cruises – to form Admiral Cruises. As already mentioned in the Effjohn chapter, Sundance Cruises was a joint venture between Sweden's Johnson Line (historically famous for its liner routes to South America but more recently involved in cross-Baltic ferries as a member of the Silja Line consortium) and Mr. Stan McDonald, who had been the founder of Princess Cruises before selling it off to P&O. Sundance had a single vessel, the cruise ferry *Stardancer*, built at Nantes in 1982 as the *Scandinavia* of DFDS's short-lived Scandinavian World Cruises operation (see above).

With a converted World War 2 troopship, a former British liner and a modern cruise ferry, the combined Admiral fleet was nothing if not diverse. To improve its market position, the company ordered a new large cruise ship, known during the design stage as *Future Seas*, from Chantiers de l'Atlantique. Not only would this vessel offer an impressive array of the modern leisure and entertainment facilities found in the ships of the sister Royal Caribbean fleet, but a unique selling point would be her futuristic 'high tech' styling with smooth, bulging forms and vast areas of glazing to let light pour into her interiors. However, by the time *Future Seas* was completed in 1990, Admiral Cruises had been fully absorbed into the Royal Caribbean fleet and she entered service as her new owners' *Nordic Empress*. The *Stardancer* was rebuilt the following year as a fully-fledged cruise ship, the *Viking Serenade*. (Eleven years later, under the name *Island Escape*, she was transferred to a new company, Island Cruises, which Royal Caribbean set up jointly with the British tour operator First Choice.)

BUILDING A UNIFIED FLEET

Meanwhile, in 1988, Carnival Cruises attempted to gain control of Royal Caribbean but Anders Wilhelmsen thwarted them by buying out the interests of Skaugen and Gotaas-Larsen in collaboration with the Hyatt hotel group. In 1993, a listing was obtained on the New York Stock Exchange and, now with increased financial muscle, Royal Caribbean powered ahead with an impressive expansion programme. Today, the Wilhelmsen family still control around 25% of the company. The majority of the company's ships remain Norwegian-registered.

The incorporation of the ex-Admiral Cruises ships *Viking Serenade* and *Nordic Empress* into the Royal Caribbean fleet was merely a diversion from the company's central strategy, which was to develop a unified group of very large cruise ships along the lines of *Sovereign of the Seas*. The intention was to give the same high level of service throughout the fleet, while standardisation of the vessels coupled with their high capacity would, it was hoped, increase their profitability. Two sister ships were

Photographed from the fantail of Premier Cruises' *Rembrandt*, the futuristic-looking *Nordic Empress* catches the early morning sunlight as she arrives at New York in August 2000 on her regular summer route from Bermuda. *Author*

ordered from Chantiers de l'Atlantique: the *Monarch of the Seas*, delivered in 1991, and the *Majesty of the Seas*, which entered service the following year. These ships displaced the comparatively small *Sun Viking*, which was sent across the Atlantic to expand Royal Caribbean's sphere of activities in the traditional European cruising regions of the Baltic and the Mediterranean. In recognition of its wider remit, the company was now re-styled Royal Caribbean International.

A series of yet larger ships followed, some built by Chantiers de l'Atlantique in France and others by Kvaerner-Masa, the former Wärtsilä company, in Finland. The new vessels were a refinement of the *Sovereign of the Seas* class. Anticipating new regulations which would require lifeboats to be placed at main deck level, and also the increasing demand for cabins with balconies, the new sextet had the majority of their public rooms located in the superstructure. Recessed behind the lifeboat promenades,

As the World's largest cruise liner, the *Sovereign of the Seas* caused a sensation at the time of her introduction into the Caribbean cruise trade from Miami. She is seen sailing from there in August 1998 after a successful decade of service. *Peter Knego*

161

The gleaming white *Splendour of the Seas* sails from Copenhagen, bathed in early evening sunlight in July 1994. *Author*

enormous double height expanses of glazing give panoramic views over the sea. To maximise the effect, the public rooms on the upper level were recessed with airy open spaces along each side. The trademark Viking Crown Lounge was enlarged and placed forward of the base of the funnel on the 69,143-ton *Splendour of the Seas* and *Legend of the Seas*. On the larger, 75,000-ton *Grandeur of the Seas*, *Rhapsody of the Seas*, *Enchantment of the Seas* and *Vision of the Seas*, it was removed from the funnel altogether and placed forward, on top of the main atrium spaces.

The *Splendour of the Seas* differed somewhat from the others by having more richly toned interiors and a greater emphasis on indoor space. She was obviously intended for the European market and indeed has become a highly popular part of the European cruising scene, with her regular Baltic cruises from Harwich attracting passengers from both sides of the Atlantic. With so many magnificent ships, Royal Caribbean has rapidly expanded its activities elsewhere. In the summer, the *Rhapsody of the Seas* cruises to Alaska, *Legend of the Seas* is based in the Mediterranean and the remainder of the fleet sails from a variety of American and Caribbean ports – Miami, Fort Lauderdale, Los Angeles and San Juan in Puerto Rico.

Meanwhile, the original Royal Caribbean fleet was phased out. The *Song of Norway* and *Nordic Prince* were sold to Airtours, the British holiday firm, in 1996 and 1997. A condition of the sale was that the Viking Crown Lounges would have to be removed from their funnels. This work altered their appearance considerably. The two sisters re-entered service on western Mediterranean itineraries as *Carousel* and *Sundream*, based at Palma de Majorca. In 1999, they were joined in the Airtours fleet by the *Song of America*, which was refurbished by Cammell Laird at Birkenhead as the *Sunbird*. In her case, removing the lounge from the funnel was deemed to be too costly, so thankfully it remains intact.

THE CELEBRITY CRUISES ACQUISITION

The ambitions of Royal Caribbean International have continued to surge ahead. In 1997, it acquired Celebrity Cruises and its fleet of five stylish, modern cruise ships – the *Horizon*, *Zenith*, *Mercury*, *Galaxy* and *Century* – from the Greek Chandris family. Celebrity has retained its identity and has embarked in its own new-building programme, beginning with the innovative, though hardly attractive, gas turbine-powered *Millennium*, introduced in June, 2000. Also built by Chantiers de l'Atlantique, the 91,000-ton *Millennium* was the first of a class of four, being followed by the *Infinity*, *Summit* and *Constellation*. Royal Caribbean's ownership of Celebrity emphasises how widely and subtly the influence of Scandinavian shipowners now reaches.

While Celebrity's luxurious ships may once have had Greek owners and have been the work of Greek and Scandinavian designers, their interiors, though undeniably impressive in their sheer scale and ostentation, are blandly international. The same has been increasingly true of much of the cruise industry. As the largest ships are based in the Caribbean in winter and elsewhere in summer, their design must appeal to a very diverse clientele with differing cultural values. This has to an extent led to a uniformity of design output with a common vocabulary of 'glamorous' touches to which designers believe passengers will respond positively, whatever their backgrounds. Polished veneers and neo-classical details are supposed to suggest heritage and quality; chandeliers and marble provide opulence; and inlaid compass designs infer maritime tradition. Yet, taken together, these gestures add up to very little that is either coherent or commendable. It is easy to become blasé about the centrally located atrium with its showy carpets, white grand piano, concealed lighting and glass lifts as the formula has become so ubiquitous.

The American-owned Carnival group, meanwhile, has become the dominant force in the cruise industry – and its ships are anything but dull and bland. Instead, they are highly ornate and very much in the post-modern 'themed' manner of Las Vegas resorts. Yet, while this brash and showy approach may be highly popular with the mass market, which doubtless feels that it is receiving excellent value for money, in terms of cultural and national identity it is entirely homogenous – a kind of globalised theme park spectacle. There are, of course, a few exceptions to this generalisation, notably the very Italian *Costa Romantica* and *Costa Classica* and the conservative but comfortable British ships with interiors by McNeece, but overall there is a regrettable uniformity about present-day cruise ship décor.

The scale alone of the interiors on recent RCCI ships impresses, even if the décor itself resembles that of modern hotels. Here we see part of the *Splendour of the Seas*' vast atrium and her dining room.
David Trevor-Jones

The *Rhapsody of the Seas* - one of four similar sisters - on an Alaskan cruise in June 1998.
Alastair Paterson

The central Royal Promenade on *Voyager of the Seas*, a 'high street' of shops, cafés and bars, is the ship's focal point. *Kvaerner Masa Yards*

THE SPECTACULAR VOYAGER OF THE SEAS

Royal Caribbean however still astonishes its passengers with the sheer scale of its projects. The most impressive addition to a fleet which is among the finest and most innovative afloat, is undoubtedly the *Voyager of the Seas* – a vessel for which one nearly runs out of superlatives. This 137,000-ton, 3,840 passenger giant entered service from Miami in the summer of 1999 and was by far the largest passenger ship the world had ever known. Built by Kvaerner-Masa at Turku and powered along by three Azipod electric motor units suspended from the hull, this voluptuous vessel has set new standards for the entire cruise industry. Apart from the formulaic components of a typical large cruise ship, the spaciousness of the *Voyager of the Seas* has enabled a number of new facilities to be offered which would be impossible on a smaller vessel.

If she was to fit into existing ports, the designers could not make the ship longer, so they were forced to build up and to compensate by making the hull wider. As most passengers now expect a cabin with a window, the solution was ingenious. Following the precedent of the two large Baltic ferries built for Silja Line in the early 1990s, the *Silja Serenade* and *Silja Symphony*, a 'walking street' of shops, bars and restaurants, known as the Royal Promenade, was devised down the centre line of the ship with a full-length atrium overhead. Cabins, located in the decks above either have a view out to sea or one overlooking this 'street'. Due to its novelty value, this design feature has meant that inside cabins are among the most sought-after accommodation on the *Voyager of the Seas*. (Incredibly, almost 50 per cent of the ship's 1,557 passenger cabins have balconies.) According to the Royal Caribbean brochure, this 'cruising innovation' is 'four decks high' and 'offers 24-hour dining and entertainment options and a world of shopping to explore.' An Irish-themed pub is located between the 'Connoisseur Club', a mahogany-lined cigar bar, and a jazz club called 'High Notes', decorated 'to evoke the swinging 'thirties'. The 'Casino Royale', named after a James Bond film, is said to resemble 'somewhere between Las Vegas and Monte Carlo.' Guests are encouraged to 'take a leisurely stroll and stop for a relaxing lunch in the tropical atmosphere of the Island Grill, followed by an intimate dinner for two at the Euro-Italian restaurant Portofino.' Onboard, it is possible to sample faux styles, customs, cultures and cuisine from around the world - indeed probably the only Norwegian items on the *Voyager of the Seas* are its officers.

The dining rooms are cavernous, multi-tiered spaces reminiscent in their scale of those on the great Atlantic liners of the 1930s. The theatre, located forward is of operatic proportions, inspired by La Scala in Milan. It is the first afloat to be able to host the most complex blockbuster musicals. An ice rink is located amidships with tiered seating on all sides. For exercise, there is what is claimed to be the largest fitness centre afloat with a running track encircling the lido area and even a climbing wall up the back of the funnel. With such a ship, Royal Caribbean's marketing slogan 'Like no vacation on earth' was hardly an overstatement. A few observers thought that the exceptional *Voyager of the Seas* might remain a one-off project but, before she even entered service, the company announced the construction of a series of equally imposing sister ships. The second of these, named *Explorer of the Seas*, entered service in the summer of 2000, followed by *Adventurer of the Seas* in November 2001 with more sisters to follow.

As if operating such a fleet was not enough, in the summer of 1999 Royal Caribbean announced the building of a further new type of large cruise liner, code-named the 'Vantage' class. An order was placed at Meyer Werft in Germany for an initial pair of 88,000 ton liners to be named *Radiance of the Seas* (delivered in April 2001) and *Brilliance of the Seas* with an option for a further two vessels. Powered by gas turbines, this new class promises to be quieter and also much more environmentally friendly than traditional motor ships. These voluptuous vessels are certainly among the most outstandingly innovative passenger ships in the world today.

Then the World's largest cruise liner, the mighty *Explorer of the Seas* arrives at Southampton en route from her Finnish builders to Miami in 2000. *Mick Lindsay*

8
Consolidation, Globalisation and New Directions

The change from distinctly Scandinavian design identities to the post-modern aesthetics of the international leisure and hospitality industry has been accelerated by the globalisation of the cruise industry. Cruise lines no longer belong to a single owner, but to large international corporations with many institutional and private shareholders. For example, today only a minority of Royal Caribbean's shares actually belong to a Scandinavian ship owner, Anders Wilhelmsen, while Norwegian Cruise Line's ultimate owners are based in Singapore and its ships are managed from Florida.

Furthermore, the mass market sector of the cruise industry, in which Norwegian ship owners in particular had once excelled, is now experiencing a phase of consolidation. Of the big players, firstly, Norwegian Cruise Line was acquired by Star Cruises. Next, in November 2001, industry observers were astonished to learn that two other leading operators, Royal Caribbean International and the P&O subsidiary, Princess Cruises, had proposed to merge to form what would become the world's largest cruise line, Royal Caribbean Princess, operating an international fleet of over forty vessels. The American-based Carnival Corporation, presently the world's largest and most profitable cruise operation, then made its own hostile (but ultimately successful) bid for Princess Cruises. The outcome of these machinations will be that three global giants will dominate the cruise industry with smaller operators left to exploit niche markets.

Yet, not withstanding these recent trends, Scandinavian entrepreneurship continues to shape the future direction and growth of passenger shipping. For example, the Norwegian 'Hurtigrute' coastal express concept has recently been exported to South America, where the sturdy 11,386 grt *Nordnorge* has been introduced on cruises in the Chilean fjords. In contrast with the mass-market megaships, which have become destinations unto themselves, the *Nordnorge* carries only 464 passengers on 16 day voyages and the emphasis is on the ports of call, enjoying the spectacular scenery and outdoor pursuits. While the *Nordnorge* brings an already proven concept to a new potential market, another recently-delivered Norwegian-owned passenger ship marks a radical shift in perceptions of what a passenger ship actually is.

THE WORLD

When Knut Kloster introduced the *Norway* to his Norwegian Caribbean Line in 1979, he changed the face of cruising. Recently, his son, Knut Kloster Jr, has overseen the construction of a ship every bit as epoch-making. On 12 March 2002, six years after the project was first announced, Kloster's company, Residensea, took delivery of *The World* – the first residential cruise ship and luxury resort, intended to carry wealthy passengers around the world, dropping anchor at exotic destinations and attending special events, such as the Olympic Games, the Cannes Film Festival and the Monaco Grand Prix. Remarkably, *The World* is the first cruise ship ever actually to have been built in Norway and she was delivered from the Fosen Mekaniske Verksteder at Rissa, near to Trondheim (although the hull was in fact constructed in Sweden at Bruce's Shipyard in Landskrona, a Fosen subsidiary).

The World contains 110 fully furnished residences and 88 guest suites. These comprise two and three bedroom apartments, each with a bathroom, dining area, veranda and kitchen. Prices range from $2 – 6.8 million (plus annual maintenance charges of up to $330,000) and the apartments come decorated in one of four intentionally vague themed styles: 'Traditional Comfort', 'Classic Contemporary', 'Continental' and 'Maritime'. Each was devised by one of Residensea's four 'international signature designers': Nina Campbell, Juan Pablo Molyneux, Luciano Di Pilla and Yran and Storbraaten. Residensea's commentary about their designs reveals much about the aspirations of *The World's* expected upwardly mobile clientele. For example, Juan Pablo Molyneux, based in New York, is said to have 'masterfully combined tasteful antiques with sumptuous fabrics to create a sophisticated Continental home in which to live, entertain and work, and best of all, travel the world. The design includes stone floors and upholstered walls, Baltic, Russian and French-style furniture, mixed with Chinese lacquer. An array of textiles and custom designed carpets will complete the residents' homes at sea. "The residences are a reflection of the owners' lifestyles and achievements including things they love: art, antiques and mementos that reflect their past," says Molyneux.' Such apparently random selections of imagery and influences, culled from the global leisure lexicon, are, as we have seen, in fact typical of many recent cruise ships.

However, *The World* differs significantly from other vessels in her general arrangement. Because she is essentially a floating apartment complex, her public rooms are considered less important than her residential accommodations, and so are unusually located on her lowest passenger deck, where a central 'pedestrian street', running the entire length of the ship, links a variety of small restaurants, shops and cafes. Because each apartment has its own kitchen there is no main restaurant, but there is a delicatessen where fresh produce and wine can be purchased. There is also an interdenominational place of worship, a 3,000-volume library and an art gallery. When *The World* entered service, Residensea claimed to have sold over 80% of her apartments, although in a difficult global economic and security climate, the firm

The unique and innovative residential cruise ship *The World* **is seen making her inaugural call at San Francisco in the early summer of 2003.** *Andy Kilk*

has since struggled to sell all of the remainder. Indeed, a press report stated in early 2003 that the original shareholders in the company had lost their entire investment. The project is also known to have plunged the Fosen shipyard into financial difficulties.

Back in Norway, meanwhile, the principal ferry operator, Color Line, has recently ordered a new vessel from Kvaerner Masa for its lengthy Oslo-Kiel route. This will be the largest cruise ferry that the world has yet seen and its owners claim that it will offer all of the facilities found onboard similarly sized cruise ships. Certainly, in external appearance at least, it will closely resemble recent new buildings for Royal Caribbean. New developments such as these suggest that the future for Passenger Liners Scandinavian Style looks bright.

Fleet List

Tonnages and dimensions are as given in Lloyd's Register of Shipping when each vessel first took the name under which it is listed.

DFDS:

OSCAR II, HELLIG OLAV and **UNITED STATES**
Completed: 1902-3.
Built by: Alexander Stephen & Son, Linthouse, Glasgow, Scotland.
Tonnage: 10,012 gross tons.
Length overall: 156.97m.
Breadth: 17.67m.
Machinery: Two 3-cylinder triple-expansion reciprocating steam engines. 8,500 IHP. Twin screw.
Service speed: 15½ knots.

C. F. TIETGEN (I) (ex **ROTTERDAM**)
Completed: 1906.
Built by: Harland & Wolf, Belfast, Northern Ireland.
Tonnage: 8,173 gross tons.
Length overall: 148.13m.
Breadth: 16.18m.
Machinery: Two 3-cylinder triple-expansion reciprocating steam engines. 5,250 IHP. Twin screw.
Service speed: 14 knots.

FREDERIK VIII
Completed: 1913.
Built by: A.G. Vulcan, Stettin, Germany.
Tonnage: 11,850 gross tons.
Length overall: 165.07m.
Breadth: 18.89m.
Machinery: Two 4-cylinder quadruple-expansion reciprocating steam engines. 11,000 IHP. Twin Screw.
Service speed: 17 knots.

PARKESTON, ENGLAND (I), **JYLLAND** and **ESBJERG**
Completed: 1925-32
Built by: Helsingør Skibsvaerft, Elsinore, Denmark.
Tonnage: 2,762 gross tons.
Length overall: 98.75m.
Breadth: 13.41m.
Machinery: Two 6-cylinder Burmeister & Wain 6150MX diesel engines. 3,254 BHP. Twin Screw
Service speed: 15½ knots.

C. F. TIETGEN (II)
Completed: 1928.
Built by: Helsingør Skibsvaerft, Elsinore, Denmark.
Tonnage: 1,850 gross tons.
Length overall: 86.74m.
Breadth: 12.22m.
Machinery: One 8-cylinder Burmeister & Wain 855-MTF-100 diesel engine. 1,950 BHP. Single Screw
Service speed: 14¼ knots.

DRONNING ALEXANDRINE
Completed: 1927.
Built by: Helsingør Skibsvaerft, Elsinore, Denmark.
Tonnage: 1,854 gross tons.
Length overall: 80.46m.
Breadth: 11.61m.
Machinery: One 6-cylinder Burmeister & Wain 6150-SS diesel engine. 1,470 BHP. Single Screw
Service speed: 13 knots.

KRONPRINS OLAV
Completed: 1937.
Built by: Helsingør Skibsvaerft, Elsinore, Denmark.
Tonnage: 3,038 gross tons.
Length overall: 99.76m.
Breadth: 13.89m.
Machinery: Two 7-cylinder Burmeister & Wain 750-VF-90 diesel engines. 4,800 BHP. Twin screw.
Service speed: 18½ knots.

KRONPRINS FREDERIK and **KRONPRINSESSE INGRID**
Completed: 1941 and 1949.
Built by: Helsingør Skibsvaerft, Elsinore, Denmark.
Tonnage: 3,895 gross tons.
Length overall: 114.48m.
Breadth: 15.20m.
Machinery: Two 10-cylinder Burmeister & Wain 1050-VF-90 diesel engines. 7,100 BHP. Twin screw.
Service speed: 20¼ knots.

PRINSESSE MARGRETHE (I)
Completed: 1957.
Built by: Helsingør Skibsvaerft, Elsinore, Denmark.
Tonnage: 5,061 gross tons.
Length overall: 121.03m.
Breadth: 16.18m.
Machinery: Two 8-cylinder Burmeister & Wain diesel engines. 7,300 BHP. Twin screw.
Service speed: 20½ knots.

KONG OLAV V (I)
Completed: 1961.
Built by: Aalborg Vaerft, Aalborg, Denmark.
Tonnage: 4,555 gross tons.
Length overall: 121.01m.
Breadth: 16.18m.
Machinery: Two 8-cylinder Burmeister & Wain diesel engines. 7,500 BHP. Twin screw.
Service speed: 20½ knots

ENGLAND (II)
Completed: 1964.
Built by: Helsingør Skibsvaerft, Elsinore, Denmark.
Tonnage: 8,221 gross tons.
Length overall: 140.0m.
Breadth: 19.33m.
Machinery: Two 10-cylinder Burmeister & Wain 1050-VT2BF-110 diesel engines. 14,000 BHP. Twin screw.
Service speed: 22 knots.

WINSTON CHURCHILL
Completed: 1967.
Built by: Cantieri Navali del Tirreno e Riuniti, Riva Trigoso, Italy.
Tonnage: 8,657 gross tons.
Length overall: 140.65m.
Breadth: 20.53m.
Machinery: Two 10-cylinder Burmeister & Wain 1050-VT2BF-110 diesel engines. 14,000 BHP. Twin screw.
Service speed: 22 knots.

KONG OLAV V (II) and **PRINSESSE MARGRETHE** (II)
Completed: 1968-9.
Built by: Cantieri Navali del Tirreno e Riuniti, Riva Trigoso, Italy.
Tonnage: 7,965 gross tons; after rebuilding in 1975 8,669 gross tons.
Length overall: 124.95m.
Breadth: 20.53m.
Machinery: Two 12-cylinder Burmeister & Wain 1242-VT2BF-90 diesel engines. 12,000 BHP. Twin screw.
Service speed: 21 knots.

AALBORGHUS (later **DANA SIRENA**, later **DANA CORONA**) and **TREKRONER** (later **DANA CORONA**, later **DANA SIRENA**)
Completed: 1969-70.
Built by: Cantieri Navali del Tirreno e Riuniti, Riva Trigoso, Italy.
Tonnage: 7,697 gross tons; after rebuilding 7,988 gross tons.
Length overall: 124.85m.
Breadth: 19.31m.
Machinery: Two 12-cylinder Burmeister & Wain 1242-VT2BF-90 diesel engines. 12,000 BHP. Twin screw.
Service speed: 21 knots.

DANA REGINA
Completed: 1974.
Built by: Aalborg Vaerft, Aalborg, Denmark.
Tonnage: 12,192 gross tons.
Length overall: 153.70m.
Breadth: 22.70m.
Machinery: Four 8-cylinder Burmeister & Wain diesel engines. 17,600 BHP. Twin screw.
Service speed: 21½ knots.

DANA ANGLIA
Completed: 1978.
Built by: Aalborg Vaerft, Aalborg, Denmark.
Tonnage: 14,399 gross tons.
Length overall: 152.9m.
Breadth: 23.7m.
Machinery: Two Lindholmen-Pielstick diesel engines. 15,455 BHP. Twin screw.
Service speed: 21 knots.

TOR BRITANNIA and **TOR SCANDINAVIA**
Completed: 1975-6, acquired 1981.
Built by: Flender Werke, Lübeck, West Germany.
Tonnage: 15,650 gross tons.
Length overall: 182.26m.

Breadth: 23.62m.
Machinery: Four Pielstick PC3 diesel engines. 45,600 BHP. Twin screw.
Service speed: 27¼ knots.

THE EAST ASIATIC COMPANY:

ST. DOMINGO (I) (later *CURONIA*) (ex-*DOUNE CASTLE*)
Completed: 1890, acquired 1904.
Built by: Barclay, Curle, Glasgow, Scotland.
Tonnage: 4,034 gross tons.
Length overall: 120.7 m.
Breadth: 13.16 m.
Machinery: 3-cylinder triple-expansion steam reciprocating engine by the builder. 479 NHP. Single screw
Service speed: 15 knots.

ST. DOMINGO (II) (ex-*RAGLAN CASTLE*)
Completed: 1897, acquired 1905.
Built by: Barclay, Curle, Glasgow, Scotland.
Tonnage: 4,239 gross tons.
Length overall: 116.89 m.
Breadth: 14.11m.
Machinery: 3-cylinder triple-expansion steam reciprocating engine by the builder. 419 NHP. Single screw
Service speed: 15 knots.

JULIETTE (ex-*DUNOLLY CASTLE*)
Completed: 1897, acquired 1905.
Built by: Barclay, Curle, Glasgow, Scotland.
Tonnage: 4,603 gross tons.
Length overall: 112.24m.
Breadth: 14.12m.
Machinery: 3-cylinder triple-expansion steam reciprocating engine by the builder. 568 NHP. Single screw.
Service speed: 16 knots.

BIRMA (ex-*ARUNDEL CASTLE*)
Completed: 1894, acquired 1905.
Built by: Fairfield, Govan, Glasgow.
Tonnage: 4,595 gross tons.
Length overall: 126.7m.
Breadth: 17.58m.
Machinery: 3-cylinder triple-expansion steam reciprocating engine by the builder. 568 NHP. Single screw.
Service speed: 16 knots

RUSSIA (later *RUSS*, later *LATVIA*)
Competed: 1908.
Built by: Barclay, Curle, Glasgow, Scotland.
Tonnage: 8,596 gross tons.
Length overall: 144.78m.
Breadth: 17.58m.
Machinery: Two 3-cylinder triple-expansion steam reciprocating engines by the builder. 1194 NHP. Twin screw.
Service speed: 15 knots.

KURSK
Completed: 1910.
Built by: Barclay, Curle, Glasgow, Scotland.
Tonnage: 7,869 gross tons.
Length overall: 137.16m.
Breadth: 17.13m.
Machinery: Two 3-cylinder triple-expansion steam reciprocating engines by the builder. 1020 NHP. Twin screw.
Service speed: 15 knots.

SELANDIA
Completed: 1912.
Built by: Burmeister & Wain, Copenhagen, Denmark.
Tonnage: 4,964 gross tons.
Length overall: 112.89m.
Breadth: 16.22m.
Machinery: Two 8-cylinder Burmeister & Wain diesel engines. 468 NHP. Twin screw.
Service speed: 12 knots.

JUTLANDIA (I)
Completed: 1912.
Built by: Barclay, Curle, Glasgow, Scotland.
Tonnage: 4,874 gross tons.
Length overall: 112.89m.
Breadth: 16.22m.
Machinery: Two 8-cylinder Burmeister & Wain diesel engines. 468 NHP. Twin screw.
Service speed: 12 knots.

CZAR (later *ESTONIA*)
Completed: 1912.
Built by: Barclay, Curle, Glasgow, Scotland.
Tonnage: 6,503 gross tons.
Length overall: 129.54m.
Breadth: 16.22m.
Machinery: 3-cylinder triple-expansion steam reciprocating engine by the builder. 889 NHP. Single screw.
Service speed: 15 knots.

CZARITZA (later *LITUANIA*)
Completed: 1915.
Built by: Barclay, Curle, Glasgow, Scotland.
Tonnage: 6,598 gross tons.
Length overall: 134.1m.
Breadth: 16.27m.
Machinery: 3-cylinder triple-expansion steam reciprocating engine by the builder. 889 NHP. Single screw.
Service speed: 15 knots.

AMERIKA
Completed: 1930.
Built by: Burmeister & Wain, Copenhagen, Denmark.
Tonnage: 10,110 gross tons.
Length overall: 141.85m.
Breadth: 18.95m.
Machinery: Two 6-cylinder Burmeister & Wain diesel engines. 1,236 NHP. Single screw.
Service speed: 16 knots.

EUROPA
Completed: 1931.
Built by: Burmeister & Wain, Copenhagen, Denmark.
Tonnage: 10,224 gross tons.
Length overall: 141.85m.
Breadth: 18.95m.
Machinery: Two 6-cylinder Burmeister & Wain diesel engines. 1,236 NHP. Single screw.
Service speed: 16 knots.

ERRIA
Completed: 1932.
Built by: Nakskov Skibsvaerft, Nakskov, Denmark.
Tonnage: 8,636 gross tons.
Length overall: 134.2 m.
Breadth: 18.95 m.
Machinery: Two 6-cylinder Burmeister & Wain diesel engines. 1,283 NHP. Twin screw.
Service speed: 16 knots.

JUTLANDIA (II)
Completed: 1934.
Built by: Nakskov Skibsvaerft, Nakskov, Denmark.
Tonnage: 8,457 gross tons.
Length overall: 133.13m.
Breadth: 18.65m.
Machinery: Two 5-cylinder Burmeister & Wain diesel engines. 1,073 NHP. Twin screw.
Service speed: 15 knots.

CANADA
Completed: 1935.
Built by: Burmeister & Wain, Copenhagen, Denmark.
Tonnage: 11,108 gross tons.
Length overall: 142.89m.
Breadth: 19.59m.
Machinery: Two 6-cylinder Burmeister & Wain diesels. 1,236 NHP. Single screw.
Service speed: 16 knots.

FALSTRIA
Completed: 1945
Built by: Nakskov Skibsvaerft, Nakskov, Denmark.
Tonnage: 6,993 gross tons.
Length overall: 138.07m.
Breadth: 19.26m.
Machinery: Two 6-cylinder Burmeister & Wain diesel engines. Twin screw.
Service speed: 15 knots.

NORWEGIAN AMERICA LINE

KRISTIANIAFJORD and **BERGENSFJORD** (I)
Completed: 1913.
Built by: Cammell Laird, Birkenhead, England.
Tonnage: 10,669 gross tons.
Length overall: 155.44 m.
Breadth: 18.59m.
Machinery: Two 4-cylinder quadruple-expansion reciprocating steam engines. 1,469 NHP. Twin screw. (*Bergensfjord* fitted with low-pressure turbine, 1931.)
Service speed: 15 knots. (*Bergensfjord* 17½ knots after modification.)

STAVANGERFJORD
Completed: 1918.
Built by: Cammell Laird, Birkenhead, England.
Tonnage: 12,977 gross tons.

Length overall: 162.30 m.
Breadth: 19.56m.
Machinery: Two 4-cylinder quadruple-expansion reciprocating steam engines. 1,567 NHP. Twin screw. 1932: Fitted with two Bauer Wach low pressure turbines by A.G. 'Weser', Bremen.
Service speed: 17 knots.

OSLOFJORD (I)
Completed: 1938.
Built by: Deschimag Werft, Bremen, Germany.
Tonnage: 18,673 gross tons.
Length overall: 179.22m.
Breadth: 22.25m.
Machinery: Four MAN 7-cylinder diesel engines. 17,600 BHP. Twin screw.
Service speed: 18³/₄ knots.

OSLOFJORD (II)
Completed: 1949.
Built by: Nederlandsche Dok en Scheepsbouw, Amsterdam, The Netherlands.
Tonnage: 16,800 gross tons.
Length overall: 175.86m.
Breadth: 22.03m.
Machinery: Two 7-cylinder Stork diesel engines. 16,350 BHP. Twin screw.
Service speed: 19¹/₂ knots.

BERGENSFJORD (II)
Completed: 1956.
Built by: Swan, Hunter & Wigham Richardson, Wallsend-on-Tyne, England.
Tonnage: 18,739 gross tons.
Length overall: 176.26m.
Breadth: 21.94m.
Machinery: Two 8-cylinder Stork diesel engines. 18,600 BHP. Twin screw.
Service speed: 20 knots.

SAGAFJORD
Completed: 1965.
Built by: Forges et Chantiers de la Méditerranée, La Seyne, France.
Tonnage: 24,002 gross tons.
Length overall: 188.88m.
Breadth: 24.46m.
Machinery: Two 9-cylinder Sulzer RD66 diesel engines. 17,650 KW. Twin screw.
Service speed: 22 knots.

VISTAFJORD
Completed: 1973.
Built by: Swan, Hunter & Wigham Richardson, Wallsend-on-Tyne, England.
Tonnage: 24,291 gross tons.
Length overall: 191.09m.
Breadth: 24.38m.
Machinery: Two 9-cylinder Clark-Sulzer RD68 diesel engines. 17,650 KW. Twin screw.
Service speed: 22¹/₂ knots.

DET BERGENSKE DAMPSKIBS SELSKAB (BERGEN LINE)

LEDA (I)
Completed: 1920.
Built by: Armstrong, Whitworth, Newcastle-on-Tyne, England.
Tonnage: 2,415 gross tons.
Length overall: 93.15m.
Breadth: 12.71m.
Machinery: Two Brown-Curtis steam turbines. 3,300 BHP. Single screw.
Service speed: 17 knots.

METEOR (I)
Completed: 1904. Acquired 1921.
Built by: Blohm & Voss, Hamburg, Germany.
Tonnage: 3,717 gross tons.
Length overall: 105.52m.
Breadth: 13.47m.
Machinery: Two 3-cylinder triple-expansion reciprocating steam engines. 235 NHP. Twin screw.
Service speed: 14 knots.

JUPITER (II)
Completed: 1916.
Built by: Lindholmens Varv, Gothenburg, Sweden.
Tonnage: 2,471 gross tons.
Length overall: 93.15m.
Breadth: 12.71m.
Machinery: One 3-cylinder triple-expansion reciprocating steam engine. 3,000 IHP. Single screw.
Service speed: 15 knots.

STELLA POLARIS
Completed: 1927.
Built by: Götaverken, Gothenburg, Sweden.
Tonnage: 5,020 gross tons.
Length overall: 136.85m.
Breadth: 15.42m.
Machinery: Two 8-cylinder Götaverken-B&W diesel engines. 5,250 BHP. Twin screw.
Service speed: 15 knots.

VENUS (II)
Completed: 1931.
Built by: Helsingør Skibsvaerft, Elsinore, Denmark.
Tonnage: 5,406 gross tons (6,269 gross tons after 1947 rebuilding).
Length overall: 128.62m.
Breadth: 16.45m.
Machinery: Two 10-cylinder Burmeister & Wain diesel engines. 12,592 IHP. Twin screw.
Service speed: 19 knots.

VEGA (II)
Completed: 1938.
Built by: Cantieri Riuniti dell 'Adriatico, Trieste, Italy.
Tonnage: 7,287 gross tons.
Length overall: 129.41m.
Breadth: 17.76m.
Machinery: Two 10-cylinder CRDA-Sulzer diesel engines. 12,400 BHP. Twin screw.
Service speed: 19 knots.

METEOR (II)
Completed: 1955.
Built by: Aalborg Vaerft, Aalborg, Denmark.
Tonnage: 2,856 gross tons.
Length overall: 90.52m.
Breadth: 13.71m.
Machinery: One 8-cylinder Burmeister & Wain 850-VF-90 diesel engine. 2,950 BHP. Single screw.
Service speed: 17 knots.

LEDA (II)
Completed: 1953.
Built by: Swan, Hunter & Wigham Ricjardson, Wallsend-on-Tyne, England.
Tonnage: 6,670 gross tons.
Length overall: 133.13m.
Breadth: 17.43m.
Machinery: Two sets Parsons steam turbines. 13,000 SHP. Twin screw.
Service speed: 22 knots.

JUPITER (III) and *VENUS* (III) see *BLACK WATCH* and *BLACK PRINCE*

FRED. OLSEN

BESSHEIM
Completed: 1912.
Built by: Nylands Mekaniske Verksted, Oslo, Norway.
Tonnage: 1,774 gross tons.
Length overall: 78.02 m.
Breadth: 11.0m.
Machinery: 3-cylinder triple-expansion reciprocating steam engine. 225 NHP. Single screw.
Service speed: 14 knots.

BLENHEIM (I)
Completed: 1923.
Built by: Nylands Mekaniske Verksted, Oslo, Norway.
Tonnage: 1,807 gross tons.
Length overall: 77.84m.
Breadth: 11.03m.
Machinery: 3-cylinder triple-expansion reciprocating steam engine. 225 NHP. Single screw.
Service speed: 12 knots.

BRABANT
Completed: 1926.
Built by: Akers Mekaniske Verksted, Oslo, Norway.
Tonnage: 2,335 gross tons.
Length overall: 82.29m.
Breadth: 12.55m.
Machinery: One 12-cylinder Burmeister & Wain diesel. 446 NHP. Twin screw.
Service speed: 13 knots.

BRETAGNE
Completed: 1937.
Built by: Akers Mekaniske Verksted, Oslo, Norway.
Tonnage: 3,245 gross tons.
Length overall: 95.74m.
Breadth: 11.0m.
Machinery: One 9-cylinder Burmeister & Wain diesel engine. 608 NHP. Single screw.
Service speed: 16 knots.

BLACK PRINCE (I) and BLACK WATCH (I)
Completed: 1938.
Built by: Akers Mekaniske Verksted, Oslo, Norway.
Tonnage: 5,035 gross tons.

Length overall: 118 m.
Breadth: 16.7m.
Machinery: Two 9-cylinder Burmeister & Wain diesel engines. 1,215 NHP. Twin screw.
Service speed: 18 knots.

BLENHEIM (II) and BRAEMAR (I)
Completed: 1951 and 1953.
Built by: John I. Thornycroft, Southampton, England and completed by Akers Mekaniske Verksted, Oslo, Norway.
Tonnage: 4,766 gross tons.
Length overall: 114 m.
Breadth: 15.9 m.
Machinery: One 8-cylinder Burmeister & Wain diesel engine. 4,600 KW. Single screw.
Service speed: 16 knots.

BLACK WATCH (II)/JUPITER (III) and BLACK PRINCE (II)/VENUS (III)
Completed: 1966.
Built by: Flender Werke, Lübeck, West Germany.
Tonnage: 9,499 gross tons. *Black Prince* 11,209 gross tons after conversion, 1987.
Length overall: 141.6m.
Breadth: 20.25m.
Machinery: Two 18-cylinder Pielstick diesel engines. 16,740 BHP. Twin screw.
Speed: 23 knots.

KØBENHAVN
Completed: 1966
Built by: Orenstein-Koppel und Lübecker Maschinenbau AG, Lübeck, West Germany
Tonnage: 3,611 gross tons.
Length overall: 93.92m.
Breadth: 16.44m
Machinery: Two 8-cylinder Lindholmen-Pielstick diesel engines. 6,500 BHP. Twin screw.
Service speed: 18 knots.

BLENHEIM (III)
Completed: 1970.
Built by: Upper Clyde Shipbuilders, Clydebank, Scotland.
Tonnage: 10,736 gross tons.
Length overall: 149.38m.
Breadth: 20.60m.
Machinery: Two 18-cylinder Crossley-Pielstick diesel engines. 13,240 KW. Twin screw.
Service speed: 23 knots.

BOLERO
Completed: 1973
Built by: Dubigeon-Normandie S.A. Prairie au Doc, Nantes, France.
Tonnage: 11,344 gross tons.
Length overall: 141.46m.
Breadth: 19.9m.
Machinery: Two Semt-Pielstick 12 PC 3V diesel engines. 24,400 BHP. Twin screw.
Speed: 22 knots.

BLACK WATCH (III) see ROYAL VIKING STAR

BRAEMAR (III) see CROWN DYNASTY

JAHRE LINE

KRONPRINS HARALD (I)
Completed: 1961.
Built by: Howaldtswerke Deutsche Werft A.G. Kiel, Germany.
Tonnage: 7,034 gross tons.
Length overall: 122.54m.
Breadth: 18.04m.
Machinery: Two 9-cylinder MAN diesels. 8,458 KW. Twin screw.
Speed: 19.5 knots.

PRINSESSE RAGNHILD (I)
Completed: 1966
Built by: Howaldtswerke Deutsche Werft A.G. Kiel, Germany.
Tonnage: 7,694 gross tons.
Length overall: 124.92m.
Breadth: 20.2m.
Machinery: Two 9-cylinder MAN diesels. 13,500 BHP. Twin screw.
Speed: 21.5 knots.

KRONPRINS HARALD (II)
Completed: 1976.
Built by: Werft Nobiskrug, Rendsburg, Germany.
Tonnage: 12,752 gross tons.
Length overall: 156.42m.
Breadth: 23.98m.
Machinery: Two 20-cylinder Stork-Werkspoor 20TM410 diesels. 24,000 BHP. Twin screw.
Speed: 22.5 knots.

PRINSESSE RAGNHILD (II)
Completed: 1981. Rebuilt 1991.
Built by: Howaldtswerke Deutsche Werft A.G. Kiel, Germany. Rebuilt by Astilleros Españoles, Cadiz, Spain.
Tonnage: 16,631gross tons. (after rebuilding 38,500 gross tons).
Length overall: 170m (after rebuilding 205.3m).
Breadth: 24m (after rebuilding 26.6m).
Machinery: Two 20-cylinder Stork-Werkspoor 20 TM 410 diesels. 23,672 BHP. Twin screw.
Speed: 21 knots.

KRONPRINS HARALD (III)
Completed: 1987
Built by: Wärtsilä A/B, Turku, Finland
Tonnage: 31,122 gross tons.
Length overall: 166.3m.
Breadth: 28.41m.
Machinery: Two 12-cylinder Sulzer-Wärtsilä 12 ZAV 40 diesels plus two 6-cylinder Sulzer-Wärtsilä 6 ZAL 40 diesels. 19,800 KW. Twin screw.
Speed: 22 knots.

I.M. SKAUGEN

SKAUGUM
Built : 1940 (rebuilt 1948).
Built by: Germaniawerft, Kiel, Germany
Tonnage: 11,626 gross tons.
Length overall: 168.1m.
Breadth: 20.3m.
Machinery: 4 4SA 9-cylinder Krupp diesels connected to electric motors. Twin screw.
Speed: 15 knots.

SKAUBRYN
Completed: 1951
Built by: Oresundsvarvet, Landskrona, Sweden
Tonnage: 9,786 gross tons.
Length overall: 139.75m.
Breadth: 17.37m.
Machinery: One 2SA 9-cylinder Götaverken diesel. Twin screw.
Speed: 16 knots.

SWEDISH AMERICAN LINE

STOCKHOLM (I) (ex-POTSDAM)
Completed: 1900, acquired 1915.
Built by: Blohm & Voss, Hamburg, Germany.
Tonnage: 12,975 gross tons.
Length overall: 167.66m.
Breadth: 18.89m.
Machinery: Two 3-cylinder triple-expansion reciprocating steam engines. 7,600 IHP. Twin screw.
Service speed: 15 knots.

DROTTNINGHOLM (ex-VIRGINIAN)
Completed: 1905.
Built by: Alexander Stephen, Linthouse, Glasgow, Scotland.
Tonnage: 10,757 gross tons.
Length overall: 158.61m.
Breadth: 18.28m.
Machinery: Three sets Parsons steam turbines. 15,000 BHP. Triple screw. After rebuilding in 1922-23 Three De-Laval steam turbines. 10,500 IHP.
Service speed: 17 knots.

KUNGSHOLM (I) (ex-NOORDAM)
Completed: 1902.
Built by: Harland & Wolff, Belfast, Northern Ireland.
Tonnage: 12,500 gross tons.
Length overall: 167.73m.
Breadth: 18.98m.
Machinery: Two 3-cylinder triple-expansion reciprocating steam engines. 1,265 NHP. Twin screw.
Service speed: 14 knots.

GRIPSHOLM (I)
Completed: 1925.
Built by: Armstrong, Whitworth, Newcastle-upon-Tyne, England.
Tonnage: 17,944 gross tons.
Length overall: 168.55m.
Breadth: 22.5m.
Machinery: Two 12-cylinder Burmeister & Wain diesel engines. 13,500 BHP. Twin screw.
Service speed: 16 knots.

KUNGSHOLM (II)
Completed: 1928.
Built by: Blohm & Voss, Hamburg, Germany.
Tonnage: 21,250 gross tons.
Length overall: 181.32m.

Breadth: 23.77m.
Machinery: Two 16-cylinder Burmeister & Wain diesel engines. 17,000 BHP. Twin screw.
Service speed: 17 knots.

STOCKHOLM (II/III)
Completed: 1941.
Built by: Cantieri Riuniti dell' Adriatico, Monfalcone, Italy.
Tonnage: 29,307 gross tons.
Length overall: 205.60m.
Breadth: 26.10m.
Machinery: Three 10-cylinder CRDA-Sulzer diesel engines. 20,000 BHP. Triple screw.
Speed: 19 knots.

STOCKHOLM (IV)
Completed: 1948.
Built by: Götaverken, Gothenburg, Sweden.
Tonnage: 11,893 gross tons. After 1953-4 rebuilding 12,644 gross tons.
Length overall: 160.02m.
Breadth: 21.03m.
Machinery: Two 8-cylinder Götaverken diesel engines. 12,000 BHP. Twin screw.
Speed: 19 knots.

KUNGSHOLM (III)
Completed: 1953.
Built by: De Schelde, Flushing, The Netherlands.
Tonnage: 21,165 gross tons.
Length overall: 182.87m.
Breadth: 23.47m.
Machinery: Two 8-cylinder Burmeister & Wain diesel engines. 18,100 BHP. Twin screw.
Service speed: 19 knots.

GRIPSHOLM (II)
Completed: 1957.
Built by: Ansaldo, Genoa, Italy.
Tonnage: 23,190 gross tons.
Length overall: 192.32m.
Breadth: 24.90m.
Machinery: Two 9-cylinder Götaverken diesel engines. 25,200 BHP. Twin screw.
Service speed: 19 knots.

KUNGSHOLM (IV)
Completed: 1966.
Built by: John Brown, Clydebank, Scotland.
Tonnage: 26,677 gross tons.
Length overall: 201.17m.
Breadth: 26.52m.
Machinery: Two 9-cylinder Götaverken VG-9U diesel engines. 25,200 BHP. Twin screw.
Service speed: 21 knots.

SWEDISH LLOYD

THULE
Completed: 1892.
Built by: Wigham Richardson, Wallsend-on-Tyne, England.
Tonnage: 1,914 gross tons.
Length overall: 86.78m.
Breadth: 11.35m.
Machinery: One 3-cylinder triple-expansion reciprocating steam engine. 1,600 IHP. Single screw.
Speed: 12 knots.

BALDER/NORTHUMBRIA
Completed: 1898.
Built by: Blackwood & Gordon, Port Glasgow, Scotland.
Tonnage: 1,486 gross tons.
Length overall: 74.22m.
Breadth: 10.39m.
Machinery: One 3-cylinder triple-expansion reciprocating steam engine. 212 NHP. Single screw.
Speed: 12 knots.

SAGA (I)
Completed: 1909.
Built by: Swan, Hunter & Wigham Richardson, Wallsend-on-Tyne, England.
Tonnage: 2,943 gross tons.
Length overall: 97.8m.
Breadth: 14.03m.
Machinery: 3-cylinder triple-expansion reciprocating steam engine. 2,500 IHP. Single-screw.
Service speed: 14 knots.

PATRICIA (I) (ex-WESTERN AUSTRALIA, ex-MONGOLIA,)
Completed: 1901, acquired 1919.
Built by: Stabilimento Tecnico, Trieste, Italy.
Tonnage: 3,285 gross tons.
Length overall: 105.09m.

Breadth: 13.02m.
Machinery: Two 3-cylinder triple-expansion reciprocating steam engines. 712 NHP. Twin screw.
Service Speed: 16 knots.

PATRICIA (II) (ex-PATRIS II)
Completed: 1926, acquired 1935.
Built by: Swan, Hunter & Wigham Richardson, Wallsend-on-Tyne, England.
Tonnage: 3,902 gross tons.
Length overall: 105.17m.
Breadth: 14.48m.
Machinery: 3-cylinder triple-expansion reciprocating steam engine. 527 NHP. Single screw.
Speed: 13 knots.

BRITANNIA and SUECIA
Completed: 1929.
Built by: Swan, Hunter & Wigham Richardson, Wallsend-on-Tyne, England.
Tonnage: 4,661 gross tons.
Length overall: 113.85m.
Breadth: 15.27m.
Machinery: Three Parsons single-reduction geared turbines. 1,043 BHP. Single screw.
Service speed: 21 knots.

SAGA (II)
Built: 1940-46.
Built by: Lindholmens Varv, Gothenburg, Sweden.
Tonnage: 6,458 gross tons.
Length overall: 126.17m.
Breadth: 16.84m.
Machinery: Four 8-cylinder Götaverken diesel engines. 8,000 BHP. Single screw.
Service speed: 18 knots.

PATRICIA (III)
Completed: 1951.
Built by: Swan, Hunter & Wigham Richardson, Wallsend-on-Tyne, England.
Tonnage: 7,764 gross tons.
Length overall: 138.39m.
Breadth: 17.74m.
Machinery: Six Parsons steam turbines. 5,406 KW. Single screw.
Service speed: 19 knots.

SAGA (III) , HISPANIA/SAGA (IV) (ex-SVEA) and PATRICIA (IV)
Completed: 1966-67.
Built by: Lindholmens Varv, Gothenburg, Sweden.
Tonnage: 8,869 gross tons.
Length overall: 141.20m.
Breadth: 20.96m.
Machinery: Four 6-cylinder Lindholmens-Pielstick diesel engines. 10,082 BHP. Twin screw.
Service speed: 20 knots.

SIGLINE

VIKING PRINCESS (ex-RIVIERA PRIMA, ex-LAVOISIER)
Completed: 1950. Acquired 1964.
Built by: Ateliers & Chantiers de la Loire, St. Nazaire, France. Rebuilt by T. Marriotti, Genoa, 1962.
Tonnage: 12,812 gross tons.
Length overall: 163.4m.
Breadth: 19.5m.
Machinery: Two 8-cylinder Sulzer diesel engines. 12,000 BHP. Twin screw.
Service speed: 16 knots.

NORWEGIAN CARIBBEAN LINE/NORWEGIAN CRUISE LINE

SUNWARD
Completed: 1966.
Built by: Bergens Mekaniske Verksteder, Bergen, Norway.
Tonnage: 8,666 gross tons.
Length overall: 139.43m.
Breadth: 20.80m.
Machinery: Two Burmeister & Wain 12-cylinder 42VT2BF-90 diesel engines. 13,200 BHP. Twin screw.
Service speed: 20¼ knots.

STARWARD and SKYWARD
Completed: 1968-69.
Built by: Weser Seebeckwerft, Bremerhaven, West Germany.
Tonnage: 12,940 gross tons.
Length overall: 160.13m.
Breadth: 22.80m.
Machinery: Two V16-cylinder MAN VSV40/54 diesel engines. 17,380 BHP. Twin screw.
Service speed: 21½ knots.

SOUTHWARD
Completed: 1971.
Built by: Cantieri Navali del Tirreno e Riuniti, Riva Trigoso, Italy.

Tonnage: 16,607 gross tons.
Length overall: 163.38m.
Breadth: 22.80m.
Machinery: Four 10-cylinder FIAT C.4210SS diesel engines. 18,000 BHP. Twin screw.
Service speed: 21½ knots.

SUNWARD II (ex-*CUNARD ADVENTURER*)
Completed: 1971. Acquired 1977.
Tonnage: 14,151 gross tons.
Length overall: 148.11m.
Breadth: 21.49m.
Machinery: Four 12-cylinder Stork-Werkspoor diesel engines. 19,860 KW. Twin screw.
Service speed: 22½ knots.

NORWAY (ex-*FRANCE*)
Completed: 1961. Acquired 1979.
Built by: Chantiers de l'Atlantique, St. Nazaire, France. Rebuilt as *Norway* by Hapag Lloyd, Bremerhaven, West Germany, 1979-80.
Tonnage: 66,348 gross tons as *France*; 70,202 gross tons when first rebuilt as *Norway*; 76,049 gross tons today.
Length overall: 315.46m.
Breadth: 33.52m.
Machinery: Four sets (originally eight) CEM-Parsons steam turbines. 160,000 shp. Twin screw (originally quadruple).
Service speed: 25 knots.

SEAWARD (later *NORWEGIAN SEA*)
Completed: 1988.
Built by: Wärtsilä, Turku, Finland.
Length overall: 216.40m
Breadth: 28.34m
Machinery: Four 8-cylinder Sulzer diesel engines. 18,476 KW. Twin screw.
Service speed: 20 knots.

DREAMWARD (later *NORWEGIAN DREAM*) and *WINDWARD* (later *NORWEGIAN WIND*)
Completed: 1992-93, rebuilt 1997-98.
Built by: Chantiers de l'Atlantique, St. Nazaire, France; lengthened by Lloyd Werft, Bremerhaven, Germany.
Tonnage: 39,217 gross tons; 50,764 gross tons after lengthening.
Length overall: 190.0m; 229.84m after lengthening.
Breadth: 28.50m.
Machinery: Four 8-cylinder MAN diesel engines. 18,638 KW. Twin screw.
Service speed: 21 knots.

LEEWARD (ex-*SALLY ALBATROSS*)
Completed: 1992 (rebuild of a 1980-built ferry).
Built by: Finnyards, Rauma, Finland (1980: Wärtsilä, Turku)
Tonnage: 25,076 gross tons.
Length overall: 187.71m
Breadth: 28.21m.
Machinery: Four V12-cylinder Wärtsilä-Pielstick diesel engines. 26,000 BHP. Twin screw.
Service speed: 21 knots.

NORWEGIAN MAJESTY (ex-*ROYAL MAJESTY*)
Completed: 1992.
Built by: Finnyards, Rauma, Finland.
Tonnage: 32,396 gross tons (40,876 gross tons after lengthening, 1999).
Length overall: 173.13m (207.26m after lengthening).
Breadth: 27.6m.
Machinery: Four 6-cylinder Wärtsilä diesel engines. 28,697 bhp. Twin screw.
Service speed: 20 knots.

NORWEGIAN SKY
Completed: 1999.
Built by: Bremer Vulkan, Vegesack, Germany, completed by Lloyd Werft, Bremerhaven, Germany.
Tonnage: 77,104 gross tons.
Length overall: 259.99m.
Breadth: 32.25m.
Machinery: Diesel-electric. Six MAN diesel engines (three 7-cylinder and three 6-cylinder) powering two electric motors. 50,700 KW. Twin screw.
Service speed: 21 knots.

NORWEGIAN CROWN (ex-*CROWN ODYSSEY*)
Completed: 1988.
Built by: Jos. L. Meyer, Papenburg, Germany.
Tonnage: 34,250 gross tons.
Length overall: 187.71m.
Breadth: 28.21m.
Machinery: Four Krupp-MaK diesel engines (two 8-cylinder and two 6-cylinder). 21,300 KW. Twin screw.
Service speed: 22 knots.

ROYAL VIKING LINE

ROYAL VIKING STAR, *ROYAL VIKING SKY* and *ROYAL VIKING SEA*
Completed: 1972-73,
Built by Wärtsilä, Helsinki, Finland; lengthened by Lloyd Werft, Bremerhaven 1981-83.
Tonnage: 21,847 gross tons; 28,221 gross tons after lengthening.
Length overall: 177.74m; 205.46m after lengthening.
Breadth: 25.2m.
Machinery: Four 9-cylinder Wärtsilä-Sulzer 92H40/48 diesel engines. 13,240 KW. Twin screw.
Service speed: 21½ knots.

ROYAL VIKING SUN
Completed: 1988.
Built by: Wärtsilä, Turku, Finland.
Tonnage: 37,845 gross tons.
Length overall: 204.21m.
Breadth: 27.0m.
Machinery: Four 8-cylinder Wärtsilä-Sulzer diesel engines. 21,120 KW. Twin screw.
Service speed: 21½ knots.

ROYAL VIKING QUEEN
Completed: 1992.
Built by: Schichau Seebeckwerft, Bremerhaven, Germany.
Tonnage: 9,975 gross tons.
Length overall: 133.80m.
Breadth: 19.00m
Machinery: Four Bergen diesel engines (two V12-cylinder type KVMB and two 8-cylinder type KRMB). 7,240 KW. Twin screw.
Service speed: 21 knots.

SUNDANCE CRUISES

SUNDANCER (ex-*SVEA CORONA*)
Completed: 1975.
Built by: Dubigeon-Normandie, Nantes, France.
Tonnage: 12,348 gross tons.
Length overall: 153.0m.
Breadth: 22.04m.
Machinery: Four Pielstick 12-cylinder diesel engines. 24,000 BHP. Twin screw.
Service speed: 21 knots.

STARDANCER – see *SCANDINAVIA*

COMMODORE CRUISE LINE

BOHEME
Completed: 1968.
Built by: Wärtsilä, Helsinki, Finland.
Tonnage: 9,789 gross tons.
Length overall: 134.32m.
Breadth: 19.91m.
Machinery: Two 8-cylinder Wärtsilä-Sulzer diesel engines. 14,000 BHP. Twin screw.
Service speed: 20 knots.

CARIBE (ex-*FREEPORT*)
Completed: 1968.
Built by: Orenstein-Koppel & Lübecker Maschinenbau, Lübeck, West Germany
Tonnage: 10,448 gross tons.
Length overall: 134.42m
Breadth: 21.5m.
Machinery: Two 16-cylinder Pielstick 16 PC2V diesel engines. 16,000 BHP. Twin screw.
Service speed: 19 knots.

CARIBE 1 (ex-*OLYMPIA*)
Completed: 1953, rebuilt 1982.
Built by: Alexander Stephen, Linthouse, Glasgow, Scotland.
Tonnage: 17,362 gross tons (22,979 gross tons after rebuild).
Length overall: 186.11m.
Breadth: 24.08m.
Machinery: Originally two sets Stephen-Pametrada steam turbines; rebuilt with four 12-cylinder Humboldt-Deutz diesel engines. 20,258 bhp. Twin screw.
Service speed: 18 knots.

ENCHANTED ISLE (ex-*BERMUDA STAR*, ex-*VEENDAM*, ex-*MONARCH STAR*, ex-*VEENDAM*, ex-*BRASIL*, ex-*VEENDAM*, ex-*ARGENTINA*) and *ENCHANTED SEAS*, later *UNIVERSE EXPLORER*, (ex-*QUEEN OF BERMUDA*, ex-*CANADA STAR*, ex-*LIBERTÉ*, ex-*ISLAND SUN*, ex-*VOLENDAM*, ex-*MONARCH SUN*, ex-*VOLENDAM*, ex-*BRASIL*)
Completed: 1958.
Built by: Ingalls, Pascagoula, Mississippi, United States of America.
Tonnage: 14,984 gross tons (23,395 gross tons after 1972 rebuild).
Length overall: 188.22m.
Breadth: 25.61m.
Machinery: Two sets, General Electric steam turbines. 35,000 shp. Twin screw.
Service speed: 23 knots.

CROWN CRUISE LINE

VIKING PRINCESS (ex-ILMATAR)
Completed: 1964.
Built by: Wärtsilä, Helsinki, Finland.
Tonnage: 5,101 gross tons (7,155 gross tons after lengthening, 1973).
Length overall: 108.27m; 128.31m after lengthening.
Breadth: 16.40m.
Machinery: One Wärtsilä-Sulzer 12-cylinder diesel engine, to which were added two 8-cylinder Nohab diesel engines at the time of the lengthening. 8,520 BHP. Single screw.
Service speed: 16$^1/_2$ knots, becoming 19 knots after installation of extra engines.

CROWN DEL MAR (ex-LAS PALMAS DE GRAN CANARIA)
Completed: 1967. Converted to cruise ship, 1986.
Built by: Union Naval de Levante, Valencia, Spain.
Tonnage: 8,983 gross tons; 16,292 gross tons after conversion.
Length overall: 130.65m.
Breadth: 19.2m.
Machinery: Two 7-cylinder MTM-Burmeister & Wain diesel engines. 16,000 BHP. Twin screw.
Service speed: 17 knots.

CROWN MONARCH
Completed: 1990.
Built by: Union Naval de Levante, Valencia, Spain.
Tonnage: 15,271 gross tons.
Length overall: 150.72m.
Breadth: 20.60m.
Machinery: Four 6-cylinder Bergen BRM9 diesel engines. 12,400 KW. Twin screw.
Service speed: 20 knots.

CROWN JEWEL and CROWN DYNASTY
Completed: 1992-93.
Built by: Union Naval de Levante, Valencia, Spain.
Tonnage: 19,089 gross tons.
Length overall: 163.81m.
Breadth: 22.50m.
Machinery: Four 8-cylinder Wärtsilä diesel engines. 17,826 BHP. Twin screw.
Service speed: 19$^1/_4$ knots.

PEARL CRUISES OF SCANDINAVIA

PEARL OF SCANDINAVIA (ex-FINNSTAR, ex-FINLANDIA)
Completed: 1967.
Built by: Wärtsilä, Helsinki, Finland,
Tonnage: 10,311 gross tons; 12,456 gross tons after rebuilding as Pearl of Scandinavia, 1982.
Length overall: 156.7m.
Breadth: 20.0m.
Machinery: Four 9-cylinder Wärtsilä-Sulzer 9ZH40/48 diesel engines. 16,400 BHP. Twin screw.
Service speed: 22 knots.

SCANDINAVIAN WORLD CRUISES

SCANDINAVIA
Completed: 1982. Converted to Royal Caribbean's Viking Serenade, 1991.
Built by: Dubigeon-Normandie, Nantes, France.
Tonnage: 26,747 gross tons. (40,132 gross tons after conversion.)
Length overall: 185.3m.
Breadth: 27.0m.
Machinery: Two 9-cylinder Chantiers de l'Atlantique-Burmeister & Wain diesel engines. 27,000 BHP. Twin screw.
Service speed: 20$^1/_2$ knots.

SCANDINAVIAN SEA – see BLENHEIM (II)

SCANDINAVIAN SUN – see CARIBE

K/S NORDLINE/COPENHAGEN CRUISE LINE

COPENHAGEN
Completed: 1974
Built by: Vickers Ltd, Barrow-in-Furness, England. Fitted out by Swan, Hunter, Newcastle, England
Tonnage: 13,758grt
Length overall: 136.30m
Breadth: 21.49m
Machinery: Two 16-cylinder Crossley-Pielstick diesel engines. 16,000 BHP. Twin screw.
Service speed: 21knots.

FLAGSHIP CRUISES

SEA VENTURE and ISLAND VENTURE
Completed: 1971-2.
Built by: Rheinstahl Nordseewerke, Emden, West Germany.
Tonnage: 19,903 gross tons.
Length overall: 168.76m.
Breadth: 24.6m.
Machinery: Four 10-cylinder FIAT C4210 diesel engines. 18,000 BHP. Twin screw.
Service speed: 21$^1/_2$ knots.

EASTERN STEAMSHIP LINES / ADMIRAL CRUISES

EMERALD SEAS (ex-ATLANTIS, ex-PRESIDENT ROOSEVELT, ex-LEILANI, ex-LA GUARDIA, ex-GENERAL W. P. RICHARDSON)
Completed: 1944.
Built by: Federal Shipbuilding & Drydock, Kearny, New Jersey, U.S.A.
Tonnage: 17,951 gross tons, later 20,071 gross tons.
Length overall: 174.66m.
Breadth: 23.04m.
Machinery: Two sets of De Laval geared steam turbines. 18,700 SHP. Twin screw.
Service speed: 19 knots.

AZURE SEAS (ex-CALYPSO, ex-SOUTHERN CROSS)
Completed: 1955.
Built by: Harland & Wolff, Belfast, Northern Ireland.
Tonnage: 20,204 gross tons.
Length overall: 184.09m.
Breadth: 23.77m.
Machinery: Two sets of Harland & Wolff-Parmetrada geared steam turbines. 20,000 SHP. Twin screw.
Service speed: 20 knots.

VARIOUS CRUISING YACHTS AND EXPEDITION SHIPS

DISCOVERER
Completed: 1974.
Built by: Schichau-Unterweser, Bremerhaven, West Germany.
Tonnage: 3,153 gross tons.
Length overall: 87.50m.
Machinery: Two 8-cylinder MaK 8M452AK diesel engines. 4,800 BHP. Single screw.
Service speed: 16$^1/_2$ knots.

LINDBLAD EXPLORER
Completed: 1969.
Built by: Nystads Varv, Nystad, Finland.
Tonnage: 2,481 gross tons.
Length overall: 72.90m.
Machinery: Two 8-cylinder MaK diesel engines. 3,800 BHP. Single screw.
Service speed: 15 knots.

LINDBLAD POLARIS
Completed: 1960 (as a ferry). Converted to expedition cruise ship, 1982.
Built by: Solvesborgs Varv, Solvesborg, Sweden.
Tonnage (after conversion): 2,214 gross tons.
Length overall: 72.10m.
Machinery: Two 6-cylinder Nohab Polar diesel engines. 3,200 BHP. Twin screws.
Service speed: 13$^1/_2$ knots.

NORTH STAR
Completed: 1966 (as a stern trawler). Converted to expedition cruise ship, 1983.
Built by: "Weser" Werk Seebeck, Bremerhaven, West Germany.
Tonnage (after conversion): 3,095 gross tons.
Length overall: 89.20m.
Machinery: Two 8-cylinder MaK 8M582AK diesel engines. 3,200 BHP. Single screw.
Service speed: 15 knots.

RENAISSANCE ONE to RENAISSANCE FOUR
Completed: 1989 – 1990.
Built by: Cantiere Navale Ferrari, La Spezia, Italy.
Tonnage: 3,990 gross tons.
Length overall: 88.30m.
Machinery: Two V12-cylinder Burmeister & Wain – Alpha diesel engines. Twin screws.
Service speed: 16 knots.

RENAISSANCE FIVE to RENAISSANCE EIGHT
Completed: 1991 – 1992.
Built by: Nuovi Cantieri Apuana, Marina di Carrara, Italy.
Tonnage: 4,280 gross tons.
Length overall: 90.60m.
Machinery: Two 8-cylinder Burmeister & Wain – Alpha diesel engines. 4,783 BHP. Twin screws.
Service speed: 16 knots.

SEA GODDESS I and SEA GODDESS II
Completed: 1984 – 1985.
Built by: Wärtsilä, Helsinki, Finland.
Tonnage: 4,253 gross tons.
Length overall: 104.80m.
Machinery: Two V12-cylinder Wärtsilä – Vasa diesel engines. 4,800 BHP. Twin screws.
Service speed: 17$^1/_2$ knots.

SEABOURN PRIDE, *SEABOURN SPIRIT* and *SEABOURN LEGEND* (ex-*ROYAL VIKING QUEEN*)
Completed: 1988 – 1992.
Built by: Schichau Seebeckwerft, Bremerhaven, West Germany.
Tonnage: 9,975 gross tons.
Length overall: 133.80m.
Machinery: Two V12-cylinder Bergen diesel engines and two 8-cylinder Bergen diesel engines. 9,891BHP. Twin screws.
Service speed: 18 knots.

SONG OF FLOWER
Completed: 1974 as ro-ro freighter. Converted into cruise ship, 1986.
Built by: Kristiansands Mekaniske Verksted, Kristiansand, Norway.
Tonnage (after conversion): 8,282 gross tons.
Length overall: 124.22m.
Machinery (after conversion): Two V10-cylinder Wichmann diesel engines. 7,446 BHP. Twin screws.
Service speed: 16 knots.

ROYAL CARIBBEAN CRUISE LINE / ROYAL CARIBBEAN INTERNATIONAL

SONG OF NORWAY, *NORDIC PRINCE* and *SUN VIKING*
Completed: 1970-72. *Song of Norway* and *Nordic Prince* lengthened 1980.
Built by: Wärtsilä, Helsinki, Finland.
Tonnage: 18,416 gross tons; 23,200 gross tons after lengthening.
Length overall: 168.30m. (*Sun Viking* 171.70m.); *Song of Norway* and *Nordic Prince* 194.32m. after lengthening.
Breadth: 24.00m.
Machinery: Four 9-cylinder Wärtsilä-Sulzer 9ZH40/48 diesel engines. 18,000 BHP. Twin screw.
Service speed: 21 knots.

SONG OF AMERICA
Completed: 1982.
Built by: Wärtsilä, Helsinki, Finland.
Tonnage: 37,584 grsoo tons.
Length overall: 214.50m.
Breadth: 28.40m.
Machinery: Four 8-cylinder Wärtsilä-Sulzer 8ZL40/48 diesel engines. 22,391 BHP. Twin screw.
Service speed: 21 knots.

SOVEREIGN OF THE SEAS, *MONARCH OF THE SEAS* and *MAJESTY OF THE SEAS*
Completed: 1987, 1991 and 1992.
Built by: Chantiers de l'Atlantique, St, Nazaire, France.
Tonnage: 73,192 gross tons (*Soveriegn*), 73,937 gross tons (*Monarch* and *Majesty*).
Length overall: 268.30m.
Breadth: 32.20m.
Machinery: Four 9-cylinder Semt-Pielstick PC20L diesel engines. 27,840 BHP. Twin screw.
Srtvice speed: 20 knots.

NORDIC EMPRESS
Completed: 1990.
Built by: Chantiers de l'Atlantique, St. Nazaire, France.
Tonnage: 48,563 gross tons.
Length overall: 210.8m.
Breadth: 30.7m.
Machinery: Two V12-cylinder and two 8-cylinder Wärtsilä-Sulzer diesel engines. 22,011 BHP. Twin screw.
Service speed: 19 knots.

SPLENDOUR OF THE SEAS and *LEGEND OF THE SEAS*
Completed: 1995-96.
Built by: Chantiers de l'Atlantique, St. Nazaire, France.
Tonnage: 69,143 gross tons.
Length overall: 264.26m.
Breadth: 32.00m.
Machinery: Diesel-electric. Five 12-cylinder GEC/Alsthom-Wärtsilä diesel engines. 54,620 BHP. powering electric motors. Twin screw.
Service speed: 24 knots (*Splendour*), 19$^{1}/_{2}$ knots (*Legend*).

GRANDEUR OF THE SEAS, *RHAPSODY OF THE SEAS*, *ENCHANTMENT OF THE SEAS* and *VISION OF THE SEAS*
Completed: 1996-98.
Built by: Kvaerner-Masa, Helsinki, Finland (*Grandeur* and *Enchantment*) and Chantiers de l'Atlantique, St. Nazaire, France (*Rhapsody* and *Vision*).
Tonnage: 73,817 gross tons (*Grandeur* and *Enchantment*) and 78,491 gross tons (*Rhapsody* and *Vision*).
Length overall: 279.1m.
Breadth: 32.2m.
Machinery: Diesel-electric. Four 12-cylinder MAN diesel engines (46,195 bhp) powering electric motors (Grandeur and Enchantment); four 12-cylinder GEC/Alsthom-Wärtsilä diesel engines (46,195 BHP) powering electric motors (Rhapsody and Vision).
Service speed: 22 knots.

VOYAGER OF THE SEAS, *EXPLORER OF THE SEAS*, *ADVENTURER OF THE SEAS*, *NAVIGATOR OF THE SEAS*, *MARINER OF THE SEAS* and sister ship.
Completed: 199, 2000, 2001, 2003 and beyond.
Built by: Kvaerner-Masa, Helsinki, Finland.
Tonnage: 137,000 – 140,000 gross tons.
Length overall: 311m.
Breadth: 38.6 m.
Machinery: Six Wärtsilä diesels. 74544 KW. connected to electric motors in pods.
Service speed: 22 knots.

RADIANCE OF THE SEAS, *BRILLIANCE OF THE SEAS*, *SERENADE OF THE SEAS*, *JEWEL OF THE SEAS*
Completed: 2001-02 and beyond.
Built by: Meyer Werft, Papenburg, Germany.
Tonnage: 90.090 gross tons.
Length overall: 293.2m.
Breadth: 32.2m.
Machinery: Two General Electric Gas Turbines 50,000 KW. One Fincantieri steam turbine, 7800 KW. 2 ABB Pods.
Service speed: 24 knots.

RESIDENSEA

THE WORLD
Completed: 2002
Built by: Bruce's Shipyard, Landskrona, Sweden (hull). Completed by Fosen Mekaniske Verksted, Rissa, Norway
Tonnage: 43,188gross tons.
Length overall: 196.35m
Breadth: 29.8m
Machinery: Two 12-cylinder Wärtsilä diesel engines. 11,880 KW. Twin screw.

Index

Aalborghus 27, 28,168
Adventurer of the Seas 176
Amerika 35,169
Anna Salén 76
Ariane 106
Azure Seas 160,175

Balder 101,172
Bayard 63
Bele 101
Bergen 53
Bergensfjord (1913) 37,38,39,41,170
Bergensfjord (1956) 7,10,44,45,46,49,50,51,170
Bessheim 63,171
Birma 33,169
Black Prince (1938) 7, 63, 64,171
Black Prince (1966) 7,11,58,62,67,68,69,71,72,73,74,120,171
Black Watch (1938) 7, 64,171
Black Watch (1966) 7,11,58,59,62,67,68,69,71,73,171
Black Watch (1972) 74,144,171
Blenheim (1923) 63,171
Blenheim (1951) 7,11,64,65,66,67,171
Blenheim (1970) 69,70,71,152,153,171,175
Boheme 145,146,174
Bolero 71,146,171
Bonheur 63
Brabant 62,63,171
Braemar (1953) 7,11,64,65,67,171
Braemar (1993) 74,150,171
Bretagne 7, 63,64,171
Brilliance of the Seas 165,176
Britannia 102,103,106,107,121,173

C.F.Tietgen (1906) 12,168
C.F.Tietgen (1928) 13,168
Canada 35,170
Caribe 145,146,174,175
Caribe 1 145,146,147,174
Copenhagen 154,175
Crown Del Mar 149,174
Crown Dynasty 74,148,149,150,,175
Crown Jewel 149,150,175
Crown Monarch 149,174
Curonia 33
Czar 35,169
Czarita 35,169

Dana Anglia 29,30,31,169
Dana Corona 28,29,168
Dana Gloria 32
Dana Regina 13,29,30,32,113,169
Dana Sirena 28,29,168
Danmark 35
Discoverer 156,175
Dreamward 138,173
Drottningholm 79,80,88,172
Dronning Alexandrine 13,168

Emerald Seas 156,160,175
Enchanted Capri 148
Enchanted Isle 147,148,174
Enchanted Seas 147,148,174
Enchantment of the Seas 162,176
England (1932) 13,168
England (1964) 6,11,20,22,23,24,25,26,29,30,32,47,113,168
Erria 34,169
Esbjerg,13,14,168
Estonia 35,169
Europa 34,35,169
Explorer of the Seas 165,176

Falstria 35,170
Frederik VIII 12,13,30,168
Fridtjof Nansen 95
Future Seas 160

Grandeur of the Seas 162,176
Gripsholm (1925) 6,80,81,82,85,87,88,93,96,121,172
Gripsholm (1957) Front cover, 53,92,93,94,95,97,100,101,146,172

Hammershus 7,8,9,10
Hellig Olav 12,168
Hispana 108,109,110,173

Irma 55
Island Venture 100,154,155,175

Java 35
Jewel of the Seas 176
Juliette 33,169
Jupiter (1916) 54,59,170
Jupiter (1966) 6,11,58,59,62,68,69,71,72,78,119,171
Jutlandia (1912) 34,35,169
Jutlandia (1934) 35,169
Jylland 13,168

København 72,73,171
Kong Olav V (1961) 20,21,168
Kong Olav V (1969) 26,29,114,115,168
Kristianiafjord 36,37,38,170
Kronprins Frederik 15,16,17,18,19,20,22,168
Kronprins Harald (1961) 76,77,78,171
Kronprins Harald (1976) 78,171
Kronprins Harald (1987) 78,172
Kronprins Olav (1937) 7,9,14,15,16,17,20,64,168
Kronprinsesse Ingrid 16,17,20,22,168
Kungsholm (1902) 79,80,172
Kungsholm (1928) 6,80,83.84,85,88,172
Kungsholm (1953) 90,91,92,93,95,96,97,172
Kungsholm (1966) 96,97,98,99,100,107,108,155,156,172
Kursk 33,35,169

Lalandia 35
Latvia 35,169
Leda (1920) 55,59,170
Leda (1953) 59,60,61,119,171
Leeward 139,140,148,173
Legend of the Seas 161,176
Lindblad Explorer 156,175
Lindblad Polaris 156,175
Lituania 35,169

Majesty of the Seas 161,176
Malaya 35
Mariner of the Seas 176
Mayan Express 32
Meonia 35
Mercur 53
Meteor (1904) 54,55,156,170
Meteor (1955) 59,61,62,171
Monarch of the Seas 161,176

Navigator of the Seas 176
Nelly 76,77
New Bahama Star 157
Nordic Empress 160,161,176
Nordic Prince 158,162,176
Nordnorge 166
Norge 53
North Star 156,175
Northumbria 101,172
Norway 124,135,136,137,158,159,160,166,173
Norwegian Crown 144,174
Norwegian Dream 138,173
Norwegian Dynasty 140,150
Norwegian Majesty 139,174
Norwegian Sea 173
Norwegian Sky 140,174
Norwegian Star 142,144
Norwegian Wind 138,139,173

Ocean Pearl 151
Oscar II 12,168
Oslofjord (1938) 40,41,170
Oslofjord (1949) 7,10,41,42,43,44,45,46,64,170

Parkeston 13,14,168
Patricia (1901) 101,103,173
Patricia (1926) 103,173
Patricia (1951) 105,106,107,157,173
Patricia (1967) 108,109,173
Pearl of Scandinavia (1967) 76,151,152,175
Pearl of Scandinavia (1988) 32
Polonia 35
Prince of Scandinavia 32
Princess of Scandinavia 32
Prins Henrik af Danmark 154
Prinsesse Margrethe (1957) 20,21,22,168
Prinsesse Margrethe (1969) 26,27,29,168
Prinsesse Ragnhild (1966) 77,78,120,171
Prinsesse Ragnhild (1981) 78,171

Radiance of the Seas 165,176
Rasa Sayang 50
Renaissance One – Renaissance Eight 156,175

Rhapsody of the Seas 162,163,176
Royal Viking Queen 143,144,156,174,175
Royal Viking Sea 141,142,144,174
Royal Viking Sky 141,142,143,144,174
Royal Viking Star 74,141,142,143,144,171,174
Royal Viking Sun 125,143,144,174
Russ 33,169
Russia 33,35,169

Saga (1909) 101,172,173
Saga (1946) 103,104,106,107,173
Saga (1966) 107,108,109,110,112,173
Saga (also 1966) 109,110,173
Sagafjord Front cover,7,10,46,47,48,49,50,51,52,53,116, 117,141,143,156,170
St. Domingo (1890) 32,33,169
St. Domingo (1897) 33,169
Scandinavia 145,152,153,154,160,174.175
Scandinavian Sea 71,152,153,175
Scandinavian Song 135
Scandinavian Star 154
Scandinavian Sun 153,154,175
Scandinavica 72
Sea Goddess I 143,156,175
Sea Goddess II 156,175
Sea Venture 100,154,155,175
Seabourn Pride 156,175
Seabourn Spirit 156,175
Seabourn Sun 144
Seaward (not delivered) 133,135
Seaward (1988) 137,138,173
Selandia 6,33,34,169
Serenade of the Seas 176
Skaubryn 75,76,172
Skaugum 75,172
Skyward 130,132,133,134,146,173
Song of America 158,159,162,176
Song of Flower 156, 176
Song of Norway 158,159,162.176
Southward 133,134,135,139,154,173
Sovereign of the Seas 137,159,160,176
Splendour of the Seas 162,163,176
Stardancer 145,154,160,174
Starward 122,130,132,133,139,144,146,173
Stavangerfjord 38,39,40,41,42,43,44,45,46,170
Stella Polaris 6,40,55,56,87,117,118,156,170
Stena Oceanica 109
Stena Saga 109
Stockholm (1900) 79,80,172
Stockholm (1941) 7,85,86,87,88,90,92,93,172
Stockholm (1948) 88,89,90,95,172
Suecia 14,15,102,103,106,173
Sun Viking 158,161,176
Sundancer 145,174
Sunward (1966) 72,108,123,129,130,131,135,173
Sunward (1973) 143,144
Sunward II 134,135,139,173
Svalbard 77
Svea 107,108,110,173
Svea Corona 174
Svea Star 146

The World 167,176
Thule 101,172
Tor Britannia 31,32,109,169
Tor Scandinavia 31,32,109,169
Trekroner 27,28,29,168

United States 12,168

Vega (1938) 15,56.57,59,170
Venus (1931) 9,56.57,58,59,67,170
Venus (1966) 6,11,62,68,69,71,72,171
Viking Princess (1950) 129,173
Viking Princess (1964) 149,174
Viking Saga 148
Viking Serenade 145,160,175
Vision of the Seas 162,176
Vistafjord 10,30,50,51,52,53,143,154,170
Vistula 13
Voyager of the Seas 127,128,164,165,176

Walrus 150
Westward 143,144
Windward 138,139,173
Winston Churchill Frontispiece,6,24,25,26,29,30,32,168